Capital and Ressentiment

Capital and Ressentiment

A Brief Theory of the Present

Joseph Vogl

Translated by Neil Solomon

polity

Originally published as *Kapital und Ressentiment* © Verlag C.H.Beck oHG, München 2021

This English edition © Polity Press, 2022

The translation of this work was funded by Geisteswissenschaften International – Translation Funding for Work in the Humanities and Social Sciences from Germany, a joint initiative of the Fritz Thyssen Foundation, the German Federal Foreign Office, the collecting society VG WORT, and the Börsenverein des Deutschen Buchhandels (German Publishers & Booksellers Association).

Polity Press
65 Bridge Street
Cambridge CB2 1UR, UK

Polity Press
111 River Street
Hoboken, NJ 07030, USA

ISBN-13: 978-1-5095-5181-1 (hardback)
ISBN-13: 978-1-5095-5182-8 (paperback)

A catalogue record for this book is available from the British Library.

Library of Congress Control Number: 2022935477

Typeset in 10.5 on 12 pt Sabon
by Fakenham Prepress Solutions, Fakenham, Norfolk NR21 8NL
Printed and bound in Great Britain by TJ Books Ltd, Padstow, Cornwall

For further information on Polity, visit our website: politybooks.com

Contents

Preliminary remark

In the title of *Capital and Ressentiment*, the conjunction "and" is subjected to critical strain. It refers to the question of how the construction of new entrepreneurial forms of power in digital capitalism combines with the erosion of democratic procedures and institutions. Here, a trail is followed that leads from the domination of the financial industry to the emergence of the platform economy and finally to the dynamics and storms on the current markets of opinion.

Several central theses determine the trajectory of the following chapters. Thus, the current Internet industry is initially understood as a renewal of a financial regime that has been taking shape since the 1970s and, over the course of various crises, has opened up a new source of value creation: the management of information of all kinds. Information has become the most important resource in contemporary capitalism. The associated business models are also the result of the close elective affinity between finance and communication technologies. What is now called digitalization is much more than just the transformation of analog values into digital formats and the spread of such technologies into all possible social, political, and economic spheres. Electronic networks have, in fact, enabled an effective fusion of the economies of finance and information, bringing about a rapid expansion of the financial sector and the hegemony of finance capitalism. On the one hand, this has created an economic power that intervenes in the decision-making processes of governments, societies, and economies across national borders. On the other hand, the privatization of the Internet, legal privileges, and the commercialization of information since the 1990s have also spawned new kinds of media corporations whose business is the appropriation of public infrastructures, the expansion of private control mechanisms, and the creation and provision of information markets. In the context of network architectures, platform industries, and digital companies, the control of societies and public spaces has itself become a corporate project. Finally, the resulting debates about fragmented public spheres and political polarization, about the erosion of democracy and the current trend toward mendacious behavior in public life are taken as an opportunity to trace the interrelationship between economic processes, individuals' relations to the world, and economies of affect. In this context, the social affect of ressentiment occupies a privileged position: in the current economic system, it functions as both a product and a productive force, and precisely with its politically and socially erosive forces contributes to the stabilization of finance and information capitalism. The aim of these theses is not to pursue a hermeneutics of epochs or embellish general diagnoses of the times. They do, however, support a concise theory of the present situation in that they relate to those circumstances and conditions that first make possible an understanding of this present period and how it is produced.

1

Monetative Power

In economic history, major upheavals are marked less by resounding events than by imperceptible twists in long-term trends. While the recent financial crisis put a resounding end to a *belle époque* of finance capitalism, a rather pedantic census has recorded several hundred banking and currency crises since the 1970s, ranging from the Herstatt bankruptcy in 1974 to the collapse of the dot-com market in 2000.[1] Such series provide ample material for attesting to a structural instability in the more recent financial system, in which turbulence and crashes have become routine and the concept of financial crisis itself has lost its power to reference the character of extraordinary market events: the "crises" have become stationary or steady-state in character. Above all, however, they reflect the gradual making of an economic regime in which, over the past four decades, the interaction of adverse circumstances, quandaries, new business ideas, rabid political interventions, and ideological upswings has led to finance capital breaking out of its welfare state containment to dictate the fate of nation-states, societies, and economies.

Against this backdrop, the quarter century after the end of the Second World War could always appear as an exceptional period, a golden but now vanished economic idyll in which, under the impression of the economic, social, and political disasters of the 1920s and 1930s, an attempt was made to save capitalism on the basis of moderate versions of the same. For, beyond all controversial assessments of this postwar period, it had to be conceded that strong unions and banking regulation, capital and currency controls, a defensive business cycle, tax and social policy, long-term investment and mass production, low interest rates and modest profit margins had led, at least temporarily, to industrial growth, wage increases, and a moderation in the distribution of wealth and income. As once envisioned by Max Weber, Joseph Schumpeter, John Maynard Keynes, or Karl Polanyi, the times of the unleashed markets of an extremist capitalism seemed to have finally found their end. Indeed, as late as 1968, there was hope that the existing economic institutions and instruments of Western industrialized countries could prevent uncontrolled inflation and depression, perpetuate economic growth, and optimize "processes in society as a whole." In short, this was an era characterized by hopes for peace and plenty, for "prosperity for all," and the prospect of defusing distributional struggles through expected growth dynamics.[2]

The erosion of these social and political compromise formulas then proceeded through a number of stages in which a dislocation in economic forces combined with a shift in political decision-making power. Both the reversal of the trend and its culmination were marked by two amply discussed dates. On the one hand, we have the end of the Bretton Woods Agreement in 1971 and 1973. This agreement represented the postwar order adopted in 1944, which, by pegging important currencies to the dollar and the dollar to gold, was supposed to guarantee stable exchange rates and thus provide safeguards for international transactions involving commodities, capital, and payments. Whatever may have triggered the demise of this financial, monetary, and economic epoch – increasing mobility in international capital movements and an expansive US monetary policy, the transformation of the US from an international creditor to a global debtor, the accumulation of foreign dollar assets, the growing US deficit due to the Vietnam War and increasing inflationary pressure, a search for higher returns on capital due to falling profit rates in American companies, export surpluses (especially in Germany and Japan), or the mismatch between US obligations and gold reserves – in any case, it marked a failure of complex constructs in fiscal policy as well as a slow but final transition from commodity money to credit money, to unbacked currency systems with fluctuating exchange rates.

This not only created new markets for new financial products, such as currency derivatives, but also initiated an almost exponential growth of the money supply in circulation.[3] Today, five trillion dollars are traded on foreign-exchange markets worldwide on a daily basis. On the other hand, rising inflation rates, stagnation, and declining productivity in the United States motivated drastic interest rate increases by the Federal Reserve under Paul Volcker between 1979 and 1981. They accomplished the feat of turning the trade deficits and foreign debt of the US to its advantage and steering international surplus capital to Wall Street with high-interest investments. Even though Volcker's decision was probably improvised and intuitive, the success of such inflation-fighting measures not only led to a strengthening of the dollar exchange rate but also to a momentous redistribution of wealth and income. While profit rates for banks and financial institutions, for securities, bonds, stocks, and large capital assets rose, and 70% of the profits from European trade surpluses flowed back onto the New York financial markets, debts became more expensive, wage increases were curbed, and the income of the manufacturing industry, small businesses, and agriculture was reduced. The growth of the financial sector and the returns on finance capital were accompanied by recession, Third World debt crises, and rising unemployment. With an invisible hand, income shares of the 55% of those households that had no financial assets or only negative ones were distributed to the top 45%.[4]

Expanding financial markets and debt economics thus secured the hegemony of US capitalism under changed auspices in the 1970s. In so doing, they provided the framework for the enactment of those liberalist programs first tested under Chile's military dictatorship from 1973 onwards and pushed through in various sequences, time spans, and versions after the political arrival of Thatcher and Reagan in the 1980s. The measures ranged from the fight against unions and labor market reforms, via the privatization of social welfare and public functions and services, to the comprehensive revision of corporate, property, and income taxes, the targeted promotion of credit and financial markets, and capital gains relief. In the process, this mixture of heterogeneous developments and concerted actions has acquired a systemic or systematic context by being flanked by prominent institutional structures. Let's take the International Monetary Fund (IMF), to name just one such organization alongside the World Bank, GATT, or WTO. It was founded in 1945 and initially had the task of coordinating international monetary policy and moderating possible tensions in the system of fixed exchange rates by means of compensatory payments. The IMF was, however, temporarily deprived of its function following the collapse of the world monetary system and the abrogation of the Bretton Woods Agreement. Its remit was then reinvented in the 1970s, and a new authority was created to monitor compliance with stability criteria in the face of floating exchange rates and also to act as lender of last resort for central banks and governments on the international financial markets.[5]

This marked the beginning of the great era of "structural adjustment programs" with which the World Bank and the IMF, with the help of the OECD, reacted to the debt crises in Latin America and Asia, linked the granting of loans to developing and emerging countries to reform conditions, generalized the corresponding socioeconomic development perspectives, and ultimately established the orientation of international economic and financial policy. The main points of the program were summarized in the Washington Consensus of 1989 and, in addition to demands for budgetary discipline, reductions in government spending, tax reforms, and privatization of state-owned enterprises, these also included market-oriented interest rates and exchange rates, investor protection, deregulation of markets, and liberalization of capital movements including the easing of constraints on foreign investment. With these guidelines for financial and economic global governance, the international financial institutions not only sought to change state structures and economic policy conditions, but also to provide targeted support for specific interest groups and agencies.[6] Even if this policy has repeatedly been declared a failure,[7] it can be seen as the blueprint for recent government experiments in which the spectrum of austerity programs tested in developing and emerging countries – stability and fiscal pact, debt brakes, budgetary discipline, privatizations – was once again executed within the eurozone.

Finally, such conditioning of political decision-making processes was also forced by a change in the function of central banks in the twentieth century. While national banks emerged from the notorious indebtedness of early modern territorial states and their management by private creditors and, like the Bank of England in 1694, were founded for the purpose of permanent state financing, that is, for the management of state deficits, these institutions gradually acquired a broader range of tasks. These tasks arose from specific historical situations and included, for example, the monopoly of note issuance and money creation, the safeguarding of the banking system, concerns about the value of the currency, the regulation of the money supply in circulation, and issues of price stability, interest rate policy, and inflation control. It was above all the banking, financial, and monetary crises since the end of the nineteenth century that determined the orientation of exemplary institutions – from the Federal Reserve System in the US (1913) to the Deutsche Bundesbank (1957) and the European Central Bank (ECB, 1992 and again in 2007) – and resulted in three main trends. They were conceived as safety nets for the financial and monetary system (1) and, at the same time, as bankers' banks, as service providers for banks and financial markets that were tasked with ensuring the provision of capital reserves in times of need and distress (2). This is also linked to the special legal status of these banks, which is characterized by a formal sealing off or immunization against other government organs (3). Based on the close coupling between central banks, credit institutions, and the financial system, the dogma of the "independence" of central banks prevailed over the course of the twentieth century, and especially by the 1990s, and perhaps most radically for the ECB: according to Article 107 of the Maastricht Treaty (1992), in exercising "the powers and carrying out the tasks and duties conferred" upon it, the ECB may not "seek or take instructions from [European] Community institutions or bodies, from any government of a Member State or from any other body."[8]

Thus, we are dealing with the creation of governmental enclaves that are independent of all other governmental bodies and, in particular, escape any control by legislative powers. This had far-reaching consequences and brought about a strict and at times constitutional separation of sovereign tasks such as money and monetary policy from the economic and fiscal policy of national governments. Invoking the liberal doctrine of monetarism, which assumes a more or less mechanical link between the money supply and economic development, this paved the way for a technocratic handling of political decisions and placed monetary policy under the idol of "governance without government." Not least, this approach programmed a radical one-sidedness, a one-sided responsibility of central banks. On the one hand, any accountability to elected governments, to a democratic electorate, was annulled. It was a matter of protecting the financial-economic market order against "the tyranny of accidental parliamentary majorities" (Knut Wicksell), and especially with regard to the euro and the ECB, no secret was made of the fact that it was a matter of removing the "bothersome democracy … from the economic system."[9] On the other hand, their deference does extend to the moods of the financial public; and to safeguard currency and monetary value they are above all beholden to those investors and actors who dictate the dynamics of financial markets. Thus, as government institutions, central banks provide a kind of minority protection for the representatives of finance against fickle democratic majorities; by means of central banks, financial markets and their agencies have become an integral part of government practice, where they manifest their parademocratic nature.

It was only with the multiplicity and interplay of such political, institutional, and doctrinal interventions that the preconditions were created for promoting what has recently become finance (or financial-market) capitalism. And it was here that the foundations were laid for that global mass experiment which, for four decades now, has focused on a "financialization" of national economies and of economic and social infrastructures as a whole. Emerging from the efforts, particularly in the US since the late 1960s, to free itself from economic and political constraints, new spheres of action were opened up for the financial sector in the exercise of political decision-making power. This was initially reflected in a two-fold expansion of financial transactions, in both growth and scope. For example, the global volume of financial operations increased more than seventeen-fold between 1980 and 2007. The volume of trading on the New York Stock Exchange multiplied from $19 million a day in 1975 to $109 million a day in 1985; trading in derivatives and securitizations increased nearly ten-fold from 1998 to 2008; financial assets reached 355% of world gross domestic product in 2007; and transactions in so-called shadow banks, that is, transactions that take place outside of regulatory requirements such as equity guidelines and minimum reserves, assumed a size of 140% of global economic output in 2008, and 150% in 2015. This was accompanied by a multiplication of debt in the public sector but, above all, in the private sector: taking the United States as an example, debt rose from 155% of gross domestic product in 1980 to 353% of GDP in 2008. In addition, and again in the US, the share of the finance, insurance, and real estate (FIRE) industries in domestic product relative to goods production grew from about 30% in the early 1960s to over 90% by around 2010.

These developments were connected with a process in which the share of industrial profits in overall corporate returns steadily declined. It fell from 24% to 14%–15% in the US in the 1970s and was overtaken by the profit share of the FIRE-related businesses in the 1990s. This was also due to a reorganization of corporate structures that manifested itself not only in mergers and concentrations, in the outsourcing of labor, and in the privileging of shareholder interests, of short-term payouts to shareholders over long-term investments, but also in the diversion of profits to financial markets and in the transformation of large corporations into financing companies: the largest share of profits of companies such as General Electric or Ford Motor Company came not from sales of industrial products but from financial services; and if, for example, Nike was able to increase its revenues by 470% between 2002 and 2005, this was not due to sales of sneakers and jerseys but to earnings from interest and dividends. In the US, half of all investment by nonfinancial firms went into the financial sector in 2000, and in 2001, more than 40% of all corporate profits were in the financial industry.[10]

Financialization has thus become structural. It enjoyed academic endorsement as exemplified by the Efficient Market Hypothesis, which attested to the perfect competition, ideal pricing mechanisms, rational modes of action, and optimal information distribution specific to financial markets. And it is characterized by the growing importance of financial-economic motives, actors, instruments, and institutions for the conditions of material production as well as for the dynamics of domestic and international markets. It shapes the way in which the accumulation of financial capital has become a dominant force in the structuring of the social and political realm.

On the one hand, the strengthening of pension funds and the financially defined provision of public services, the molecularization of competition and the promotion of precarious forms of employment, and the increase of debt risks through consumer credit, credit card systems, education costs, and mortgages have guaranteed an increasing inclusion of populations in the value creation process of financial markets. The functioning of the capital market requires a constant tapping into new resources and leads to a claim that is sometimes explicitly stated: "The world needs our leadership";[11] this is how Larry Fink, the CEO of the world's largest asset manager, Black Rock, put it, summarizing the financial industry's vision of the future.

On the other hand, the systematic strengthening of financial markets and their institutions has proven to be a program of income and wealth redistribution that has now been sufficiently documented. The figures and dynamics are widely known and resemble each other in most contemporary industrialized countries. Thus, the expansion of capital markets has led to a release of divergent forces. It has also led to the fact that, in Europe, for example, since the turn of the millennium, the volume of private wealth has been four to six times the total annual national income and that the return on capital has significantly exceeded the long-term growth rate of economic output. This was reflected in the disparity between low and high incomes, between wages and capital gains.[12] Between 1988 and 2008, 44% of income growth was generated by the richest 5%, and almost 20% by just 1% of the world's adult population. From 1999 to 2009, the incomes of the bottom 10% of households in Germany shrank by 9.6%, while those of the top 10% grew by 16.6%; real incomes of wage earners declined by about 3% between 2005 and 2015. In 2007, 10% of the richest households in Germany owned two-thirds of total private net wealth, 1% owned more than one-third of it, and the top 0.1% held a 22.5% share. By contrast, the entire bottom half only accounted for 1.4% of total private net wealth. The situation was even more pronounced in the US, where 43% of total household net wealth was concentrated in the richest 1% of the population and 83% in the richest 10%. The share of total income held by the poorest 50% of the population fell from 20% in 1980 to 12% in 2018, accompanied by a reduction in real minimum wages since the 1980s. Moreover, countries with particularly dominant financial industries, such as the UK and the US, are now among those Western societies with the lowest levels of upward mobility.[13]

Even after the last financial and economic crisis, this trend has continued. According to a study by the International Labor Organization (ILO), in 2019 10% of those with the highest incomes commanded 49% of the sum of global wages, with the bottom half sharing only 6.4% and the bottom fifth less than 1%. This also relates to the stagnation or decline of low incomes in the years after 2008. In Germany in particular, 10% of the richest households have benefited almost exclusively from the swelling export surpluses of recent years, and more than half of the increase of three trillion euros in private wealth resulting from the real estate boom in the same period benefited the richest 10%, while almost 40% of the population has no assets or only debts. In 2020, the German Institute for Economic Research (DIW) determined that the richest 1% of the population owns around 35% of individual net wealth, while the richest tenth owns over 67% and the bottom half only 1%. Moreover, the 45 richest households have as much wealth as the weaker 50% combined.[14] Apart from the fact that financial crises are always accompanied by a redistribution from the bottom to the top, a development can be observed, both in general and at the latest since the beginning of the 1980s, in which the growth of the gross domestic product (GDP) in Western industrialized countries, and especially in the US, has become decoupled from the growth of the incomes of 90% of the population. This ultimately raised doubts about whether the calculation of GDPs could in any sense still provide meaningful economic and wealth indicators without first taking into account concrete wealth and income distributions.[15] Such a hyperconcentration of income and wealth is not only an indicator of the economic transformations of recent decades. The connection between overaccumulation and inequality also indicates a subordination of social and economic reproduction to the reproductive cycles of finance capital. In this, a gradual change in the organization of techniques of governance can be discerned, which has led to the status quo of a reign of finance, with at least *five basic features*. First, the term "finance economy" today cannot be taken to refer either to a purely economic state of affairs or to a specific market system. The protracted process of establishing the current financial regime cannot be grasped in terms of a dogmatic opposition between state and market or politics and economics. Moreover, the so-called liberalization of markets, and especially of financial markets, since the 1970s cannot be understood simply as a withdrawal of regulatory authority. On the contrary, it has been demonstrated that the demand for regulations, for regulatory practices, instruments, and agencies has increased in proportion to the privatization of state functions and enterprises.[16] It is precisely the vehement assertion, reinforcement, securing, and legitimization of market mechanisms that has brought to the fore a plethora of public, semi-public, and private institutions that are evidence of a multiplication and dispersion of governance functions and are embodied in international committees, associations, treaties, and lobby groups. They operate, as it were, pluralistically and on different levels; and as elements and forms of a finance-economic global governance, they characterize more than just a regime that could be brought about, starting from North America and Europe, on the initiative of the leading economic powers. Much more, the mutual interpenetration of nation-state bodies, international organizations and networks, private agencies, corporations, and market processes has resulted in a multilayered web of regulatory regimes of varying density and scope. Market forces are pushed through a proliferation of regulatory instances, while, conversely, market dynamics and actors call for a consolidation of regulatory systems. Governance functions and market-based modes of action have entered into a bipolar internal relationship, defining an economic and financial system that deserves the title of *regulatory capitalism*.[17] The liberal fiction of "free," "efficient," or "unregulated" markets that are supposed to be able to evolve happily and autonomously apart from government intervention loses any analytical value here. It is precisely the liberalization of markets and financial markets that has given rise to a global program of regulation and re-regulation. As a form of power of its own variety, the financial regime has thus taken on a diagrammatic character: it structures an immanent space in which sovereign prerogatives, governing actions, business transactions, and market operations are intertwined. The supporting or static structures of political architectures, such as those of the nation-state, are honeycombed by the dynamic axiomatics of finance capital, which breaks free of territorial ties and manifests itself as "a cosmopolitan, universal energy which breaks through every limitation and bond"[18] by generating its own rules and dependencies.

Thus, with the processes of financialization, the transition from a geopolitical to a geoeconomic order has been completed. In this process, the financial regime has installed itself as a power operating inter- or transgovernmentally, of ill-defined legal and institutional location, which supplements or replaces the formal authority of governments, undermines the distinctions between public and private, and intervenes directly in national economies, in the governmental policies of old nation-states. As a special technology in the exercise of governmental power, the financial regime can thus secondly claim the character of a *fourth power*, asserting itself as a *monetative power*[19] (with special escalation potential) that joins the trinity of legislative, executive, and judicial governmental powers.

The crisis management since 2007 has demonstrated just how the formation of reserves of transnational sovereignty has combined with the agencies of monetative power. Eurozone policies, in particular, have been distinguished in their operations by their bracketing of legal considerations and parliamentary participation, as well as by their suspension of formal procedural channels and democratic conventions. Various bodies such as the "Troika," the "Quadriga," the "Institutions," or the "Eurogroup" have not only imposed the usual packages of measures on European debtor states, which a good-humored financial world has given the suggestive acronyms of PIIGS or GIPSI (i.e., Portugal, Italy, Ireland, Greece, and Spain). These measures include privatizations, savings, staff cuts, streamlining of the healthcare system, labor market reforms, cuts in social benefits, wages and pensions, or the restriction of trade union rights. On the contrary, to satisfy the interests of bondholders, sovereign powers were also exercised by means of direct interventions in national budget, tax, and labor legislation, interventions that were not necessarily covered by the legal framework of the eurozone. This seems all the more remarkable given that some of these bodies themselves were at best improvised and informal in character, initiating legislative processes as ill-defined executive bodies. The so-called Eurogroup, for example, which consists of the finance ministers of the euro states, the ECB president, the EU commissioner responsible for economic and financial affairs, and a representative of the IMF, monitors compliance with stability criteria as well as the budgetary policy and public finances of the euro countries, but is not provided for as a separate entity in European legislation and is not accountable to any regular European institution including parliament. When asked about the legitimacy of the decisions of the Eurogroup and its president during the negotiations on liquidity assistance for Greece, the following response was immediately issued: "... the Eurogroup does not exist in law, as it is not part of any of the EU treaties. It is an informal group of the finance ministers of the eurozone member states. Thus, there are no written rules about the way it conducts its business, and therefore its president is not legally bound."[20]

It is not surprising, then, that public and private representatives of the financial regime sometimes complained about democratic overreach, reminding us, for example, that "[e]lections cannot be allowed to change economic policy" or that democratic constitutions represented "legacy problems of a political nature" and were "incompatible" with current financial-economic necessities.[21] These concerns also articulate the tension between democratic procedures and a financial order whose global economy of power has been reproduced in Europe. From the struggle against legal and political hurdles in the adoption of the first bailouts to the special governing powers of various EU institutions, figures of exceptional political power have emerged that transcend national borders. As if heeding Milton Friedman's advice to seize upon economic crises as opportunities to implement that which is politically unpalatable,[22] the window of opportunity afforded by the last crisis was used to expand these actors' room to maneuver, set political priorities, secure the interests of the financial industry, and reorder decision-making power despite constitutional concerns. Moreover, the associated exceptional powers were immediately made permanent: be it through the European

Stability Mechanism (ESM), the special purpose vehicle established under Luxembourg law, whose entities enjoy complete immunity when deciding on emergency loans and whose directives are outside all parliamentary and judicial control; or be it through the European Fiscal Compact and the reform of the Stability and Growth Pact, which, in special situations, empower the EU Commission and the European Council to directly intervene in the budgetary policies of individual states. In this way, European legislative procedures were circumvented along the lines of an "unwritten emergency constitution." Within existing legal systems, a *legally nonformalized secondary structure* has been created that functions as an extraordinary operational reserve for stationary or steady-state crisis situations.[23] To this day, it is part of the orientation of the European art of government that the violation of economic austerity criteria is vehemently sanctioned, while the breach of constitutional and democratic norms is rather discreetly admonished, and it was probably this crisis policy that was essentially responsible for the unleashing of centrifugal forces in Europe.

Against this backdrop, the gap between the euro countries widened after 2008; between Italy and Germany, for example, the difference in gross national product has since increased by 8,000 euros per capita per year.[24] Such distortions continued, albeit under different ratios and auspices, in the spring of 2020. Thus, in the shadow of the pandemic emergency and extraordinary situations associated with it, and under the EU's watchful eye, not only were authoritarian structures solidified here and there, in Hungary or Poland, but at the same time existing financial-economic mandates and rules were again suspended. The irregular interventions and the purchase of government bonds by the ECB to prop up the euro, the diverse national rescue packages, and the projects to nationalize wage payments and losses have demonstrated that debt brakes, the Stability Pact, the Maastricht criteria, or the "black zero" (balanced budget) are not at all technical or technocratic frameworks, but action programs for achieving political goals, and can simply be ignored if priorities change. But apart from the fact that past austerity dictates in countries such as Greece, Spain, or Italy have proved to be crisis or shock amplifiers, lending by the European Investment Bank (EIB) and the European Stability Mechanism, as well as the notorious vetoes against Eurobonds and concerted borrowing, have directly echoed the old post-2008 debt policies. They have weakened the position of the so-called southern countries vis-à-vis the financial markets and further exacerbated the associated breaking points and forces of divergence within the eurozone. As early as April 2020, risk premiums on Roman sovereign bonds had soared, and just at the crest of the first Covid-19 wave, rating agencies urged a rapid reduction of Corona debt with the usual threat of credit rating downgrade.[25]

On the one hand, then, the financialization processes of the last four decades have led to a financial-economic global governance that, with the close intertwining of business routines and regulatory systems, of public and private regulatory instances, intensified the interdependence between political institutions and economic dynamics and took on the format of a separate government function. On the other hand, they reinforced the capacities with which the issues of the financial sphere occupy the social and political field. Thirdly, the cycles of international capital reproduction determine the way politics and society interpret themselves and their situation. They dictate the agenda of the "competitiveness" of institutions and states and fulfill the liberal hope of employing financial and foreign-exchange markets as "judges over governments,"[26] i.e., as adjudicators of budgetary and investment decisions.

What has come to be understood as an "erosion of statehood" or political "globosclerosis"[27] is reflected less in a weakening of governmental practices than in a restructuring of their goals, maxims, and procedures. In the intensified interconnectedness of regulatory capitalism, the accent of regulatory practice shifts; direct intervention and administrative command structures are augmented by an indirect system of incentives and inducements. As early as the 1980s, the American economist and political scientist Charles Lindblom had recognized the governmental dimension of markets in the establishment of *automatic disciplining mechanisms* that limit political and legal leeway with the grim scenarios of capital flight, interest rate disadvantages, investment abandonment, economic stagnation, and rising unemployment. Decision patterns are aligned with the anticipation of market preferences. Since then, the liberalization and opening of markets, from the financialization of the global economy to the structuring of the euro area, have generated a new enclosure or containment milieu in which the *financial market in particular acts as a prison* for political systems and government activities. Here it holds that "no market society can achieve a fully developed democracy because the market imprisons the policy-making process."[28] Modern market and economy-driven societies did not become "post-democratic" at some point; their ground plan and architecture have always been defined by the limitation of the scope of popular sovereignty and democracy. The reality of "market conforming" or "liberal" democracies is defined by the way in which markets seize or embed themselves in the institutions and subjects of these democracies. As the markets of all markets, financial markets in particular are arenas in which the flagrant unleashing of financial-economic forces is combined with the consistent construction of strict relations of dependency. So-called market discipline has become a fundamental criterion of policy and has tightened the interventional capacity of the financial regime.

From this perspective, the post-2007 turmoil does not appear as a major and tumultuous rupture, but as a continuation and restoration of a financial system that has been forming since the 1970s. In order to save the most recent form of finance capitalism, the course of events could not be left to the financial markets alone, and fourthly, the dramaturgy of the economic crisis has proven to be a *consistent consolidation of the financial regime and its structures*. What began as a liquidity problem in mortgages and financial markets in 2007 and transformed into a sovereign debt crisis led to a quandary in which debt was to be nationalized, banking institutions recapitalized, but government budgets supported only subject to certain conditions. This was particularly evident in the euro area. For as much as, for most euro countries, the liquidity crisis did not begin with budget deficits but with the implosion of financial markets,[29] the subsequent escalation process prioritized above all the vital interest of creditors in the profitable circulation of government debt. Private bank defaults were paid for by borrowing from private banks, and holders of government bonds were privileged in the servicing of their debts; moreover, the prohibition of direct government financing by central banks and the ECB's supply of cheap money to private institutions gave sufficient reason to pass this money on with added interest to finance government budgets. This triggered a capital cycle that, with the bold nationalization of private losses, was able to finance investors back into the position of creditors of last resort. The temporary inclination of finance capital to socialize itself was combated at great expense using public funds. In this respect, debt brakes, stability mechanisms, fiscal pacts, and deficit procedures can also claim the fiscal merit of securing the confidence as well as the prominent position of private creditor power and, moreover, of generating reliable public debtors who, in the event of a crisis and while limiting their fiscal sovereignty, give priority to the portfolios and claims of their creditors.

The transfer of the risks of the finance economy from markets to states, social systems, and populations has thus been successful. While, especially in Europe, shrinking economies, budget cuts, rising unemployment, cuts in social benefits, and stagnating or falling wages after 2008 may justify talk of an internal colonization of local societies, at the same time the attractiveness of financial markets has been increased. Already in 2009, Wall Street had one of its best years ever, and global assets grew by nine trillion in 2010, reaching a peak of $121.8 trillion. At the same time, the "bonus season" was more favorable than ever, generating $117 billion in 2008 and $145 billion in 2009 for the managers of the largest investment banks, asset managers, and hedge funds. Goldman Sachs alone posted stock profits of $13.4 billion in 2009 and paid out $16.2 billion in bonuses and compensation to its staff. In 2010, there were more millionaires worldwide and more wealth in their hands than in 2007, and while another sixty million people had fallen below the absolute poverty line, the volume of international derivatives trading was already greater in 2011 than in 2007.[30]

Economic policy has dedicated itself to the concerns and needs of private creditors and financial firms; and so it was only logical that erstwhile notions and ideas for reorganizing the financial markets, such as a financial transaction tax, higher taxes on capital gains, restrictive capital adequacy rules, changed incentives for investment and compensation, a ban on certain financial products, or the institutional separation of commercial and investment banking, were not implemented, or hardly at all, or at best in inconspicuous doses.[31] This goes hand-in-hand with the observation that the dogmas of macroeconomics and its representatives also recovered very quickly from the intellectual challenges of the crisis years. While as late as 2008 the "whole intellectual edifice" of finance, including its models and forecasts, was seen to be collapsing,[32] it was only shortly thereafter that all doubts were dispelled. As former Federal Reserve Chairman Ben Bernanke remarked in 2010 on behalf of a good part of his guild: "I don't think the crisis by any means requires us to rethink economics and finance from the ground up."[33]

Theoretically, politically, and practically, the finance industry's room to maneuver has been secured under difficult conditions, ratifying in this way a situation in which states and societies have proven themselves to be reliable buttresses for the instabilities of the financial system. Crisis events have been responded to by taking care of their causes; and an automatic enrichment mechanism has been installed in which lower wage and income strata are available as potential net payers for the owners of financial capital. The redistribution of interest payments upward is matched by a redistribution of financial risk from top to bottom. One result could be noticed in the aftermath of the euro crisis: the weakest countries and population groups had borne the costs of the crisis. By means of such socioeconomic hedging, populations themselves were used as minimum reserves for the transactions of the financial markets, and the structural instabilities of these markets were offset using stable enrichment structures: what can be called "primitive accumulation" was made permanent and, with the differentiation of zones of exploitation and centers of accumulation, established a new class struggle in which the interests of mobile investor groups or "supercitizens" are pitted against earthbound state or subcitizens.

However, in the shadows of these events, dynamics had made themselves felt that testify to significant shifts in the status and significance of monetative power, dynamics that have begun to occupy economists intensely. For example, the processes of financialization have already ensured that the axis and well-established interplay between central and commercial banks have inevitably declined in importance. Until the second half of the twentieth century, banks were at the center of the financial system, guaranteeing the extension of credit, the provision of liquidity, and the management of payment flows, escorted in turn by central banks and their reserves. Bank liquidity was tied to governments or central banks, which set growth and money supply targets. In contrast, the expansion of financial markets and the multiplication of private credit instruments weakened the overall strategic linkage between central banks and the credit system.

Whereas in the US of the 1950s, for example, more than three-fifths of credit was provided through commercial banks, this volume shrank to one-fifth around the year 2000. Toward the end of the 1990s, the volume of debt securities of all kinds comprised 163.8% of US GDP, while bank reserves accounted for only 0.5% of it; in Germany, the corresponding ratio was 85.4% to 2.5%.[34] Key moments of money creation, liquidity provision, and credit activity have shifted to financial markets, where they are in turn dominated by a closely networked financial oligarchy consisting of twenty to thirty large corporations. Thus, fifthly, there has been a transition from a government-controlled to a market-controlled financial system,[35] which has meant that the "intermediate targets" for the central banks' steering mission, namely discount or interest rates and bank reserves, have themselves lost their direct effectiveness. Targets are now addressed less directly and less via banks, and more indirectly and via those financial markets which, with their transactions and with their volume, essentially determine credit, interest rates, and the price of money itself. It was necessary to acknowledge an escalating privatization of money creation and a multiple "decoupling"[36] between central bank instruments and market movements: control over systemic risks and the volume of money in circulation, over long-term interest rates and over credit volumes was attacked or faded away.

This has ultimately resulted in a dilemma of financial or monetary policy. While, according to prevailing dogma, economic growth is generated by low interest rates and cheap money, it is precisely the application of this doctrine in the crisis interventions since 2008 that has provoked strange market behavior. For, on the one hand, discount and interest rate pressures, "quantitative easing," and the stimulation of money supply growth, together with the resolute purchase of debt instruments, failed to bring about any particular movement in inflation rates and credit behavior. There were increasing signs that the development of the financial system had impaired the effectiveness of pure monetary policy. In the summer of 2019, the ECB had to concede that even the reduction of the prime rate to zero and the deposit rate to –0.4% had not led to a pleasing economic outlook or to the targeted inflation in the euro area. This corresponds with the general observation that the hyperfinancialization of economic activity in general hinders or minimizes long-term growth opportunities.[37] On the other hand, vast amounts of cheap money have created incentives to expand "fragile activities," increase risky investments, and compensate for minimizing growth risks by increasing speculative risk potential. In 2017, for example, less than one-third of European banks' loans were invested in nonfinancial firms.[38] In addition, the skyrocketing of real estate prices worldwide documents that efforts to finance growth are primarily fueling financial and real estate markets, where they are building up future risk cascades. Here, too, one is confronted with the unreasonableness of lost illusions: for example, when the ECB in July 2019, through its Systemic Risk Committee, somewhat euphemistically referred to "signs of overvaluation" of residential real estate[39] and thus indirectly warned against the consequences of its own monetary policy. The hypertrophy of finance capital after 2008 has opened up a horizon in which – at the limits of what monetary policy can do – the increase in systemic risks can no longer be compensated for by growth prospects. Perhaps this has indeed brought about a changed situation in the development of the latest iteration of finance capitalism: contrary to some hopes,[40] however, it will again not succumb to its own contradictions, but will instead seek out profitable escapes and new methods of value creation.

2

The Information Standard

On the Episteme of the Finance Economy

Neither the precondition for such value creation nor the dominance of the modern financial regime can be explained, however, without the symbioses and convergences between finance capital and information technologies. The tight interconnectedness of commercial businesses and news publishing has been documented from late medieval merchant letters to the emergence of news agencies. Moreover, the dynamics of banking operations and especially of stock-exchange trading have always been defined in terms of their dependence on media infrastructures. The commercial deployment of postal riders or carrier pigeons, and of optical or electromagnetic telegraphs, all came about in the pursuit of marginal advantages in market information. It manifested itself both in the overlapping of financial and press metropolises and in the tendency toward technologically driven acceleration. It was chiefly bankers who, from the mid-nineteenth century onward, financed new telegraph lines between financial centers, became their main users, sometimes opposed state monopolies, used business news to promote trade, stoked channels with economic and stock-exchange data, and, in doing so, accounted for between 40% and 60% of all telegraph traffic. Right up to the laying of undersea transatlantic fiber-optic cables around the turn of the twentieth century, it was the needs of the finance economy for acceleration, as in high-frequency trading, that drove the expansion of global networks.[1]

In this context, it was once again in the 1970s that financial markets were able to expand through a dynamic merger of business information and information economy, and, in so doing, mobilize privileged venues. To cite one of the most prominent examples, the creation of the electronic stock exchange Nasdaq in New York, for instance, initially dates back to the 1920s, a time that resulted not only in the Great Depression but also in new and promising interest groups such as that of securities traders. Starting in the 1930s, the US National Association of Securities Dealers (NASD) had been especially concerned with those stock and capital transactions that were conducted off of the trading floor in amorphous networks and over-the-counter between individual investors and brokers. In 1971, around the end of the Bretton Woods Agreement, NASD created the National Association of Securities Dealers Automated Quotations, or NASDAQ, an automated quotation information service for securities traders. It began as an electronic display system, a news agency operating in real time for a few thousand club members, which acquired the reputation as the first computer network – initially still linked via telephone lines. It subsequently developed into a platform on which brokerage firms operated electronic trading systems, enabling online investment, direct buying and selling of stocks, and, since the 1980s, the automatic processing of orders. The organizing of price information was transformed into an automated brokerage system; market information was no longer merely transmitted, but immediately evaluated and modified by means of buying decisions. This replacement of traditional floor trading by mainframe computers did more than just interconnect buyers and sellers without human intermediaries and minimize transaction costs. More importantly, the accompanying relaxation of stock-exchange laws, the lowering of access thresholds for individual investors and day traders, and the proliferation of private electronic communications networks with some 300,000 terminals all contributed to Nasdaq's emergence from over-the-counter trading: it became the scene of a stock market that was as volatile as it was fast-growing. By the end of the millennium, this had nourished the vision of an inclusive financial engine "available to anyone, anywhere in the world 24 hours a day."[2]

The adoption of information technology modernization by the finance economy was complemented by targeted investments made by the financial industry in the IT sector. In this context, initial public offerings (IPOs), which, since the 1980s, have been driven primarily by technology, media, and software companies as well as by Internet start-ups, provided particular momentum. "New markets" were not only stimulated by expanding companies such as Netscape, Microsoft, Cisco, Intel, or Oracle, but also by the alliance of Nasdaq premieres and so-called venture capital. The relaxed listing requirements facilitated accelerated IPOs, often accompanied by baroque advertising campaigns. Even for companies that had previously made no profit or only losses, they sometimes triggered stock price jumps of several hundred percent per year and contributed to the Nasdaq index increasing by 80% and market capitalization by more than 350% in the late 1990s alone. As early as 1994, Nasdaq's trading volume exceeded that of the old New York Stock Exchange (NYSE); moreover, Nasdaq's merger in 1998 with the American Stock Exchange, which was, among other things, specialized in financial products, also created access to trading in financial derivatives and listed investment funds. The example of Nasdaq could be seen as the creation of a "market of all markets" and the largest global "liquidity pool,"[3] whose systemic importance was also manifested in the crash of April 2000, with the destruction of two trillion dollars in stock values within a week. It owed this immense development to an effective combination of communications technology, finance, and information economy. The Nasdaq could thus become a synonym for the boom and bust of a new economy.

Such interlinkages of information and finance can also be practically demonstrated in the cycle of corporate shareholdings. For example, let us take the Reuters news agency: it was founded in the mid-nineteenth century as a service provider for financial information, then expanded its range to include journalistic news of all kinds, becoming one of the largest agencies worldwide. Nonetheless, the 1960s saw it on the verge of bankruptcy. However, after the end of the Bretton Woods Agreement, fluctuating exchange rates and various financial instruments opened up broader scope for speculative trading. Then, in the early 1970s, Reuters began to specialize in financial news on foreign exchange, securities, and money markets by means of a new screen technology (Videomaster) and an electronic communications system, Reuters Monitor Money Rates. After gaining subscribers and achieving high increases in profit, the company was admitted to both the London Stock Exchange and the New York Nasdaq in 1984. Parallel to this, the electronic trading system Institutional Network Corporation (Instinet) started operations in 1969. Even before Nasdaq was launched, it had begun decentralized trading in securities between banks, investment funds, and insurance companies, considering itself to be a competitor to traditional stock-exchange transactions on the NYSE. As probably the oldest of the electronic communications networks, it was involved in setting up Nasdaq, coordinating, as a brokerage firm, supplies and demands for securities. It was ultimately bought by Reuters in 1987. Thereafter, with a steadily growing market share, Instinet ended up handling 15 to 25% of Nasdaq's trading volume. As in many other similar or related cases, such as the takeover of the Dow Jones Industrial Average by Rupert Murdoch's News Corporation in 2007, this could also be seen as an example of the way in which the consolidation of the financial regime since the 1970s owed much to the interconnection of information and financial markets, to an interlocking of media and financial companies.[4]

Such consortia, like the functioning of Nasdaq, which one might want to designate as the first worldwide network, as a precursor of the Internet, as well as a prototypical platform company,[5] have not only functioned as drivers of financialization and ensured the notorious expansion, proliferation, and acceleration of financial operations. They also point to a technical, economic, and strategic elective affinity between communications media and financial markets that has intensified since the structural changes of the 1970s and found its privileged arena in electronic trading systems. This involves, not least, a two-fold, self-reinforcing movement at the heart of recent finance(-market) capitalism, in which the informatization of financial markets is combined with a financialization of information on the basis of network technologies. This suggests that, in addition to knowledge breakthroughs in cybernetics and information technology, it was primarily work commissioned by the finance economy that contributed to the theoretical and systematic virulence or dissemination of modern conceptions of information. The alliance of media technology and finance, in any case, finds its critical factor, or commitment, in the operational status of "information."

In the process, various technical and theoretical lines of convergence had initially emerged. For example, the Nasdaq system was set up by companies such as Bunker Ramo Corporation, a Pentagon supplier specializing in military electronics, and equipped with the latest UNIVAC mainframes, tried and tested in air traffic control systems or in the personnel management of the US military. But apart from this fact, the installation of Nasdaq also coincided with a period characterized by a wide-ranging coming-to-terms with conceptions of information. On the one hand, the fierce promotion of military information and communications technology under the Cold War was complemented, at least since the 1980s, by a US policy that, under Reagan, emphasized consistent privatization of telecommunication infrastructures, funding cuts for public networks, and restrictions on noncommercial uses. On the other hand, expanding fields of application have demanded a theoretical overhaul of models of information: be it in cybernetics, where information has been used since the 1940s as a measure of organization and ordering patterns in various systems: technical, physical, biological, psychological, and social; or be it in mathematical communications theories, which have been concerned with questions of signal transmission and noise suppression with a view to setting up fire control systems or electronic networks. Against this background, a scientific and cultural dispersion of the concept of information could be observed, as well as the emergence of an "information discourse" ranging from game theory, via research in physics and genetics, to the question of data processing in the economic and social relations of so-called "post-industrial" societies. The concept of information in mathematical information theory, from Claude Shannon and Warren Weaver to Norbert Wiener, had been radically narrowed, having been separated from any content or semantic dimensions and reduced to the stochastics of sign combinations. At the same time, it diffused into all possible fields of knowledge as a metaphor for controlled communication processes and advanced to a new "substance-concept" that is as universal as it is fuzzy.[6]

It is therefore not surprising that this information discourse has not only led to an efficient interlinking of information technology and the financial market, but also to a special challenge for the informational framing of financial market theories. The reorganization of capital markets since the 1970s created the conditions for the rapid adoption of recent technologies and established a reciprocal influence between system architectures. The financialization of the world economy cannot be separated from processes of informatization, and the upswing enjoyed by the concept of information has arguably led to a far-reaching epistemic and dogmatic shift in financial economic knowledge. The role of information has to be understood as inherent, as basic, to developments in the finance economy. From this perspective, financial transactions should function as information processing, market behavior as a controllable feedback process, and the market itself as a computer, as a calculating control system. In other words, concepts of information define the epistemic character of knowledge in financial economics. The formal way in which economics moved closer to information-based concepts involved questions about the commodity character of information, about a stochastic modeling of the world, and about the market as an information-processing machine. A first and essential step toward this fusion of neoclassical economics, cybernetics, and information theory was already taken in postwar liberalism and especially by Friedrich Hayek. The conception of market operations as a "mechanism for communicating information"[7] was marked by a consistent replacement of ordering concepts by system concepts and of figures of "knowledge" by matters of "information." Here, the market itself emerges not only as an information processor but also as an arena for the coordination of events constituted by a series of precognitive, that is, reflex-based and preconscious reactions to price signals. Prices contain the most important information for the self-reproduction of the economic system and, through feedback and balancing mechanisms, the market ultimately functions as "the most mechanical or exact" of "all the signaling systems produced by society."[8]

Such considerations could be seen as a starting shot for the "information economy."[9] It was joined by those prominent attempts that were christened the *efficient market hypothesis*.

The latter provided an essential theoretical link that could both mediate between the finance economy and information technology as well as integrate the concept of information into the modeling of capital markets. Since the 1960s, these attempts have involved the application of neoclassical interpretations of market mechanisms and competition to financial transactions, claiming precisely to find in them dynamics that represent market activity par excellence and in the greatest purity. According to these considerations, financial markets, unencumbered by transportation and by the complications of production, are ideal settings for price formation mechanisms and perfect competition. In this context, a capital market that is "efficient" in the long run is characterized by the fact that under favorable competitive conditions "all available information is freely available to everybody, there are no transaction costs, and all market participants are price takers." Moreover, the effectiveness of "homogeneous expectations" is assumed, which means that all participants agree on "the implications of available information for both current prices and probability distributions on future prices of individual investment assets." Companies make reasoned decisions about investments, and consumers can presume when choosing among the securities or company holdings "that security prices ... 'fully reflect' all available information." Prices embody or compress information about information. In concrete cases, this means, for example, that stock prices or the price of securities of all kinds are the adequate expression of the conjectures that analysts, investors, or management hold about future returns and profit prospects. Only a market "in which prices fully reflect available information" can be called efficient.[10] The value of things is nothing other than their price, which is articulated as information about aggregated value estimates.

If the financial market is imagined as a frictionless and self-referential universe in which information translates into prices and vice versa, this efficient process implies another condition that defines the status of information concepts in the modern finance economy. Namely, the hypothesis of efficiency implies that a stochastic random movement, as it were, is installed inside this market process. In the 1960s, for example, a dissertation from 1900 was rediscovered in which the mathematician Louis Bachelier, under the supervision of Henri Poincaré, formalized the oscillation of stock-market prices along the lines of molecular drift (such as that of Brownian motion). In his *Théorie de la Spéculation*, successive price changes are linearly independent and determined by identically distributed random variables; and the sum of speculative actions follows a motion analogous to the distribution or diffusion of particles in gaseous mixtures.[11] It was not until the second half of the twentieth century that such considerations were given a plausible framework, that is, one that enhanced their resonance. This enabled them to merge with considerations of the relationship between information content and noise in message transmission[12] as well as with models of consistently efficient financial markets. Indeed, if the prices of this market contain all relevant information at any point in time, their change is due only to new, that is, unpredictable, information that requires new or unpredictable decisions.

The path that prices take between different points in time now falls – like the question of data transmission in general – into the domain of probability calculus and stochastics and resembles a random walk, a nonlinear random path. Random movements have become a feature of efficient markets, the *random walk theory* a necessary complement of the *efficient market hypothesis*. And this means that where all entrepreneurs have equal access to all circulating information, every selective profit opportunity is immediately exploited, by whomsoever. Provided that each of these operations is immediately reflected in market prices, price variations themselves can only appear unpredictably, i.e., aleatorily. Market reason entails that pieces of information – the events of price differences – cancel each other out by being exploited. Moreover, competition among profit-maximizing interested parties is supposed to cause speculation in the individual to thwart the speculative character of the whole, and arbitrage is supposed to abolish the effects of arbitrage and destroy the scope for overvaluation and undervaluation.[13] On the one hand, then, the rationality or efficiency of financial markets means that betting on future price movements is arguably akin to a chimpanzee throwing darts at the stock-market section of a newspaper while blindfolded; the more efficient the markets, the more random the oscillations generated there. On the other hand, a kind of equilibrium is established here, in which the random fluctuations arrange themselves around a mean value and eventually follow that of a normal distribution.

Efficient markets could thus be identified as the privileged domain of econophysics and as the basis of modern financial market valuation methods. Against this background, models were ultimately developed at the beginning of the 1970s that make particular reference to the information economy of trading in derivatives; that is, those products that are at the center of recent financial markets, and which are intended to minimize the risks of speculative transactions by means of other speculative transactions. One of the most prominent of these models, which was worked out by the mathematicians and economists Robert C. Merton, Fischer Black, and Myron Scholes between 1969 and 1973, leading to Nobel Prizes, has become a standard program of financial economic transactions. It tracks the valuation of financial options using geometric Brownian motion and has provided essential structure to the transfer between economic theory, financial markets, and information technology. On the one hand, it aims to apply the aforementioned initial conditions: profit-oriented entrepreneurs, efficient markets, uniformly distributed and generally available information, frictionless transactions, and ultimately continuous price variations that conform to the pattern of a normal distribution. On the other hand, it is a matter of calculating from existing prices, for instance for stocks and loans, that price horizon that can become the motive for the valuation of a present future from a future present. The present price of a derivative – more precisely: of a stock option on the future purchase or sale of an asset – is justified if a possible future of the underlying value is reflected in it. Only through an inversion of this kind are uncertain prospects transformed into the probability of future presents; and only this replication of future courses can justify the expectation that the risks of fluctuating rates and prices can be hedged and balanced by trading in these risks. This is also the crux of the solution proposed by Black, Scholes, and Merton. While, for example, the current price of a security, its base or issue price, the interest rate, and the maturity or term of an option may enter the calculation procedure as more or less known quantities, the degree of possible deviation, that is, the volatility of the underlying values, remains the precarious unknown in the calculation of the option price.

At the center of the operation there is a famous differential equation that aims to capture stochastic processes with a function for logarithmic normal distributions and in turn reveals itself to be a version of equations for heat conduction and diffusion in statistical mechanics.[14] Put in simplified terms, by means of this operation, the unknown future volatility is calculated according to the price amplitudes and random movements of underlying values in comparable historical periods. It is not necessary to guess the data and hits of possible futures, but only to calculate an oscillatory space within which they could take place, one way or the other. In this way, the assumption is built into the calculation that the future unpredictable will behave according to the distribution of past unpredictabilities: one does not know what will happen, but one assumes that the unforeseen or unpredictable will at least reproduce existing expectations.[15] However original the system of formulas devised by Black, Scholes, and Merton may have been; however much it was anticipated by isolated and forgotten attempts from the turn of the twentieth century; and however singularly it may hold its own in a series of contemporary attempts;[16] the success of this computational model was guaranteed not least by the following: as an essential element of the discourse, it responded to the problematic situation of finance economics in the 1970s and was able to build a bridge to the informatization of financial markets. This bridge linked liberal market theory, mathematical formalization, and information technology.

However, such "super perfect-market" models[17] had not initially provided a description of real market conditions, but at best ideal abstractions. As little as theories of efficient markets, for example, correspond to the reality of imperfect market situations, it is all the more the case that they operate with a concept of information that itself disregards physical realities, such as the inconveniences of production, wear and tear, or transport. Instead, it occupies the position of a Platonic eidos or an Aristotelian form. In much the same way that for Norbert Wiener, according to an oft-quoted remark, information is nothing but information, thus being neither "energy" nor "matter" and eluding all materialistic grasp,[18] it has been emphasized that liberal, self-regulating price systems represent an ideal type and cannot really be found in the unwieldy material world.[19] In keeping with its origin in the Latin *informare*, "to form," "shape," or "give form," the concept of information here, separated from its physical representation, refers to an entity with its own laws and its own internal logic. On the one hand, in the information economics of such models, from the hypothesis of efficient markets to the Black-Scholes formula and all its variants, one is forced to recognize purely theoretical products. On the other hand, these theoretical products also document the performative quality of the calculation, since, by means of it, financial products now generate the condition of their own possibility and appeal to a market on which their own informational rationality will one day be able to be put into effect. In this respect, one has spoken of an adaptation of financial-economic reality to economic theory, for instance, of the gradual emergence of a special "Black-Scholes world" that did not yet exist in the 1970s: with the establishment of protocols according to which the markets themselves will then operate.[20] As a product of discourse, the system of formulas functions as a kind of enacted theory, offering a compelling argument for the trading of financial products and, in so doing, justifying its own theoretical implications.

In this way, this circular process points to a practical component that has determined the functioning of financial economics since the 1970s. For, with the models of efficient markets and their financial-technical offshoots, financial markets become not only objects of mathematical and information-theoretical formalization, but at the same time specific media-technical formats whose dissemination history then coincides with the stages of computer history and the development of information technologies. This ranges from the first ideas for the establishment of electronic market communication in the 1960s to the opening of computer-based stock-exchange trading, the creation of electronic trading systems and stock-exchange platforms; all the way to online brokerage and the opening of the World Wide Web for stock exchanges and financial transactions in 1993. Indeed, since the 1980s, more than 80% of all IT products and services have been purchased by the financial sector alone.

If the emergence of a financial machine can be discerned in this, in which a large part of world social welfare is to be decided,[21] then this apparatus, this device, for the trade in capital values becomes as essential as it is effective. A formalization like the Black-Scholes model appeals, as it were, to the implementation of an informational technique. Thus, option pricing was first calculated on stationary computers and the corresponding tables were then distributed in a laborious manner as hard copies to interested traders and subscribers. As early as 1974, Texas Instruments supplied a calculator programmed to a concise form of the valuation formula that offered the corresponding results for day trading. And, at the latest, since the emergence of automated exchanges for options and futures in the 1980s, an effective fusion between financial theory, information technology, and mathematics (for instance, in terms of probability distributions) has taken place. Insofar as the idea of efficient markets requires efficiency in information processing, an imitation of theory by economic reality can indeed be recorded here, or at least the hope that "reality will eventually imitate theory."[22] Only under new technological conditions does the institution of this market take place. Information technology has made possible, as former Federal Reserve Chairman Alan Greenspan once remarked, "the creation, valuation, and exchange of complex financial products on a global basis heretofore envisioned only in our textbooks," and derivatives are "the most evident of the many products that technology has inspired."[23] Financial theory, formalization, and technical implementation enter into a productive union here, in which the invention of new financial instruments and the installation of corresponding markets mutually validate the *raison d'être* of the other. Financial innovations are reflected in information systems, which then create the need for technological platforms. And that means: The consortium of the finance economy, information theory, and technology provides the prospect that maximum liquidity, optimized price discovery, and efficient data flow can come together in the consolidation of financial markets. By means of information, the scope for economic action is coupled with the operative possibilities of technical systems, and finance in particular seems to be inspired by the hope of making social processes programmable by means of information theory. The "automatic subject" of capital (Marx)[24] has fulfilled the desire for its own automation.

Thus, in the interplay of the aforementioned components (financial transactions, new calculation methods, and information technologies) a historical transformation can be seen in the financial markets, leading from currency standards of every kind to an *information standard* as the basis of world finance. The stabilization of the credit economy and currency systems is no longer made dependent on a conversion into gold or commodity money, but is thought of and structured as an ongoing exchange between money and information. Prices in financial markets are understood to be a consolidation of available information about assets and, at the same time, serve to compile information about the future of prices. Thus, in payment transactions, information about money has become more important than money itself. The market installs an automated system of information and marks units of value as units of information; information itself has congealed into a form of value. Efficient markets are markets for the efficient distribution of information; competition appears as a call for informational competition. If the international finance economy can be grasped as a technically implemented financial theory, payments and capital movements take on the function of an information-producing apparatus.

Against the backdrop of institutional and structural changes since the 1970s, more recent financial theories are thus grounded on information economics. Moreover, insofar as a reciprocal reinforcement of technical and economic process forms can be noted here, the question is once again posed of the quality, logic, and function of the concept of information implied therein. In this context, it seems worth noting that the question of the consistency of "information," in the broadest sense, has been at the center of attention since the earliest reflections on financial and stock-exchange transactions, and has triggered a certain perplexity about how its cognitive content, its epistemological status, could be grasped at all. Thus, in Joseph de la Vega's series of dialogues *The Confusion of Confusions* (*Confusión de confusiones*) from 1688, the example of the Amsterdam stock exchange and its "puzzling business" was used to reflect on the meaning of "information" (*información*) from various parts of the world, which in the form of "unexpected news" (*noticias*) and "important news" (*novedades*), such as "messages," "correspondences," "reports," "letters," "private letters," or mere "rumors," has a direct impact on the rise or fall of stock prices. Precisely because it always remains unclear which exact effects trigger favorable or unfavorable messages, and whether and how certain causes lead to such and such consequences on the stock market,[25] a theory of information inspired by financial economics has been developed. According to Joseph de la Vega, stock-exchange transactions are "time transactions" in which prospects of future profits or risks are traded, so much so that "the expectation of fact" must make a greater impression than "the fact itself," and the difference between established facts and merely possible ones must disappear. Relevant pieces of stock-market information are always related to uncertain futures; they thus turn out to be an indistinguishable conglomerate of veritable statements, conjectures, speculations, rumors, opinions, and opinions about opinions. They provoke judgments, moreover, not only about how to evaluate news, but also about how others evaluate news; how to form "a safe judgment about the prevailing current" of opinion. On the one hand, no "scientific knowledge" is alien to the stock-market business "in order to arrive at a correct decision in the case of important news": it includes recourse to the accumulated knowledge of politics, geography, nautical science, arithmetic, rhetoric, and jurisprudence in equal measure. On the other hand, such knowledge is beset by adversities that erase the difference between what is known and what is opined and run counter to the logical principles of sufficient causes and mutually exclusive opposites. In a reversal of the scholastic *cessante causa cessat effectus*, on the stock exchange the "effect" does not necessarily disappear with the "cessation of the cause." Moreover, "[w]hile philosophy teaches that different kinds of effects also arise from different kinds of causes, on the stock exchange, on the same news, some sell and others buy, so that here one cause has different effects."[26] The substance of stock-market information is thus constituted in the form of a "stock-market opinion" or "stock-market atmosphere," which, in the course of speculative dealings, in the "foaming of the waves of speculation," cannot distinguish the factual content of news from the event of its disclosure. Nor can the latter be distinguished from its evaluation or the evaluation of evaluations; it experiences its "truth" precisely in the fact that the difference between the "most real" and the "most false,"[27] irrespective of sufficient causes, cannot really be maintained. The event of information lies not so much in this or that state of affairs, but in the tension that manifests itself between existing expectations and the surprise effects of news. Applied to current circumstances, this means, for example, that unusual but fake news generally triggers more violent reactions among investors than the usual stock-market news does.[28]

The genesis of an effective concept of information in financial economics thus seems to be inseparable from the "confusion of confusions" with which news systems function as opinion generators and precisely in this way fuse with the rationality of stock exchanges and financial transactions. This can serve as the basis of a corresponding information theory and requires the acceptance of the fact that the financial market serves to procure liquidity, that this only functions via speculation and that this in turn proceeds in a mirrorlike fashion. If in the financial business, as already explained by Joseph de la Vega, the real facts consist in expectations of facts and contaminate news with opinions, then it holds for the concept of information effective in this realm that it can only be grasped as a function of a self-reflexive tendency in financial activity.[29] Insofar as the purchase of financial assets takes place as a purchase of expected returns, payable prices are set in anticipation of foreseeable prices. The course of events is determined not by what was or what is, but by what could, might, or probably will be. The financial market functions as a system of anticipations that stakes economic behavior on second-guessing what the market itself thinks the future may bring. Current expectations thus do not simply anticipate future events; rather, future events are co-constituted by expectations of future events and consequently acquire virulence in the present. Present events are produced by "before-hand" effects, as *hýsteron próteron* of their own future. With that, we find ourselves caught up in a game of exponentially raised expectations in which players observe each other's observations and anticipate each other's possible anticipations.

This mirrorlike or reflexive structure thus means that information circulating on the market is justifiable only in "doxological," not epistemological terms. It is not possible to ascertain or ground the "real," "true," or "fundamental" value of things. Instead, valuations emerge from opinions mirroring opinions about opinions. Financial markets operate as an ongoing balancing act in an environment where the pressure to conform is all-pervasive. Resonances of collective views, congealed into norms, circulate in the form of prices; and to the extent that an opinion is articulated with each payment about what general expectation generally expects to occur, decision-making and judgment profiles are increasingly conventionalized. That is not to rule out speculations against the market or isolated actions on the part of skeptics or "contrarians." In this respect, it is even possible to detect an affinity with the relationship between opinion and fashion, given that the establishment of fashion trends likewise requires a faintly paradoxical attitude of clinging to the transient and conforming to the extravagant.

Put in Kantian terms, the form taken by this economic judgment therefore has little in common with cognitive judgments. If anything, it displays an aesthetic character, since judgments of taste (according to Kant) stake a claim to "general validity" by invoking an "indeterminate norm" that, itself conceptually indeterminate, could "demand universal assent."[30] Here, one can probably draw a line from the insights of early stock-market treatises to that Keynesianism whose interests focus primarily on the financing structures of financial markets. It is not by chance that John Maynard Keynes sought to illustrate their choreography with the notorious image of beauty contests. According to this, prices, like the "prettiest faces," are determined by "the competitor whose choice most nearly corresponds to the average preferences of the competitors as a whole; so that each competitor has to pick, not those faces which he himself finds prettiest, but those which he thinks likeliest to catch the fancy of the other competitors, all of whom are looking at the problem from the same point of view."[31] Current market opinion is based on "what average opinion expects average opinion to be," and judgments are made on the assumption that a majority of judgment acts will coincide in them. Or, to put it another way, we have here an infinite game of mirrors without a fixed anchor point "in which anyone's luck or fortune depends solely on the interpretation of that which others are thinking, on what others are thinking about one's behavior, on what others will think about the reaction with which one will respond to what others are thinking about the behavior one might express, etc."[32] Insofar as financial markets operate as systems for the production of financing prices, they may be understood as mechanisms for the autopoietic production of *doxa*, in which rational expectations and preferences are only truly rational if they directly coincide with common opinion and find consensus in normative ideas. Financial truths are built on conventions, conventionalism dictates the episteme of markets, and every theoretical justification only ratifies this doxological[33] substrate.

That is why the financial-economic concept of information itself invites a significant (de)differentiation of differences. Thus, the market, qua subject of available and circulating information, reduces the older, Platonic or Aristotelian, distinction between knowledge, belief, and opinion and proves to be a machine for generating normalizing trends. This is also the basis for the quantifiability of economic processes; as Gabriel Tarde once remarked, it captures the "agreement of collective judgments," the mechanisms of the many and their conformist opinions and beliefs.[34] This has come to a very specific head in the question raised by recent financial theories about the relationship between price formation and information. Indeed, insofar as prices – according to the widely held *efficient market hypothesis* – "assemble the information and opinions of market participants," providing in this way "the best estimate of 'value,'"[35] they function as information about information and can reduce all possible kinds of information to the form of information itself, namely price differences. The latter represent a change in assumptions, valuations, opinions, or expert appraisals about the circulating financial products that trigger purchases, which, in combination, are supposed to, in turn, provide efficient markets with their adaptive organizing patterns. Stock exchanges and financial markets must therefore not only be regarded as the first, exemplary, and coherently organized opinion markets; rather, the substrate of opinion as such[36] has itself become a central functional element in them, and has ultimately stimulated those considerations that equate the circulation of opinions and the "economics of free speech" with the latitude afforded to money markets (cf. pp. 86–87).[37]

Accordingly, information could be defined here in general terms as an event that selects certain states of a system, thus exerting selective influence on system behavior and bringing about change. As an indicator of change and "difference that makes a difference" (Gregory Bateson), it manifests itself in those irritations that have the character of the unexpected, of novelty, surprise, or simply statistical rarity, and thus trigger adaptive responses; for example, the fluctuation of securities prices or currency rates provokes certain market reactions. Here, the magnitude of information is determined less by semantic contents than by the difference to prevailing structures of expectation and can thus be understood as a distinguishing factor that remains unaffected by other distinctions, such as those between what is given and what is not given, what exists and what does not, or what is asserted and what is proven. Information manifests itself as a modified or new representation of what is the case or what is believed or asserted.[38] Insofar as prices thereby function at all as information for and about economic communication processes and thus as economic realities, cumbersome procedures for their justification or substantiation are inevitably pared away and make "further investigation of the origins" of prices appear neither necessary nor meaningful. At most, such research or exercise of memory is outsourced to statistical accounting through data aggregation; a price-oriented market system itself can then operate, de jure, without historical ballast and thus delegate its decisions to algorithms.[39] The "truth" of information is represented by specific contents only insofar as a difference to what is expected or shown (i.e., to expectations or indications) is manifested in it. Under these conditions, capital markets can indeed be understood as signal-processing systems. They reduce knowledge to information and information to price differences, calling for the exploitation of information and price differences. With their profit expectations, they install an automatic financial mechanism in which information generates prices, prices generate purchase decisions, and these in turn generate information, prices, and decisions.

Under conditions of information technology, financial markets have installed themselves as opinion markets. The international effectiveness of these opinion markets has been ratified in part by the fact that the effective ranking of financial products of all kinds (whether bonds or creditworthiness) by private rating agencies has been equated in legal terms with journalistic opinion pieces and cannot be held accountable for misjudgments,[40] even though these rankings have dictated the fortunes of national economies since 2008. However, while the concept of information in financial economics makes the difference of knowledge unrecognizable in the processes of price formation, even orthodoxy in economics has expressed a certain level of distrust and called for a broader concept of knowledge. In so-called fundamental analysis, the determination of financial values is not simply left to pricing by market dynamics, but is made dependent on an extensive discussion of manifold, heterogeneous, quantitative and qualitative, micro- and macroeconomic factors, including productivity, earnings positions, cost structures, expectable dividends, current account balances, equity ratios, management quality, business cycle developments, and purchasing power. Thus, a paradigmatic conflict between doxological and epistemological approaches has grown up within the spectrum of financial economic doctrines. Whereas in the analysis of production capital, for example, one encounters moments of resistance from knowledge of concrete production relations including local or regional circumstances, such factors become obsolete in the coordination and valuation procedures of financial markets. Here, a systematic confrontation is emerging in which market valuations and book values of companies increasingly diverge and create referential confusion about actual value relations.[41] The self-assessment of the financial system cannot be separated from the systematic production of specters of value and referential illusions. The increasing disconnect, moreover, between financial quotations and overall economic activities has found its most recent expression in those euphoric price jumps and gains with which stock markets have reacted to the pandemic, rising unemployment, and prospects of depression since the spring of 2020.[42]

Against this background, prevailing market opinions or (price) information data do not distinguish themselves from knowledge, but knowledge distinguishes itself from information and, even if the cumbersome collection of fundamental data asserts itself as a conservative and routine method for assessing and justifying the share prices of capitalist companies, it nevertheless opens up a horizon that allows for a theoretical escalation. According to this, knowledge, in contrast to information, would be linked to operations that interrupt the automatable reaction cycle of information and prices, which unlike informational models are not scalable but are committed to an open research process, and thus, last but not least, that lead into a field of ambiguous history. The processing of information produces fast and flagrant solutions, which can therefore also be processed by algorithms, if algorithms offer programmed instructions for completable, well-defined, and predetermined steps for the solution of problems. The connection between the financial market and information technology (with more than 70% of all financial transactions now controlled by algorithms) can thus be understood as the pulse of a "solutionist" dynamic, for which all possible states of affairs can be transformed into processes with calculable solutions. The question of knowledge, on the other hand, turns apparent solutions into uncertainties and unsolved problematic situations, and follows an anti-algorithmic path. In contrast to information, knowledge would therefore be definable less by the brevity or the givenness of results, data, effects, or facts, but rather by those lengthy procedures and pathways that follow a work of exploration along the lines of foundational questions, that follow the track of "irreduction" and modes of continuous problematizing. Information is knowledge minus evidence and justification, but knowledge itself is committed to the uncertain outcome of vetting procedures. The end of giving grounds or reasons can only result from abstaining from giving further grounds or reasons. Experts, as Robert Musil once said, "never get to the end of anything."[43]

3

Platforms

The state of the current financial regime is thus characterized by the convergence of two lines of development. On the one hand, the reorganization of financial markets since the 1970s and the financialization of the world economy had led to a dominance of financial-economic cycles of reproduction, the effects and consequences of which cannot be grasped in purely economic terms. In the nexus of political institutions, international organizations, globally operating corporations, and market processes, a transgovernmental power had formed that intervenes directly in the decision-making processes of governments, societies, and economies without regard to nation-state borders. Yet the very crisis policies of the years after 2007 had proved to be not an interruption but an exacerbation of a long-term trend. They consolidated a financial system whose inherent instability could be compensated for by a redistribution of burdens and by the robust development and exploitation of socioeconomic resources.

On the other hand, this transition from a government-based to a market-based financial system would not have been possible without the informatization of capital markets. Under the conditions of electronic and digital media, a fusion of financial transactions, stock-market trading, information theory, and communications technologies has taken place. A process that today is still rather inadequately termed "digitalization" is characterized by more than just the transformation of analog values into digital formats and the diffusion of such technologies into all possible social, political, and economic spheres. First of all, notorious changes in modes of production and communication, in corporate structures and management, in ownership and labor relations had to be addressed here. But apart from this, global digitalization effects are due not least to a mutual entanglement of the financial and information economies and their consolidation that since the 1980s has led to the expansion of the financial sector and the hegemony of finance (or financial-market) capitalism.

Moreover, a policy of low key interest rates and cheap money had created favorable opportunities for value extraction in recent decades, contributing to cyclical momentum in financial, real estate, and technology markets. Here we have a situation in which the volume of circulating money and the expansion of capital markets have become decoupled both from investment in the industrial sector and from the dynamics of economic growth, and in which rising rates of profit have, in general, confronted declining rates of investment.[1] And precisely such a situation was bound to raise the question of as yet untapped sources of value creation or the production of surplus value, and hence of how to overcome the limits of capitalist expansion. Against this backdrop, the informatization of the financial sector and the financialization of the information economy have finally created the preconditions for the establishment and imposition of business models for which the title of an "Internet" or "platform economy" has been circulating for some time.

The name of the company was already emblematic. By the end of the 1990s, *Priceline* had not merely become a synonym for "name your own price" and thus for a patented auction model with which potential buyers of airline tickets could voice their price ideas for such tickets via an Internet platform and then receive suitable offers from airlines for previously unused seats on the desired routes. Rather, the example of the Internet company Priceline.com, founded in 1997, dealt with the intricate question of how exactly this pricing as a business might relate to the valuation of the business model itself. Equipped with professional expertise from a wide variety of industries, ranging from the advertising industry to media, finance, and technology companies all the way to Hollywood, this question was posed in a particularly urgent manner in March 1999, when the company prepared for its own launch on Nasdaq. This followed the example of a series of exceedingly auspicious IPOs, such as those of American Online, Yahoo!, or eBay. On the one hand, at the opening party, which was held with the charm of a glamorous high-school ball in Manhattan, interested investors were promised a revolutionary corporate program that, financed by the investment bank Morgan Stanley and operated with a staff of fewer than two hundred people, would overturn not only the business of airline tickets, but possibly also the trade in automobiles, mortgages, insurance, financial services, real estate, hotel rooms, or even the rest of the world of goods: an homage to the new idol of "disruption." On the other hand, Priceline had been forced to sell the said tickets below cost until now and, in combination with development and advertising costs and the issuing of stock options to airlines, the company had incurred a loss of $114 million in 1998 alone. And what's more, the prospectus, the document that corporations are required to file with the US Securities and Exchange Commission (SEC) for an initial public offering, included the following warnings, written in all caps: "We are not profitable and expect to continue to incur losses," "[o]ur business model is novel and unproven," "[o]ur brand may not achieve the broad recognition necessary to succeed," and "[w]e may be unable to meet our future capital requirements."[2] So the difficult question remained: How was one actually to achieve stock-market profits while announcing failure and registering flagrant losses, with more expected?

In any case, on the morning of March 30, 1999, at the start of Nasdaq trading, an event was triggered whose momentum simply outstripped the series of older cases. Ten million shares of Priceline.com, which were initially to be offered for between seven and nine dollars each, came onto the market at a value of sixteen dollars each, quickly rose to a price of 85 dollars and, at the close of trading on the same day, were quoted at 68 dollars each, i.e., a plus of 425%. This gave the company a capitalization of nearly ten billion dollars, exceeding the combined stock value of United, Continental, and Northwestern Airlines. Moreover, just a few weeks later, Priceline shares ended up trading at $150 apiece, giving the company a valuation higher than the entire US commercial airline industry.

This lofty leap in price cannot be understood merely as the result of a euphoric stock-market boom (complete with "herd instinct") toward the end of the 1990s, which made perplexed commentators reflect on the "absurdity" of the information and pricing mechanisms on the technology exchanges. As the so-called dot-com bubble, it came to a temporary but abrupt end with the collapse of 2000, the market rate of Priceline had then itself crashed by 97% to a price of less than $2 per share.[3] Instead, and much more, Priceline.com and related companies, as well as their IPOs and their business ideas, must be regarded as outstanding examples of why, since the 1990s at the latest, financial experts, investment bankers, venture capitalists, and visionaries of the finance economy have reacted with regard to new Internet and platform companies "excited[ly] about Internet investment opportunities and the performance of the stocks" and at the same time somewhat "nervous[ly] about the valuation levels." One might even see in this a "fundamental change in American capitalism," or at least a time when it was worthwhile to act "rationally reckless" and once again blatantly engage in land grabbing – "a land-grab time."[4]

Even if one had to concede that this new market and its potential would be difficult to assess and define, an extremely efficient fusion between finance capital and new corporate formats seemed to be in the offing here. And these were, at any rate, encouraging prospects for investment companies and venture capital, with which the formation of the Internet moved to the center of finance-capitalist interests and foreshadowed hitherto unknown opportunities for value creation. Venture capital invested in IT, technology, and Internet companies quadrupled between 1996 and 2000; more than 50,000 newly founded companies were financed with more than $256 billion, with the mission to commercialize the Internet; in 1999 and 2000, 80% of venture capital was spent on such projects; between 1997 and 2000, the price of technology stocks gained on average 300%, leading to a market capitalization of $5 trillion. Even the subsequent rise of Chinese platforms such as Alibaba and Tencent owes much to the investment of foreign (including American and Japanese) venture capital and has led to the listings of these companies on Nasdaq.[5] The alliance of Internet and finance has invoked the vision of a new global start-up era and has apparently proved as profitable as it is resilient.

This is all the more surprising, however, since for decades it had been nearly impossible to direct profit interests to emerging network technologies. While stock-exchange businesses had been pushing for the expansion of electronic platforms since the 1970s (cf. pp. 21–22), the computer networks for packet-switched data transmission that had emerged from military research did not initially arouse any investing curiosity. At the end of the 1960s, IBM rejected an offer to equip the ARPANET with computer technology, and a little later, the telecom monopolist AT&T considered participation in the network to be unprofitable. Indeed, no private company at all was tempted to make commercial use of the networks developed between military and academic institutions until after the 1970s. Only after the old ARPANET had been shut down, after software solutions had successfully integrated, standardized, and homogenized diverse network forms into a supernet (for example, through the data formats and protocols HTML, HTTP, HTTPS, and URL), after several hundred billion dollars in public funds had been invested in network technology, and after the National Science Foundation Network (NSFNET) had provided the basis for a universally accessible and rapidly growing network structure, did the private management and operation of these public resources gradually become attractive. In the early 1990s, the first little-noticed proposals and working papers for privatizing the Internet emerged; the restrictions on NSFNET, which specialized in "research and education," were relaxed and its data lines were opened to private Internet service providers. After secret negotiations between the government and private companies, the Telecommunications Act of 1996 was finally passed in the US, pursuing deregulation of the American telecommunications market and delivering the coup de grâce to the public domain of network communications. Privatization led to the concentration of market power and re-regulation in favor of the interests of large corporations; the contemporary Internet was born not with the development of network technologies but with the transformation of public services into capitalist corporate structures (cf. pp. 87–93 below). This turn of events has also given rise to the genre of eulogies and funeral orations with which older net activists continue to lament the loss of once cherished hopes for democracy in network societies.[6]

The genealogy of the Internet thus does not go straight back to a military-industrial institution born of the Cold War; rather, it traces a line that stretches from financial markets and stock-exchange transactions to shadow banking and over-the-counter trading, from electronic and computer-based trading systems to the privatization of information technology infrastructures. On the one hand, it has been possible to demonstrate that the essential building blocks of hardware and software in the field of information or Internet technology – from the first network projects to touch screens, from Internet protocols to microprocessors, from operating systems to email programs – emerged from military spending and government subsidies for academic and semiprivate research; and the business success of so-called venture capitalists from Silicon Valley in particular stemmed not least from the fact that they invested in the now market-ready technologies from a safe distance and often decades later. Such developments have confounded the notorious legends with which a heroically minded capitalist spirit has always tried to convince itself and others of the adventurous momentum of its investments, of its bold promotion of technological novelties, and of the subtlety of its financial-economic support for the incredible inventiveness of garage startups. Like other market settings in the history of capitalism, the digital and Internet market was prepared, shaped, and prevailed with the support of great political energies, and the story of the emergence of digital networks must therefore be corrected somewhat and told as a variation on that plot that moves from socialized investment risks to privatized returns.[7]

On the other hand, it was the occupation of pre-existing digital networks by finance capital that first enabled the emergence and expansion of the contemporary Internet. The robust privatization of network architectures has created the preconditions for the interests of finance and stock markets to be directly reflected in the formats of technology and Internet companies, and it is probably this alliance of finance capital and information in the so-called platform industries that has contributed significantly to the most recent mutation of finance capitalism, starting in the 1990s. On the one hand, this mutual affection is about a common preference for brokerage and intermediary services, with which – on financial markets as well as on digital platforms – techniques, procedures, and intermediary infrastructures are organized to create value between supplies and demands of all kinds. For not only do financial products share with other digital goods the materiality of software-driven data objects, with data brokers active in both cases, both finance and the Internet industry rely equally on algorithmic market operations.

Thus, it could be shown that both markets are structured by products characterized by unlimited scalability, easy distribution, and nonrivalry (i.e., lack of scarcity). The auction procedures by which, for example, advertising space, search terms, and linguistic material are auctioned and priced in the first place at Google are similar to the operations that determine the pricing and marketing of financial derivatives. Something similar holds for the algorithms that automate the prediction of demand trends at Amazon or the behavioral forecasting at Facebook, and the "viral" distribution of content follows the operations of high-frequency trading.[8] On the other hand, finance and platform companies are linked by relationships of historical filiation and common growth dynamics. If indeed the origin of platform businesses can be traced back to the logic of finance and stock-exchange trading,[9] this is not least due to the business models with which the digital economy provided finance capital. These models provided finance capital not only with new resources and opportunities for expansion, but above all with support in the securing and stabilizing of hegemonic structures.

Let us take the temporary success of Priceline.com as an example or emblem of what will later, above and beyond all differences, also constitute a common denominator of companies such as Google, Amazon, Facebook, Apple, Uber, Airbnb, TaskRabbit, and Foodora. On this assumption, a first financial-economic attraction of platform and Internet companies lies in the outsourcing of costs associated with the maintenance and the worrisome overhead of all varieties of fixed capital. This involves the material resistance of those constant varieties of capital that are characterized by wear, tear, and by finite lifespans in general. It is the egg of Columbus of platform businesses that one can offer car trips without owning vehicles, accommodations without owning real estate, room maintenance without cleaning buckets, meals without kitchen furnishings, or air travel without maintaining and operating aircraft. At most, there is a need for oversight of how so-called "independent contractors" maintain and monitor their own, usually modest, fixed capital themselves. It is precisely, in fact, the abandonment of the means of production (embodied by this fixed capital) that has contributed to the miraculous magnitudes by which the market or stock-market value of Priceline, Uber, or Airbnb has outstripped that of traditional businesses such as airlines, BMW, or Hilton Worldwide.[10]

But it is not only the fact that platform businesses, like financial markets, could be said to enjoy equally low levels of friction and high levels of information efficiency, as well as significant reductions in transaction and opportunity costs.[11] The production of notorious network effects represented another attraction for investors from the financial sector. These effects consist in the fact that users, directly or indirectly, generate more users, and that on platforms an increasing number of users produces increasing numbers of further users. Thus, these users, as it were, yield interest and, by way of positive feedback effects, follow the power law and produce exponential curves – the favorite diagram of such companies. Moreover, networks with linear growth of nodes exhibit nonlinear or convex growth curves of links. This ideally pierces or eliminates barriers to growth and minimizes marginal costs. To manage additional cab rides or accommodations, it is no longer necessary to expand the vehicle fleet or the real estate portfolio, but only one's computer capacities (although the stimulation of business sometimes makes it expedient to simulate growth oneself and, as with Uber, to have phantom cabs drive around).[12] Marginal costs tend toward zero. Ultimately, we are dealing here with effects that economists have identified as a specialty of platform businesses and as a special version of "economies of scale." Such effects occur in industrial mass production on the supply side and enable, for example, costs to fall as production numbers rise, resulting in competitive advantages. Conversely, platform economies in information networks are characterized by "*demand* economies of scale,"[13] by effects, in other words, with which user activities increase the utility of such activities within the platforms and reinforce the effectiveness of pull factors and inclusionary forces.

On the one hand, this favors dynamics in which network effects produce highly concentrated market structures and these, in turn, produce further network effects. For this reason, platform and Internet companies are said to have an intrinsic, quasi-natural tendency to form monopolies or oligopolies. This was particularly evident after the slumps of 2000 and 2008, which triggered, in addition to market adjustments, a wave of mergers and acquisitions. In an environment of cheap money and low interest rates, they supplemented the financial and real estate booms with a technology boom and, moreover, led to the market-dominating positions of corporations such as Apple, Alphabet, Facebook, and Amazon. (Since 2012, Google, i.e., Alphabet Inc., has acquired on average a company a week.)[14] This has probably also created a feedback or echo chamber in which a change in capitalist mentality is beginning to emerge, especially in the United States. Here we find surprising pronouncements that hold against the old liberal fetish of competition the new libertarian blessing for the monopolist: "Start small and monopolize" (Peter Thiel). According to this, the departure from the "delirious chaos of ... competition" – as with Google – benefits the "concern" for workers, products, and the "world" as a whole. Indeed, precisely because the existence of one's own company is no longer endangered by troublesome competitors, one can commit oneself to a "moral" upswing in which "monopoly profits" free one from the "struggle for survival" and mere "money-making." With a "handful of monopolists," the disruptions of capitalism now become truly "creative," ultimately forming a progressive social force.[15] For good capitalists competition was always a burdensome and annoying affair better left to others – smaller businesses or wage earners. In the same way, blunt language from the hearts or character masks of these new industries expresses an inclination toward the rule of a new monopoly capital that with the recent "creative disruptions" does not mean the demise of capitalism, but its continued existence. Or, to put it differently and directly: "Actually, capitalism and competition are opposites. Capitalism is premised on the accumulation of capital, but under perfect competition all profits get competed away."[16]

On the other hand, it is precisely these promises of growth and market dominance that have lured investing finance capital and seduced it into those alliances in which IPOs are not used to finance profitable companies, but, quite the opposite, companies are used to finance profitable IPOs. As was well-rehearsed during the dot-com boom, this initially involves short-term investments of venture capital and private equity as well as the creation of portfolio companies by means of which quick profit payouts or exit profits can be made in accelerated IPOs, especially on Nasdaq. The interest in selling services or products takes a back seat to the inclination to fuel gains in share prices (and has made entrepreneurial mirages like Wirecard AG[17] first possible). This follows the guiding principle of growth before profit (*get big fast*). Questionable or nonexistent profitability plays little role here. (Uber's cab rides have been just as loss-making so far as Amazon Prime's delivery services, not least because of high advertising costs.) What drives the market value of companies is the hope of so-called disruptions and "monster markets," that is, the prospects of monopolistically or oligopolistically subverting expanding markets with tumultuous and destructive entries into them. It is no coincidence that in the fourth quarter of 1999, for example, 97% of the revenues of typical dot-com companies was spent on sales and marketing. Investments in advertising and marketing, when maximizing branding and mind share by generating attention and popularity, are intended to generate the promise of maximized market shares, in order to then fuel market valuations with these promises. Here, too, the tendency is to leave the valuation of companies solely to opinion markets, brand awareness, and marketing-based asset valuation models.[18] If the latest examples of the capitalist "law of increasing firm size"[19] can be discerned in this, dynamics of market capitalization and value extraction are also being forced by practices that have been evident since the 1980s in general, and later in technology and Internet companies in particular. It is a matter of provoking such price increases with large-scale share buybacks, a practice that economists have been unable to avoid labeling as anything other than consistent price manipulation.[20] Companies such as Microsoft, Intel, and Cisco, for example, spent about $112 billion between 2000 and 2007 on so-called research and development, but $167 billion on the repurchase of their own shares: an attractive spectacle for the gilded eyes of shareholders and investors and an indication of the irresistible propensity with which finance capital is attracted to these markets by the increase in finance capital.

However, other strategies and means of externalizing avoidable costs attract particular financial economic attention. This concerns, first, the notorious procedures of tax avoidance. Unlike manufacturing industries, technology and Internet firms, much like financial institutions, do not need to transfer cumbersome hardware such as factory equipment, but usually only easily movable intellectual property or intangible items, across borders in order to establish themselves in zones with favorable tax laws. According to the US Securities and Exchange Commission (SEC) filing of March 2016, for example, Apple has 92.8% (or $200.1 billion), Google 58.7% (i.e., $42.9 billion), and Amazon still some 36.9% ($18.3 billion) of its capital reserves parked offshore and with foreign subsidiaries. Between 2008 and 2014 alone, the volume of foreign assets held by companies in the US already increased by 25% to a total of about $7.6 trillion. Moreover, in times of cheap money, it is more profitable to finance investments with debt rather than with the repatriation of foreign capital together with the corporate taxes due on it.[21]

In the case of platform companies in particular, simple transactions therefore turn out to be complex but efficient events that pursue a cross-border shifting of profits (in OECD jargon: "base erosion" or "profit shifting") and are usually indebted to the outdated state of tax legislation for internationally operating corporations. A meticulous and exemplary examination of Uber's business in Belgium, for example, revealed the following typologically relevant payment movements. To simplify somewhat, if you use an Uber app for a ride there, you do not come into contact with any employee or representative of the company; instead, the payment is automatically processed through a Dutch subsidiary (Uber B. V. in Amsterdam), which passes on 80% of the invoice amount due to the Uber driver via another Dutch sister company (Rasier Operations B. V., which is also the contractual partner of the drivers). Of the remaining 20%, Uber B. V. transfers 99% as a license fee to Uber International C. V., again a subsidiary of Uber, which, with its headquarters in Bermuda, is not subject to taxation in either the US or the Netherlands (and is also not subject to taxation on the group of islands in the Atlantic). This means that if the cost of the ride in Belgium is about €50, €40 goes to the driver and €10 to the Dutch subsidiary, which transfers €9.90 to Uber International (Bermuda). This leaves 1% of the revenue, or €0.10, which is then taxed at 25% in the Netherlands. Thus, while the Uber driver, following the lowest income tax rate in Belgium, should pay at least 25% of €40 (i.e., €10) in taxes, 0.025% (or €2.5 cents) of the Uber revenue (i.e., of €10) is paid in taxes in the Netherlands. No taxes, however, are paid in Belgium, because there the mere provision of service is not considered the permanent establishment of a company and is therefore not taxable. In addition, Uber International (Bermuda) was granted the rights to use the intellectual property, that is, the apps, in a contract with Uber Technologies (San Francisco, CA, USA), for which, in turn, royalties of 1.45% per transaction are due to the US American parent company and are only then subject to taxation in the US.[22] The remainder, 98.55% of €9.90 and thus an amount worth approximately €9.76, remains untaxed in the British overseas territory. Or to put it another way: of Uber's total revenue, only 2.4% is declared taxable at all – a tax reprieve that is only enjoyed by licensable data products.

More generally, two financial economic consequences can be linked to such an accumulation of offshore capital, which did, after all, earn Uber a mention in the 2017 Paradise Papers. As Nick Srnicek notes in his study of the economics of "platform capitalism," on the one hand, US technology companies in particular have accumulated huge sums of investment funds through tax avoidance strategies. Combined with low interest rates and loose monetary policy, and with an eye on tidy returns, this was bound to lead to risky financial investments and thus to an increase in systemic risks. On the other hand, the associated loss of tax revenues exacerbates the state of public budgets, restricts the scope of fiscal operations, and compels the adoption of an unorthodox monetary policy. Thus, it seems that platform companies constitute an essential element in the architecture of the current financial regime: "Tax evasion, austerity, and extraordinary monetary policies are all mutually reinforcing."[23] The structure of platform and Internet firms makes the unchallenged siphoning off of profit easier and blocks the intervention of tax policies into the processes of accumulation – a business privilege that makes such firms two-fold crisis winners, especially in light of the financing of the recent pandemic emergencies.

Such fiscal advantages are complemented by structural conditions and operations that guarantee, in platform firms, a hyperexternalization of labor and a systematic extraction of surplus labor, despite the glad tidings from California. The first thing to note is that wage earners are generally not benefiting from the booms of the smart economy and its companies. It proved possible to greatly reduce their employment figures in comparison with other industries and in relation to sales and market value. For example, while the three largest Detroit automakers had 1.2 million employees and a market capitalization of $36 billion in the late 1990s, with revenues of $250 billion, in 2014 the three largest Silicon Valley companies had revenues of $247 billion and a market capitalization of $1.9 trillion, with 137,000 employees. In line with these proportions, WhatsApp, with 55 employees, was sold to Facebook for $19 billion, and Instagram, with thirteen employees, for $1 billion; moreover, Amazon, with just over 800,000 employees, has a market value of $1.2 trillion – a third of Germany's domestic product – as of April 2020.[24] Such numerical ratios are attributable to a consistent outsourcing of labor – completing a trend that has been accelerating since the 1970s. This refers not only to the outsourcing of production sites, such as the notorious Foxconn factory with its low wages in Shenzhen, China, where the Apple group has its gadgets assembled under early capitalist working conditions. It is much more the case that the contraction of regular employment relationships – only 10% of those working for Apple are permanently employed – is based on the architecture of such economic forms. They have created informal, "atypical," or precarious labor markets with freelancers, contractors, and subcontractors. This, in turn, has triggered discussions about whether the staff of this gig economy consists of entrepreneurs, subcontractors, pseudo self-employed, piecework or part-time workers, or simply of day laborers and "disposable workers."[25] In any case, the impressive reduction of labor costs by about 30% is due to the fact that platform companies were able to remove payments for social security, overtime, sick leave, training, occupational injuries, and so on from their ledgers. The labor charter of these companies has proven to be a declaration of independence from those who are dependent on them, from societies and from populations.

Thus, there can be no talk at all here of an often announced "end of work." It is much more the case that the release of those working from permanent working relationships in favor of unstable ones is supplemented by an expansion of opportunities for value extraction. This is something that can be especially exploited in online communications in Web 2.0, by search engines and social media on the Internet. Admittedly, it is debatable whether the random activities of random users on the Net – on websites or platforms, in chat rooms or when microblogging – can correspond to an economically concise concept of work. Nevertheless, it is undeniable that value-creating activities are conducted in this way, more or less unnoticed, whose effects converge, under the conditions of information technology, with the process of a "surplus value" generated by "surplus labor." As much as repeated use increases utility for users and may be felt by those users to have useful "social" advantages, this optimizes just as much the operations of corresponding platform providers (such as their algorithms, decision models, and applications). In profitable platform companies, the costs of the free services offered are inevitably lower than the value added by the input of information from users.[26] The surplus for the users is, of course, exceeded by the surplus generated by the economies of use.

The fact that this is a technically complicated setup of production processes, but one that, in business terms, is as simple as it is striking, has been documented by the successes of corporations such as Google, Facebook, and others, which derive some 90% or more of their revenues from advertising income.[27] The first step is to quantify, aggregate, filter, analyze, and transform the traces of information left by online behavior in such a way that patterns are actually extracted at all from preferences, search queries, appetites, self-presentations, disputes, intimacies, or social contacts. From these patterns, products or goods are then extracted for sale to customers from the advertising industry, who are particularly interested in individually and micrologically addressable campaigns. Along the lines of the older concept of the "prosumer" – referring to the extra work done by the consumer qua producer (for example, in putting together bookshelves sold to them by furniture companies) – the apt neologism "produser" has been introduced for this and related activities. It refers precisely to the production activity performed imperceptibly or incidentally as part of the behavior of users on the Net.

Unlike industrial production, these activities for producing digital content – variously termed "immaterial," "free," or "informational" – are characterized by ubiquitous access and low thresholds of entry, by being informal, occasional, and without temporal or spatial constraints, and by their reference to anything that can be performed online. If activities of this kind, i.e., produsage, can be defined as "the collaborative and continuous building and extending of existing content in pursuit of further improvement,"[28] then the transition from specific producers to random users has become blurred and fluid. In any case, it refers to a value chain at the beginning and end of which there are content or informational artifacts that can be optimized. However, this is not simply a disappearance of "alienated" labor, whereby the Net would have become the preserve for that freedom "to do one thing today and another tomorrow" and to "hunt," "fish," or "criticize" there as one wishes.[29] That this is not the case is guaranteed by barriers or pathways in which older separations of the means of production from the producers are repeated and, if you will, made unrecognizable and sublimated. First of all, one of the pull factors of platforms and social media on the Internet is to nourish worries about the loss of social, economic, or professional advantages, and, more generally, of any and all sorts of opportunities. But apart from this, "extraction architectures" are installed that are designed to accomplish a congruence of surveillance and opportunities for profit by tracking minimal movements, such as clicks or browsing behavior, or the creation of tags or links. To cite a flagrant example, as recently as 2010 it was discovered that when the Google Toolbar was used for searches directly from one's browser, all URL data, including search paths, websites called up, and searches on competing search engines, were transmitted to Google. This tracking function, moreover, could no longer be disabled, not even by turning it off.[30]

Let us take this as an example and as a micro-model for the procedures of produsage in general. In this way, it provides, on the one hand, information about the nature of the associated production processes and products. For when the activities of users of all kinds are tracked and transformed into data, these effects, contrary to the literal meaning of "datum," are not simply a "given." Instead, under the technical conditions of Web 2.0 and platform communications, all data produced by the trackable online activities of the entire network population should be understood as data that has always already been extracted, as metadata, and thus as relational objects in which data is already correlated and collated with other data and lends itself to further processing.[31] Users, produsers, and produsage produce data extraction and, if one has repeatedly spoken of raw products or raw materials in view of such products, this has to be understood in a strict, economic sense: as an "object of labor" that "has undergone some alteration by means of labor," as an object of labor already "filtered through labor,"[32] as a means of production that has itself been produced (through user activities). Users produce what corporations sell.

On the other hand, the value creation associated with these operations owes much to the construction of a strict information asymmetry, in which the multiplication of low-threshold information offerings to users, such as maps, street views, navigation aids, databases, libraries, communication services, and so on, is combined with a strict barrier to access to the informational goods fabricated by users. Information is a nonrivalrous good and, unlike other goods, is not consumed or made scarce by consumption or use. For this reason, its commodity form must be safeguarded by the deliberate production of scarcity and precisely by protecting collected information or data from the data sources themselves. In a legal battle involving countless lawsuits and a fierce degree of advocacy, data refineries such as Google have so far been able to defend themselves against breaches of this protective wall and thus against an endangerment of their own operating model. Behind a screen of seemingly open and heterarchical relationships, the network is "arborized" or hierarchized by the business of platform and Internet companies, transformed into strictly and hierarchically ordered tree structures. Anyone who surfs around on the Internet, for example, and in the process practices what former Google boss Eric Schmidt prompts us to call "customer satisfaction," is thus separated *not only* from the means of production (the companies' hardware and software) and the means of production thereby produced (the raw materials produced by his or her activities, i.e., the data or metadata). *More importantly*, the associated production process itself remains consistently beyond his or her reach, hidden, inaccessible, and opaque. Such persons find themselves in the economically interesting position of having possibly done no work at all, but having nevertheless imperceptibly or unconsciously carried out "surplus labor." Thus, a confiscation of temporal resources takes place that cannot be measured in countable quantities of surplus labor and is, in a strict sense, both immeasurable and excessive. One could speak here of the siphoning off of a behavioral surplus value, of a vital quantum, or of the effectiveness of a "laboring unconscious" under network conditions. And it is therefore not surprising that it is precisely the investing financial industry that exerts pressure on platform companies like Google to increase the "effectiveness" of the monitoring, tracing, and tracking procedures installed.[33] In the process, older and clear-sighted demands made by an "economic imperialism" that individuals manage or capitalize their time have been realized in a surprising way. As early as the 1960s, Gary Becker pointed out, against the backdrop of long-term increases in labor productivity and shrinking workweeks, that with the inclusion of human capital, "the allocation and efficiency of non-working time may now be more important to economic welfare than that of working time" itself. In other words, it is a matter of setting such incentives that the difference between labor and leisure time becomes economically irrelevant.[34] Working time never ends.

With the informatization of the finance economy, but also with the occupation of the information economy by finance, current "digital" or "information capitalism"[35] has arguably become the latest iteration of finance (or financial-market) capitalism. While the transformation of financial markets since the 1970s created the economic conditions for the development of Internet firms, the establishment and privatization of the Internet opened up new opportunities for finance capital that inspired fruitful structural alliances between finance and the platform economy. This has several consequences. The outsourcing of the expense of maintaining fixed capital and labor; the minimization of transaction, opportunity, and marginal costs; self-reinforcing network effects; a tendency toward monopoly; and intensified value extraction have initially suggested that with the appearance of the platform economy, there has not only been an apparent commercialization of once public domains and goods, but also the most recent surge of "primitive accumulation." Here it should be recalled that Hannah Arendt, following Rosa Luxemburg, had already taken the term coined by Marx out of its historical and systematic context. There it had been a one-time predatory act and "fall from grace" in the transition to the capitalist mode of economy. Arendt, however, applied it to the aggressive approaches used for resolving recurring crises of accumulation. Just as in other historical cases, here it was a matter of creating new opportunities for exploiting the constant "production of excess capital" (such as the opportunities offered to nineteenth-century imperialism).[36] In the same manner, in light of the repeated or steady-state financial crises of recent decades, the problem has again arisen: how can the immanent limits of capital accumulation be overcome and the realization of surplus value (together with the dynamics of the system) be guaranteed by expansion into as yet unexploited territories or reserves?

Against this background, the technological and financial-economic architecture of platform companies in particular has enabled a production of surplus value that combines external and internal "land grabs," that is, external and internal access to entities that have not yet been commodified.[37] On the one hand, the current geo-economic order is characterized by a juxtaposition of different modes of production, in which the latest methods of capital accumulation are intertwined with archaic procedures of exploitation. For instance, before one can put one's hands on a smartphone with the latest operating system from a quasi-monopolist in California (which will later be disposed of as electronic scrap in Ghana or Nigeria), a dozen different minerals from various continents must be procured and processed. For example, cobalt from the Democratic Republic of Congo is mined, sometimes with child labor, and sometimes under the coercion of militias or criminal gangs. It is then shipped via smelter industries in India, Malaysia, or Thailand to manufacturing plants for the assembly of the devices under ruthless working conditions, for instance, in China.[38] It characterizes the current state of capitalist production that it is able to organize a simultaneity of the non-simultaneous, coordinating different historical stages of value extraction as in a diagram.

On the other hand, with the platform economy and the production of informational goods, finance capitalist expansion has progressed to an internal land grab, to the management of new social resources. What has been called in this context, following David Harvey, "accumulation by dispossession" or "digital dispossession" does not only concern the separation of the producers or users from the means of production of the Internet and platform companies. Rather, with the forms of produsage, regions previously unoccupied and not yet shaped by markets have been seized and incorporated into the capitalization process. Previously, new zones of human and social capital were opened up under the financialization of the economy: for example, through the privatization of public infrastructures, social systems, or pension and preventative services of all kinds. Now, in a similar way, the production of raw data material has transformed everyday online behavior and modes of communication (as well as other remnants of economic wastelands such as street routes, house views, or movement patterns) into the source of a permanent extraction of surplus value.[39]

Even if the business models of the information and platform industry can only be understood under the condition of financial-market (or finance) capitalism, it must nevertheless be conceded that the technology sector (from computer production to telecommunications to information services) can report high growth rates and a rapidly increasing market capitalization, approaching the market size of the finance and insurance sector. However, the sector itself accounts for only a small part of total economic activity and represents, for example, just under 7% of value added by private companies and 2.5% of the workforce in the US.[40] Its significance can therefore not be measured by a sectoral analysis alone. Rather, its importance lies in the fact that its products and effects cross all economic and social, public and private spheres and thus ensure the governmental effectiveness of information or finance capitalism. If the question is "of knowing how far the market economy's powers of political and social information extend"[41] under the regime of finance, then the associated claim to hegemony can be understood as the realization of a previously announced program of the new "control societies" (Gilles Deleuze). At the end of the 1980s this could at best be discerned only in its broad outlines. Mutations were recognized in which processes of financialization and informatization were linked with a crisis of the milieus of enclosure, an erosion of institutional entities, a reign of the short-term and of a multifaceted zeal for reform. These processes were further linked with a logic of modulation and the replacement of borders by passwords, with breathing factories, soulful enterprises, and a refined control of open spaces.[42] The new control societies have now become concrete in the operations of the platform industry. As control is capitalized, what is at stake is nothing less than the consequences that changing corporate structures and business models have on governance.

4

Control Power

Thus, the consolidation of the financial regime through the platform industry cannot be understood solely as an economic event. Rather, the economization of information owes much to the ability of digital technologies to guarantee a mutual convertibility of power and capital and, with the expansion of business sectors, to tap into the productive forces of new technologies of governance. In his study critiquing digital capitalism, Philipp Staab made important reference to these interconnections and identified in the emergence of "proprietary markets" an essential linchpin for the expansion of information-economic forms of power. Just as the financialization of the world economy was a reaction to growth weaknesses and accumulation crises since the 1970s, the current setup of leading companies in digital capitalism – for example, Google, Apple, Facebook, or Amazon – has emerged from increasing market saturation, from the shocks of 2000 and 2007/2008, and from a symbiosis with the financial industry. Their setup is also a response to the problem of capitalizing nonrivalrous, nonscarce goods, that is, to the question of how the general availability of information products produced at minimal marginal cost can be profitably made scarcer. Unlike the monopoly firms of industrial capitalism, the new digital monopolists do not operate in markets; rather, they become integrated into the existing economic and financial order by establishing themselves as markets, much as the brokerage of private electronic exchanges and trading platforms once generated and institutionalized specific financial markets.

In the process, as a result of replication and proliferation, diverse business practices have become more and more similar. There is a tendency for data-generating applications to proliferate and permeate the entire operational field, from software to hardware, to the supplying of the analog world. Search engines are expanding into hardware manufacturing, e-commerce and financial markets; mail-order companies are operating search engines, clouds, and banking; smartphone manufacturers are entering the market with streaming or financial services, while social media are in turn offering data, information, and financial products and dabbling in payment systems. However, these are precisely the products and services being used to sell infrastructures and thus dependencies, and the resulting "sociotechnical ecosystems" or "meta-platforms" are characterized by the fact that they structure the commercial Internet as a system of hierarchized markets. These companies have pursued aggressive expansion strategies, continuously broadened the spectrum of their offerings through investments and acquisitions, and achieved a broad inclusion of users and consumers through network effects. They mediate between producers and consumers, they generate and manage competition, and they generate income from commissions, and from granting and controlling market access. They therefore operate not in a value-creating but in a value-extracting way, generating profits as rents as do financial markets; they can achieve a progressive "expansion of market function" with insignificant marginal costs through the combination of "proprietary infrastructure" and scalable digital goods. In short:

> The leading companies of the commercial Internet are not so much producers operating in markets as markets in which producers operate. This is largely what feeds their power. As market owners, they watch over who gets access to the market in growing areas of the economy and under what conditions this occurs ...[1]

In the process, the introduction of power structures on the commercial Internet is guaranteed above all by an expansion, differentiation, and intensification of various controls on information. These controls generate those asymmetries that ensure the scarcity of nonscarce informational goods. These include data controls: the extraction and appropriation of user, seller, and market data; access controls on market participation, which relate to the exclusion of competition and to the variation of gateways and thresholds for producers and consumers, suppliers, and users; associated price controls, ranging from the prioritization of one's own offerings to product copying and to the personalization of purchasing prices; and finally, performance controls, which install continuous evaluation and assessment procedures on products, services, and work processes. Platform companies thus prove to be standardized techno-economic systems that centrally control the decentralized coordination of interfaces distributed in a network-like way. The machine operations linked to them, such as tracking, tracing, targeting, ranking, scoring, mapping, and profiling, can be understood as elements of an algorithmic management that transforms the mass of communication events on the platforms into patterns and sorts them, for example, according to significant frequencies, relationship densities, trends, or expected trajectories.[2] While liberal market theories have been grappling with solving and remedying problems of asymmetric information distribution in markets since the 1970s, here we have just the opposite case: the systematic production of such informational asymmetries. With the business strategies of platform companies, control over information and markets has become a defining productive force, reinforcing that geo-economic order that is characterized less by competing corporations than by "bundled strategies"[3] of solvent financial investors.

The proprietary markets of the platform industry thus have nothing to do with the liberal model of allegedly neutral markets, which one sought to regard as subjects of superior knowledge and which were to be approached by market participants with gestures of humility. In addition to quite dramatic economic and political interventions such as the private appropriation of transmission networks or the abolition of net neutrality in the US at the end of 2017, some systemic, technological, and structural moments have enabled and guided the specific methods of control used by platform companies. Just as for Norbert Wiener, communication and control in a technological sense were already two sides of the same coin, an intrinsic, nonarbitrary connection between decentralized digital networks and control can first be noted at the micro-technical level of machine operations. This applies, for example, to the way in which digital Internet protocols operate. In other words, it applies to those ensembles of rules and regulations that govern the connections and information flows between individual – human or nonhuman – agents within networks. Here they guarantee smooth data transfer, the encoding and decoding of information packets, and a universal and uniform network standard. Protocols operate at the level of code, ensuring the translation of immaterial numerical information into the materiality of signals. With protocols, the network becomes an information-processing machine and information itself becomes the agent, executor, and substance of network communication.

In a distributed network, where there are neither centers nor satellites and all nodes are supposed to communicate with each other, two "protocological" operations are combined that, in technological terms, are, according to Alexander Galloway, opposed to one another. On the one hand, at the level of transmissions and Internet protocols (i.e., at the level of the Transmission Control Protocol [TCP] and IP), monitoring or control power (*Kontrollleistung*) is distributed to autonomous local sites, thus enabling "rhizomatic," non-hierarchical network communication – from endpoint to endpoint, and from computer to computer. On the other hand, at the level of address management, as in the assignment of network addresses and network names in the so-called Domain Name System (DNS), strictly defined and tree-like hierarchies are introduced, whose databases are stored on a few, mostly private, root name servers, located, at least initially, primarily in the US. Thus, when working through the various and nested protocol layers in protocol-like steps: from the dimension of the application, through the levels of transport and addressing in the Internet, to transmission in physical media, transmission processes are directly linked to various, flat and hierarchical, horizontal and vertical control operations. This suggests the following theses: That the instances of control and command in network communications are not external, but intrinsic, endogenous, and thus co-active; that as networks become more decentralized, those control procedures that guarantee the network's function as a network also increase in volume; that the effectiveness of decentralized control manifests itself in the logic and structure of protocols; and, finally, that increased data traffic also accumulates control processes.[4] The functioning of digital protocols is thus not merely a matter of arbitrary and external control of distributive networks. Protocols can rather be understood, in Bruno Latour's terminology, as "inscriptions" with which information is made mobile, stable, and combinable as "immutable mobiles."[5] The forces of decentralization, opening, networking, and self-organization themselves become a controlling program.

"Control," derived from the French *contre-rôle*, a "counter-role" or a "counter-register" for checking in an original register or for administrative comparison with existing items, initially means nothing more than the continuous checking and safeguarding of individual work steps. In contrast, the core of a special and new variety in the microphysics of power can already be noted with the technological arrangement mentioned above. According to this, the control power (*Kontrollmacht*) would not be characterized simply by superordination and subordination, nor by centralization or panoptic architectures. It should not be confused at this technical level with simple surveillance. Derived from cybernetic control programs, it is rather measured by the success of transmission processes, by the logistical solution of transmission tasks in general, and is articulated in a communicative imperative: with digital protocols, improbable communications are not only made possible and probable, but directly determined; and with the dictate against *not communicating*, with the release and increase of network activities, abilities for flexible adaptation to open milieus and to contingency are produced, as well as greater leeway for mobility. At the same time, however, those surpluses of control are produced which make possible an administration of addresses, the organization of multiplicities, a coordination of the heterogeneous, and a standardization based on procedural rules. Implicit in the concept of control is the expansion of communicative free spaces through networking; it is defined as a calculable distrust in the success of network operations; and the technical setup of the Internet installs communication, connectivity, compatibility, and interactivity *as* control.

That these are political technologies in the strict sense of the word, which offer a linchpin for asymmetrical distributions of power, is already suggested by the episodic and exemplary disputes that arose, for example, in the allocation of IP addresses in the Domain Name System. The policy of the California-based Internet Corporation for Assigned Names and Numbers (ICANN), which develops Web standards and coordinates the allocation of IP addresses as a non-profit organization alongside other bodies, has been beset by a number of critical issues since its foundation in the late 1990s and following the privatization of the Internet. These issues included unclear relationships with US governmental authorities, the balance between business mandates and social concerns, or the different relationship to the public and private, sponsored and unsponsored Top Level Domains (TLPs, i.e., the highest level of the address name such as .com or .uk). They also included the geographical location of root servers, funding issues, and the international composition of the Board of Directors, along with the more or less democratic procedures for electing them. Here IP addresses have turned out to be scarce or disputed commodities, and the allocation of country-specific codes has proved to involve eminently political decisions. In 2002, for example, when a member of the Board of Directors took legal action to force the publication of annual reports, the elected directors were simply removed, leaving the impression that more is known about the conclave that elects the Pope in Rome than about ICANN's internal decision-making processes.[6]

If the political and polemics-generating dimension of network architectures is already manifest in such disputes, then the protocological arrangement of the Internet itself can be understood as an "abstract machine" for the production of control codes, which are concretized in the various economic, political, and social structures of the control society. This abstract machine links coding processes with material flows and sets up positive feedback loops between extensive use/communication and control; it operates below the visible levels of application and, as a machine unconscious, as it were, is not perceptible as a restriction on communicative latitude. In this context, what Gilles Deleuze and Félix Guattari once called abstract machines are neither to be understood as transcendent ideas nor as the base or ideological superstructure of societal forms. Rather, they can be understood as potentials or capacities that realize themselves under certain conditions – though never completely – and thus align and structure the manifold of social forms. They proceed with selective and combinatorial procedures, they select and pave the way for the assembly of concrete machines, they simultaneously establish functional interconnections between disparate techniques and institutions, and in this way traverse the social field as a whole. Panopticism, for example, could be understood as an abstract machine of older disciplinary societies that coordinates individuals and masses and, through institutional formats, creates "a cartography that is coextensive with the whole social field."[7] Abstract machines install themselves as a program for the collection, formation, and updating of heterogeneous social forces.

Therefore, as little as the logic of the abstract machine of control societies should be confused with concrete, spatio-temporal exercises of power – such as observation, tracing, or surveillance – it is not power-neutral itself and, as a political machine, has sorted out specific affinities and alliances: it functions as a "distributed management system that [inserts] control within a heterogeneous material milieu." One of the founders of network and protocol technology, Tim Berners-Lee, had already noted an analogy between networks and market economies: "[i]n a market economy, anybody can trade with anybody."[8] Indeed, it is precisely the particular achievements with which digital protocols have driven the expansion of global networks by means of universality, homogenization, normalization, and standardization of codes, and a leveling of content, that reveal perfect conditions for market structures under information standards. This suggests that it was the technological infrastructure of the Internet that enabled the privileging of new economic dynamics, as happened at the nexus of web technology and financial markets or at the intersection of digital networks and platform economies. The commercialization of the Internet since the 1990s has thus not only led to a mutual reinforcement of communication processes and market forces, but above all has forced network architecture to adopt to the control structures of the most recent forms of capital.

It was only in the socioeconomic milieu of proprietary markets and the business models of platform companies that the synchronicity of communication and control gave rise to the form of concrete machines in which informational goods are then simultaneously produced as efficient surveillance products. This is true for the advertising business of search engines and social networks as well as for the centralization of data extraction in cloud platforms or for the recording of payment flows through payment systems. It should be noted that such surveillance goods are not distributed through coercive measures but through "control contracts," in exchange for benefits, gratifications, and rewards, with cost-free services and applications of all kinds, from navigation apps to infection warnings. The watchword of control is its voluntary character. In this context it could be termed, somewhat pointedly, "surveillance capitalism" and is characterized by governmental efficiency and even behavioral programming procedures. However, this "surveillance capitalism" has produced, not least of all, those private–public interdependencies that are embodied, for example, in the seamless transitions between technical, business, and official strategies of control. The ties between intelligence agencies, ministries, and the military or health authorities, on the one hand, and platform companies such as search engines, social media, and mail-order companies, on the other, range from the founding of joint startups to paid search assignments, direct sponsorship, data analysis, and data exchange, all the way to contracts for the use of private cloud services, ties that are supplemented by informal agreements and arrangements. These collaborations and alliances are well documented,[9] and alongside of Google, Amazon Web Services, Apple or Facebook, a particularly significant example is perhaps represented by the software company Palantir Technologies. Founded in 2003, it took its fantasy-inspired name from the "seeing stones" in Tolkien's *The Lord of the Rings*, and exemplifies like no other organization the modular transitions between finance or information industries, security services, and state authorities. Financed by private investors, venture capital, and the CIA, it works with the financial industry and with media companies (such as Thomson Reuters), with US intelligence agencies and immigration authorities, with public health departments in the US and UK, and with police forces from the US all the way to Hesse or North Rhine-Westphalia in Germany. It provides data analyses that relate, among other things, to pattern recognition and software glitches, to the prediction of stock-market trends, purchasing behavior, epidemics, terrorist actions, or crime in general.[10] As little as such customer orders, transactions, and linkages can be attributed to any particular sector – public or private – as much do they document, in exemplary manner, the ways in which the governance control functions of the information and finance industries permeate the social field. Unlike the older "panoptic" disciplines, which related to the contours and boundaries of compact institutions such as factories, schools, asylums, hospitals, or prisons, the most recent processes of control can only be grasped through functional de-differentiation. They organize connections or couplings that cut across and beyond multiple institutions, subsystems, or sectors, shaping in this way business domains that range from security services to health policy, from financial products to education, from science to military reconnaissance, from policing to marketing.

If the recent capitalist land grab by platform companies was accompanied by the establishment of new governance structures and an intensification of control practices, the convergence and success of these processes were, however, only guaranteed by the opening up and occupation of areas with little or no legal regulation. One could argue that existing legislation, from tax and labor law to copyright and media law, at best met the standards of older industrial capitalism and failed to reflect the current relations between Internet technology, information goods, providers, and users. The rapid development and expansion of the information industry has, according to common wisdom, simply outrun the protracted attempts at legal and democratic adaptation, and the new corporate strategies have themselves relied on the erosion and thinning of legal regulation. In the US in particular, the relentless liberalist attacks on "authoritarian," "tyrannical," or "dictatorial" state restrictions on postwar capitalist commerce were a precondition for the most recent transformation of corporate structures, and they were supplemented in the 1990s by a number of initiatives and by arguably the "most important law" to empower nascent technology firms.[11] This does not just refer to the sale of the basic public network to a consortium of large IT companies in 1995, or the removal of market barriers and the consequent privatization of the

Internet through the Telecommunications Act of 1996, which revised the earlier Communications Act of 1934. Instead, what is also involved here is Section 230 of the Communications Decency Act, which, in response to controversial legal cases, represented a radical break. It may serve us as an example of how legislative processes can not only be utterly timely, but are themselves capable of shaping the technological era. Here, Internet providers are no longer defined as publishers but as mere intermediaries, as neutral mediators, or brokers, and are freed from any responsibility for posted, offered, published, and circulating Web content (cf. pp. 87–89). What was initially conceived as a legal measure to promote Internet technologies became a condition for the rise of companies such as Google or Facebook and, with the granting of liability privileges, was ultimately transformed into a shield protecting monopolistic interests.

Together with the advance into legally undefined territory, platform companies were thus protected by law against legal interventions in their business model. Moreover, this legal exception or immunization has been supplemented to this day by the constant political pressure with which companies like Facebook, Google, and others oppose possible legal restrictions on the collection and extraction of data. For example, as Mark Zuckerberg once remarked, privacy should no longer be claimed as a special "social norm."[12] And from this perspective, the conservative insistence on this or that constitutionally guaranteed right must seem an anachronistic claim, comparable at best to the economically foolhardy demand that Henry Ford should have produced the Model T "by hand."[13] Hostility to the law becomes a modernization program. The lowering of legal barriers has stimulated the cycle between information extraction and capital gains. It is therefore not surprising that intelligence services in particular have developed a burning desire for the lawless spaces of the platform industry; they are attracted by such private data treasures whose retrieval, unlike in the case of government institutions, is not hindered by special constitutional, legal, or democratic reservations. In the wake of 9/11, for example, an "unprecedented" collaboration between NSA and Google came about, and programmatic considerations have left no doubt about it. As former NSA Director Mike McConnell remarked in 2010:

> [I]t must shape an effective partnership with the private sector so information can move quickly back and forth from public to private – and classified to unclassified – to protect the nation's critical infrastructure. ... Recent reports of a possible partnership between Google and the government point to the kind of joint efforts – and shared challenges – that we are likely to see in the future. ... [S]uch arrangements will muddy the waters between the traditional roles of the government and the private sector. ... Cyberspace knows no borders, and our defensive efforts must be similarly seamless.[14]

The weakening of legal regulation has made platform companies, in particular, attractive to government institutions; the arcana of information are administered in gray zones between private and state.

It is therefore no coincidence that the social dynamics of technological developments are held up against the old or outdated institution of law. This follows the libertarian dream of creating idyllic, or Californian, enclaves beyond the rule of law, where experiments can be carried out in a liberated entrepreneurial milieu, untroubled by historical regulatory ballast, testing a possible society of the future. It is precisely a long history of the legal privileging of capital that has motivated an aversion to the law and nourished the claim to privileged reserves, to places set aside for experimentation.[15] This means that, in pushing back state legal rules, one hopes for a release and independence of private control procedures that follow a special logic of justification.

In this context, one may first recall that efforts have long been underway in financial markets to expand the possibilities for, and the forms of, a private creation of law. Thus, in twentieth-century liberalism, there was extensive discussion about the development of private law independent of national jurisdiction, which would protect the world market from government intervention and allow the special "rights of capital" to be anchored in national legal systems. The overall issue here was the way in which individuals and institutions, public and private actors conduct and regulate their transactions in the sense of a *lex mercatoria*. It was then argued, in the name of a liberal legal tradition, that it is precisely economic relationships, operations, and contracts that constitute a productive model for the spontaneous and independent development of law-like orders.[16]

In view of the proliferation of international agreements and transactions in the finance economy, the status of private law "beyond the state," its relationship to national legislation and public law, its legitimacy, validity, mode of procedure, and autonomy, its legal character in general, are at stake. Apart from general questions about the extent to which private law transcends the confines of state jurisdiction or offers a welcome accommodation to the realities of globalized markets, the appeal to regulations based on private law has been used to claim an autonomous normative rationality and specific value systems that unfold their attractiveness precisely where the reliability and clout of political structures are absent.[17]

Ultimately, however, it has been possible to see in this context a change in normative orders as a whole and a shift in the treatment of questions of social and economic decision-making. These are changes that manifest themselves not only in a privatization of legal rules under pressure from an international financial industry, but also in a transition from legal coordinates to an organizing function based on paralegal codes.[18] Here, a confrontation is emerging that involves the way in which systems and organizations reproduce themselves. On the one hand, for instance, you have the legal clarification of situations of social conflict: such a clarification is not directly derivable from its premises; it can neither be grasped by any kind of strictly deductive logic nor by any automatic processes of subsumption. Instead, it always operates in the open realm of the undecided. By contrast, one has to understand code in general as a script that formulates unambiguous execution rules for the processing of determinate steps for the solution of problems of whatever kind. Unlike natural languages, the code's order is characterized by a semiotic law of value that subjects the materials of signs to the format of information and transforms statements – arbitrary series of symbols – directly into actions. Code can become machine language because it does what it says. Rule by code is characterized by an advantage over other symbolic orders in its ability to execute its rules and, especially in terms of the standards of network communication, the code has the force of law.

In this way, we have "problematizing" and "solutionist" procedures that are quite fundamentally opposed to one another (and which have also been discussed in the legal sciences, for example, with regard to the question of the status of decision-making robots).[19] Against this backdrop, the structure of a new "polis of solution" has been formed: a regime and sociotope in which the control code has become the model for solving questions of social decision-making. This governance dimension is premised on the assumption that all complex social situations can either be translated into clearly defined problems that will then receive determinable and predictable solutions, or that they should be understood as more or less transparent, self-evident processes that can be optimized by using the right algorithms.[20] Such considerations are neither utopian nor dystopian; rather, they set the entrepreneurial reality of the Internet, the digital world, and the platform economy as social reality par excellence. On the basis of the control logic of codes, a new spirit of digital capitalism has been identified for which, on the one hand, a machinic surplus value or a surplus value of code arises from the control of information (and where human labor is at best tolerated as a supplement in this process). On the other hand, the combination of entrepreneurship and technology claims the privilege of finally solving those problems "that have plagued humanity for centuries," replacing "old institutions and old rules ... with computation."[21] The capitalization of information is realized in the governmental form.

Admittedly, the polis of solution and its sociotope still have an embryonic character and are arguably approaching future fruition with different speeds, variants, degrees of force, and alliances in various parts of the world. Nonetheless, a tendency can be discerned in which the historically variable – critical or conflictual – relation between capitalism and constitutional democracy threatens to turn into one of blunt opposition. This is evident not only in recent forms of governance, in the proliferation of control practices, and in the multiple and informal mergers between public and private powers under a regime of finance and information. It is also evident in a dynamic with which pseudo- or parastatal structures are themselves being established in the realm of platform capitalist enterprises. Thus, proprietary markets and infrastructures have already reinforced a development with which the more or less sharp boundaries between political or state supervision and market processes migrate into the inside of market activity itself. By so doing, it gives shape to a form of enterprise that can be addressed as the return of early capitalist, mercantilist consortia under current conditions. The great trading companies of the seventeenth century, such as the Dutch Vereenigde Oostindische Compagnie or the British East India Company, were geared toward eliminating competition and monopolizing long-distance trade, and in this way linked private business activity with sovereign powers and capital interests with the exercise of sovereign rights. Similarly, the "privatized mercantilism" of the platform industry is also characterized by directing investments toward monopoly formation, the restriction of competition, and the control of social infrastructures.[22] In this manner, fields are occupied, which as reserves of sovereignty, core political functions, or welfare state tasks were part of the domains of modern forms of state and range from the care of public goods and the satisfaction of protection and security needs to the financing of education or social welfare systems. Thus, it is perhaps possible to speak of platform sovereignties and a "state-ification" of information machines. Last but not least, the pandemic emergency since the spring of 2020 has made visible the extent to which the expansion of platform companies (as the essential winners in epidemics) and the associated transfer of power have for some time already been witnessed in a range of other fields. These include public services, involve an intertwining with sovereign and administrative tasks, but also applies to the business of healthcare, medical care, and a general need for preventive services. Amazon and Apple operate clinics; Amazon also offers health insurance and continuous medical monitoring; Google and Apple cooperate in developing disease apps; Facebook provides disease prevention maps, supplementing healthcare policy monitoring with a Covid-19 alert; and Google's Project Baseline, a comprehensive data collection on the sleep rhythms, excreta, blood pressure, pulse rate, and tear fluid levels of clinical and outpatient patients, combines entry into the healthcare market with the offer of a universal preventive medical service.[23] The liberal phobia against the provider state has morphed into the libertarian celebration of the caring corporation.

In view of the expansion of such parastatal corporate structures, it seems only logical to try to close the circle of financialization, informatization and control power, to connect the private takeover of sovereign powers to the economic order as a whole and to perfect the transition from a government-controlled to a market-controlled financial system. Just as the financial industry was attracted by the opportunities of the information economy, platform companies now pushed their way into the financial business. In particular, they took on a leading role in the highly profitable projects to create private payment and money systems, insofar as the latter were aimed at denationalizing currencies. For example, the provision of payment services, along with investment funds and financial instruments, has long been among the key drivers and components of American and Chinese platform companies. They offer the advantage of providing the most reliable data for the targeted placement of products and advertising. At the same time, they enable the centralized monitoring of decentralized international payment traffic; for example, Alibaba's Alipay or Tencent's WeChat Pay in China, and Visa, Mastercard, PayPal, Apple Pay, or Amazon Pay exclusively in the US.[24] PayPal had already set out to create a kind of "Internet currency" to replace the US dollar in international payments and undermine state currency monopolies.[25] In a continuation and intensification of such projects, the overlapping of private economic and governance practices in the platform economy has ultimately spawned new financial-economic initiatives that are expected to generate further profitable pushes for inclusiveness. One such venture, for example, which initially attracted attention as a provocative business idea or "ingenious marketing ploy," has now taken its first step toward realization: on May 16, 2020, the Geneva-based Libra Association formally applied to the Swiss finance regulator FINMA for a license to operate a payment system, clearing a key hurdle to the establishment of a global cryptocurrency by the Facebook organization (now Meta Platforms, Inc.).[26] It is presently unclear how this Libra project, in planning since 2019 and renamed Diem in December 2020, will intervene in the dynamics of the current financial system. It is unclear whether it will turn out to be a relative of the Bitcoin system, a low-cost payment service, a pseudo-bank, or an assault on state currencies. In any case, with its orientation and organizational form, it already attracts attention as an undertaking that aims to consolidate a market-based financial system by providing it with new private modes of control: a conception in which concrete ideas about the pseudo- or parastatal expansion of Facebook/Meta manifest themselves. In any event, what has been written down in the various working papers, drafts, outlines, and exposés of the Libra Association since the summer of 2019 foreshadows great promise for the finance economy and invites a provisional viewing of a possible or probable future for control societies.

In this context, it is fair to assume that one of the preconditions for such projects, like the more than 2,000 cryptocurrencies in general, lies in the past and in a tradition of liberal monetary theories that have been cultivating their aversion to national monetary policy since the 1930s. The proposals, for example, put forward by Chicago economist Henry S. Simons in 1936, in what remains a prominent contribution to the establishment of a "new 'religion of money,'" envisioned delegating the banknote monopoly away from central banks and back to the Treasury, reducing monetary interventions, fixing the money supply for the long term, securing bank deposits with 100% backing, minimizing short-term money contracts and their associated monetary surrogates, and limiting monetary policy overall to controlling the price level.[27] The aim here seems to have been to set firm rules against momentary monetary policy interventions and discretionary decisions, rules under which free entrepreneurship could operate in free markets with expectable market mechanisms. If this was the case, what was envisioned here was no less than a containment or elimination of those "authorities" embodied in national and central banks. On the outer edges of such considerations was Friedrich Hayek's radical demand to dispense with central banks and state monopolies alike, to leave the creation of "honest money" entirely to the markets and the stabilization of the price level to privately owned free banks and the forces of competition. If money is nothing but an innocent commodity alongside other commodities, old national currency monopolies can be safely denationalized or depoliticized and the privatized currencies handed over to the "control of value by competition."[28] Finally, the legacy of this monetary liberalism is arguably laid claim to by those declarations of independence made by blockchain technology in which state phobia gets translated into the high note of promised freedom:

> The time has come to challenge the State's monopoly on the fabrication of money and the control of currency flows; to deconstruct the link between geography and money (that is, to deconstruct money's national – or, in the case of the Euro, international – assignation); and to put an end to the privilege enjoyed by central banks and all the organisms that depend on them.[29]

On the one hand, a project such as the planned Libra/Diem currency ties in with the neoliberal call for the privatization of currencies. With the guiding principle of an "Internet of money," it pursues the construction of a "financial ecosystem" that would bypass or break through the financial axis between central and commercial banks and offer itself as a decentralized network for private payment and financial services. Facebook's up to three billion users are to form the basis for a frictionless global financial system, freed from politics and intermediaries, that builds technologically – in parallel to distributive networks – on the functioning of distributed ledgers (account ledgers managed in a decentralized manner) as in blockchain transactions. Particular importance is attached to developing and emerging countries in which, for instance in Africa or Asia, rudimentary political and economic institutions as well as a lack of the infrastructures of financial technology favor the establishment of a generally accessible global financial network with "distributed governance," that, as it is said, "empowers billions of people." With "distributed forms of governance," the financial-economic inclusion of hitherto uncovered populations should increase to a comparative degree and holds out the prospect of "more inclusive financial options for the world."[30] It is not surprising that liberal money experts consider this a particularly "cool idea."[31]

On the other hand, this demonstrative orientation toward decentralized networks is linked to an organizational form that relies on clear exclusions, hierarchies, and forms of centralization. Apart from the fact that Facebook, with its subsidiary Calibra, has claimed the "leadership" role in the implementation of the project, the composition of the founding members and of participants eligible to vote is as exclusive as it is significant. They come almost exclusively from the financial sector as well as from venture capital, platform, technology, and telecommunications companies, and they are strongly networked with each other. Moreover, they are distinguished by their fulfillment of demanding admission requirements: for voting membership in the Libra Association (since December 2020: the Diem Association), for example, minimum investments of ten million US dollars in the so-called Libra Reserve (or Diem Reserve) are required as well as a company value of at least one billion US dollars, a customer balance sheet of 500 million US dollars or a nomination to the Fortune 500 list. It is therefore again the "technology companies and financial institutions" that are entrusted with the obvious "solutions to help increase economic empowerment around the world."[32]

This combination of open and closed, flat and hierarchical structures characterizes the entire payment system, which can be used to tap low-income households worldwide as a new financial-economic resource. Thus, the stablecoins issued by Libra/Diem, which can be purchased through distributed outlets using ordinary means of payment, are initially backed in the corresponding reserve by a stock of "secure and stable assets,"[33] consisting of bank deposits, interest-bearing government bonds, and short-term invested securities – all denominated in reputable national currencies. As such, this reserve forms the backbone of the corporate cartel, as well as of the system as a whole, and is characterized by several distinctive business features. First of all, one can see in it the shape of an investment or money market fund, the volume of which is composed of the investments of up to a hundred members and, above all, of those depositories into which the funds generated by the sale of Libra/Diem to users flow. The resulting capital stock could, according to various estimates, range from several hundred billion to a few trillion US dollars and would secure the Libra/Diem Association a place in the group of the largest asset managers (money market funds) in the world (or make its capital stock comparable to the net asset purchases of the European Central Bank's asset purchase program).

Moreover, the returns, which consist of interest on the assets and transaction fees for payment services and which (again according to estimates) could reach several billion US dollars per year, will be passed on to the members of the Libra/Diem Association as dividends, after deduction of operating costs. The various drafts of this project immediately sought to clarify:

"Users of Libra do not receive a return from the reserve."[34] This means that what one is dealing with here is nothing other than profits from money creation. In other words, this represents a mintage or seigniorage, which is supposed to result, as it once did in the principalities of early modernity, from the toils or privileges of the issuance of money. Thus, the issuance and circulation of Libra is not merely operated as a fund or investment business, guaranteed and controlled by the financially powerful corporations of the Association; rather, it introduces a system of private money creation that carries out a strictly asymmetric distribution of capital. Two classes of owners or participants are clearly distinguished from each other, and the dispersed owners or users of Libra/Diem coins around the world stand in contrast to the owners of the platform, the currency, and the entire system itself.[35] An inclusive global payment and financial network is dominated by a small group of companies and investors, and the privatization of money creation is also achieved technically and institutionally.

The planned currency is thus not, as announced, "designed and governed as a public good" but, on the contrary, as a monetary system that is privately owned by influential investors. The decentralized payment system, together with the technology of distributive networks, is recentralized by way of the shareholders.[36] This also includes combining the announced facilitating of international payments with the appropriation of user data, and combining money functions with network services, while transferring them to a common agency. This is the task of Calibra, a subsidiary of Facebook, which was itself renamed Novi in December 2020: here, payment operations are combined with messaging functions such as Instagram and WhatsApp; the platform integrates the distribution of digital coins with the collection and extraction of user data involving, for instance, payment and goods traffic, purchasing behavior, creditworthiness, payment history, income, and assets. This access to the information in users' digital wallets is guaranteed by a so-called "open identity standard," which carries out electronic personal identification in keeping with transparent financial transactions and stores this information on central databases in the United States.[37] The precondition for this is once again indebted to the control logic of Internet protocols, as implemented by blockchain technology. This is not merely about the use of distributive network architecture and the supposed elimination of third parties and intermediaries, but primarily about a reordering of the social contract. Thus, the cryptographic operations used to process and authenticate the list of records or blocks in a decentralized manner have the character of smart contracts, in which the consent of all participants or fellow players is automatically documented with every transaction.

On the one hand, this process of machinic consensus-building through transmission protocols follows a self-executing contract profile that bypasses conventional juridical authentications, creates tension with existing national legal structures, overhauls legal encodings with digital ones, creates pseudo-legal obligations, and as such offers itself as an ideal institutional design for the supply of free markets. Denationalized private law becomes automated, as it were.[38] On the other hand, this creates machine structures that are quasi-sovereign, and of ultimate authority, whose procedures combine the decentralization of control with the executive upgrading of the code. The Libra or Diem system thus promises not only to fill a gap in the infrastructure of the international financial economy. Rather, it reveals the development of a *parasitic technology* in the strict sense of the word, in which the creation of channels for financial transactions is directly linked to interceptions and extractions. The promise of broad financial inclusion of world populations without assets and without bank accounts is contrasted with strict exclusions manifested in the monopolization by Facebook and the Libra/Diem Association of the information and capital gains derived from the process.

However, the heated debates surrounding this ambitious project are still accompanied by the unanswered question of what financial-economic format it actually represents. As little as there is doubt about the novelty of the venture, there is still much puzzlement about what kind of economic, institutional, and legal coherence the platform and the payment method have. Whether, for instance, the Libra/Diem Association is a network, a platform, a payment service, a fund or an investment company, a financial service provider, a banking institution, or all of the above or none of the above, or whether it has the characteristics of a central bank. Moreover, could the evocative names Libra and Diem, which reference a Roman imperial unit of measurement and an epochal invocation of a new "day," respectively, perhaps even intend to refer to a cryptocurrency, blockchain, digital money and e-money, financial instrument, corporate money or a virtual currency unit with all the usual monetary functions? All of these considerations and definitional efforts are summarized most succinctly by the statement that the project is "completely at odds with everything" that the ingenuity of financial industries and regulators has brought forward so far.[39] Thus, it must be conceded that the hybrid construction, which oscillates between payment service, investment fund, and bank and currency system, initially eludes all national and supranational supervisory bodies and, at the very least, does not fall within the direct remit of the regulatory authorities for banks and credit institutions. Here, too, it is a matter of occupying legally undefined territory: for the application for the licensing of a payment system presented in Switzerland in the spring of 2020 involved a project conceived of as far more than just a payment service. Against this background, Facebook's reassurances that it is "committed to working with authorities to shape a regulatory environment that encourages technological innovation while maintaining the highest standards of consumer protection" can be understood as its attempt to test the reach of existing regulations and to shape the regulatory framework toward its own interests.[40]

Thus, it is not so much the notorious questions of currency stability, potential money laundering, or terrorist financing that have made the project a challenge to governments, central banks, and regulators. Rather, economic experts have little doubt that such new forms of money are likely to become "the central lynchpins of large, systemically important social and economic platforms" that will inevitably transcend national borders, redefine the relationship between payments and user data, and ultimately "reshape … the architecture of the international monetary system, and the role of government-issued public money."[41] This marks the latest upheaval in the matter of economic governance. It means, first, that the cartography of national currency units is being duplicated by a geo-economic distribution of "digital currency areas" (DCAs). Here, transactions are guaranteed via private means of payment that are either valid within commercial networks, as in the Chinese example of Tencent and Ant Financial, or form as convertible and competing currencies, as in the case of Libra/Diem. On the one hand, this involves an inversion in the hierarchy of financial transactions: payment systems are no longer dependent on intermediation between banks; rather, it has been possible to subordinate traditional banking functions to the financial technology of payment services and platform companies. On the other hand, the horizon is opening up for digital "dollarization." To the extent that private means of payment and units of account, such as Libra/Diem, circulate on digital networks across national borders, they must be seen as having the capacity to operate simultaneously in different currency systems and possibly displace or replace national currencies with digital corporate or platform money.[42] Through such modes of intervention, platform economies are part of a development in which political geography turns out to be a palimpsest: it is overwritten by proliferating enclaves and exclaves, by migrating economic and commercial zones, privatized currency areas and networks, and characterized by fluctuating hegemonies in its financial regime.

It is not surprising, then, that Mark Zuckerberg, at a painstaking hearing before the US House of Representatives in October 2019, sought to allay such concerns about the dignity of state-owned currencies and, in reference to inevitable Chinese competition, touted the pleasant prospect for himself and for Facebook/Meta that it is precisely Libra that will be able to continue to guarantee US supremacy in the financial sector. Indeed, shortly thereafter, the original plan to secure the Libra currency by pegging it to a basket of diverse and stable currencies (multi-currency: US dollar, euro, yen, British pound) was replaced by a privileged tethering to the dollar (single currency), which in this way could retain its status as the lead or reserve currency in international payments, with all the economic and political advantages that entails: "I believe it will extend America's financial leadership."[43] Even if the exact interaction between the dollar, other individual currencies, and Libra has yet to be specified and the implementation of this financial-economic experiment remains unclear, even if the tactical renaming of Libra to Diem aims to camouflage the links between Facebook and the currency project, the project is nonetheless presented with undisguised promises of power politics. Against this backdrop, it can be understood in its current form as the systematic continuation and capstone of a development with which (US) platform capitalism secures its business models by controlling proprietary markets and, in turn, attempts to stabilize them with the expansion of pseudo-state structures – the latest stage in perfecting the governance practices of the financial regime. The aim of Libra/Diem was to establish more than just a US-dominated global currency and a proprietary infrastructure for financial services of all kinds. Instead, in designs such as those of the Libra/Diem Association, a private reserve system has taken shape that bears similarities to traditional central banking structures by issuing private fiat money and thus claiming monetary prerogatives or quasi-sovereign powers such as money creation and note issuance. The lines of development here seem to be converging in a geo-economic order of privatized economic spheres or domains subject to the control of investor groups and their particular interests, spheres which replace the scope of public regulation with private governance and power apparatuses. In any case, it cannot be precluded that this project represents more than just an instructive snapshot of current financial-economic dynamics. Rather, with its implementation, it may well reinforce existing trajectories of power and adhere to an escalating curve, culminating in an efficient detachment of the net citizen from the state citizen that results in a more or less voluntary accession of entire populations to a private "online state." Capitalism, Fernand Braudel once said, always triumphs when it becomes the state.[44]

What has already started to take shape in the processes of financialization, namely a creeping drift of monetary sovereignty from central banks to financial markets (cf. pp. 18–19), finds ratification in the blueprint of the Libra/Diem project through a new type of organization. On the broader horizon of these considerations, it is not only a question of the way in which the entrepreneurial occupation of pseudo- or parastatal structures is now also reflected in a possible reorganization of financial, monetary, and currency systems. Rather, one could speak of another "great transformation." According to Karl Polanyi, since the end of the eighteenth century, economic relations had been disembedded from their social relations and, instead, these relations had been integrated into a capital-driven market economy. A new metamorphosis now seems to be in the offing, in which the financial and monetary system itself will be oriented toward a private capitalization of information. This embedding of all social relations in the so-called "ecosystem" of digital capitalism does not necessarily hold out the prospect of a withering away of the state. However, the latest twists and turns of the financial and information regime are proving to be both part and anchor of a transnational power of governance in which network technologies, corporate structures, processes of wealth accumulation, and control practices are merged with one another. In them, the erosion of democratic rule of law combines with the expansion and diffusion of private executive powers. What once began as a portal for rating the prettiness of Harvard students now presents itself as a prototype for the entrepreneurial expansion of global powers of control.

5

Truth Games

Against the backdrop of recent financial and economic crises and in the search for new sources of value creation, more than just a close alliance of finance and information economies has emerged. By means of network technologies, the financialization of information and the informatization of finance have led much more to new corporate structures in the platform industry, whose business model consists of the appropriation of infrastructures, the extension of entrepreneurial governance, and the capitalization of governance technologies and control mechanisms. The cultivation of capitalist property rights in the sense of the *dominium* has allied itself with the rudiments of *imperium*, and what has repeatedly been called the erosion of an order based on the modern territorial or nation-state and its associated force of law has made room for the systematic establishment of private parastatal authorities. Their most recent form may perhaps be seen in a kind of statehood of information machines and in "platform sovereignties" whose specific form of power is guaranteed by an overlapping of technical, economic, and governance structures, a synergy of network communication, economic imperatives, and permanently granted legal exemptions.[1] Questions about the status and consistency of sovereign rule are being reordered in the face of its fragmentation.

Even if a fundamental transformation in the mode of reproduction of the economic and financial system is discernible here, some of its central elements in practical and in theoretical terms are not entirely new. On the one hand, it brings to mind the older contours of a capital-driven colonial system, as it was tried out, for example, in the former crown colony of Hong Kong after the collapse of the British Empire. Under changing conditions, the survival of imperial components was secured, the sovereignty of capital was guaranteed by free trade policies, low corporate taxes, and strict banking secrecy, by the absence of representative government, and by limiting democratic intervention, and all this with great economic success. Since the late 1950s, such former British colonies as Hong Kong, Bermuda, Cayman Islands, and Singapore have laid the basis for a network that has allowed capital transactions to take place apart from, and in circumvention of, national legislation and have been able to furnish international finance capitalism with an infrastructure. On the other hand, the libertarian immunization of authoritarian forms of enterprise can also be understood as the implementation of economic policy slogans that have been circulated by diverse types of (neo)liberalism since the 1960s. For, contrary to the general consensus, postwar liberalism by no means favored the freeing of markets from the superior power of the state. Rather, the projects of deregulation and privatization, as well as the widespread respect paid to inviolable market laws, were accompanied by programmatic ideas that involved protecting capitalist economic processes against overly democratic interference. The calls for vigilant and active politics were concerned not only with defending free markets but also with creating a regulatory framework to shield private capital rights from interference by the inconvenient decisions of political majorities.[2]

Thus, out of concern for the survival of capitalism, the variants of an authoritarian liberalism were linked to the design of robust global executive strategies. Moreover, it was precisely this preference for the prerogatives of capital and finance that was combined with a peculiar game of truth that was supposed to be reserved for the dynamics of the market and competition. If Friedrich Hayek had already linked the tireless invocation of the market as a sovereign subject of knowledge with the call to the rest of the world to humbly embrace their ignorance and to submit to the "impersonal forces of the market,"[3] then, in a consistent extension of this line, US doctrines in particular have offered concise versions of the predictive powers inherent to market processes. From its privileged position vis-à-vis other instances and institutions of knowledge production, the market – unsurprisingly – offers a universal agency of evaluation. This agency should be installed as the "touchstone" for the tenability, accuracy, and "quality" of circulating "ideas"; it should provide a "genuinely representative agency," a mode of representation that is better able to ensure the coordination of divergent positions and opinions than other, more formal, political decision-making processes such as elections, the party system, or parliamentary government. Freedom of opinion is economic freedom, and the market alone produces those reliable patterns of order that will allow competing economic citizens to come together in almost ideal political "unanimity."

Yet it is precisely in the United States that this hymn to the virtues of the market has led to an idiosyncratic interpretation of the First Amendment, with its reference to freedom of speech and assembly. For liberal inspirers such as Milton Friedman, this did not merely mean the congruence of free markets and free speech, in which the power of public persuasion merges with the power of financial solvency. Rather, it held out the prospect of a particular payoff in financial-economic terms. In this view, the favor of the First Amendment was also to be found in claiming freedom of speech for the "monetary system" as a whole, and in justifying the unleashing of the "finance and investment business" as well as the taming of authorities such as the Treasury Department and the Federal Reserve System. The regulation of capital movements is simply incompatible with the right to free speech, and the equation of money markets with an "economics of free speech"[4] is also legitimized by the fact that mainstream, normative reinforcements and normalizing trends will eventually prevail here as well as there.

The liberal validation of circulating speech by money and capital, and vice versa, could not eliminate financial institutions such as central banks, but it had established efficient alliances with that mode of legal reason that gives concise forms to economic life. This was realized by closely linking property rights and the freedom of speech with the US Supreme Court ruling, as early as 1978, that the freedoms guaranteed by the First Amendment had to be extended to private corporations as well. The public activities of corporations, foundations, and businesses in election campaigns and political disputes should enjoy "the same protection as individual speech under the First Amendment," and it was in the interest of society as a whole not to legally impede the "free flow of commercial information."[5] In effect, this defined investments as speech or expressions of opinion, and, at the latest, a momentous 2010 ruling removed the last barriers keeping investors from engaging in political actions and programs. With the Supreme Court's decision in Citizens United v. Federal Election Commission, limits on campaign financing, on financial contributions to so-called Super PACs – political action committees supporting parties and candidacies – were understood as a restriction on free speech in the "uninhibited marketplace of ideas," in a market that itself is supposed to function as a privileged generator and distributor of available knowledge. This did away with the distinction between fictitious persons (such as corporations) and natural persons (such as eligible voters) with regard to freedom of speech; it interpreted political forces as economic ones and election campaigns themselves as market operations, and extended the call for the deregulation of markets to the arenas of political debate as well. But, apart from all this, investing capital was now itself granted the position of a shareholder in free speech, a subject of speech in need of protection: operations involving capital are brought under the protection of the Constitution as expressions of opinion, and just as there cannot be "too much speech," so capital flows are now to pour into the pool of the public, unimpeded as is the torrent of speech that they have financed.[6]

After all, it was the Internet and platform companies that were affected by these referential confusions between opinions and markets, speech and rates of return, and in this context the guarantees of the First Amendment, arguably, should be seen as effective instruments for shaping business practices. Such issues, at any rate, have been at the heart of laws that are in line with the general tendency of liberal jurisprudence. Together with the rabid privatization of public communications networks through the Telecommunications Act (1996), they intervened in the fate and fortunes of the Internet industry (preceded as they were by fierce privatization campaigns and corresponding calls to "proselytize" for the deregulation of telecommunications).[7] They can be seen as examples of how inconspicuous and barely noticed legal modifications achieve incalculable effects through systemic catalysts. It is not without irony that the impetus for this legislation, the aforementioned Communications Decency Act, came from an initiative to combat pornographic network content, only to then become a key cornerstone of unregulated network communications. While the intended ban on the dissemination of "offensive" material was overturned by the Supreme Court with reference to the First Amendment, it was precisely this dissemination logic on the Net that was redefined by the bipartisan amendment itself. Legal rulings formed the background to this, rulings that were controversial if not outright contradictory. Whereas the online portal CompuServe had been acquitted of charges of defamation in 1991 because no review of the posted content had been carried out, a court case in 1995 had reached the opposite decision: here the Internet service Prodigy had been convicted on a similar charge, precisely because it had edited and redacted the posted content and followed self-imposed guidelines. To resolve such legal inconsistencies, the Act had then become "one of the most valuable tools"[8] for guaranteeing free speech on the Internet; and coupled with the stated intent "to preserve the vibrant and competitive free market that presently exists for the Internet and other interactive computer services, unfettered by Federal or State regulation," and indeed "to the benefit of all Americans," the corresponding Section 230 of the Communications Decency Act of 1996 states: "No provider or user of an interactive computer service shall be treated as the publisher or speaker of any information provided by another information content provider."[9] Loosely paraphrased, this means that (with a few exceptions) no provider or user of an interactive computer service can be held responsible for the distribution of any information, such as text, images, or videos, that is posted by another provider.

These regulations established a kind of "Internet exceptionalism," were soon adopted with some modifications in the European Union (through the "Directive on electronic commerce"),[10] led to the adaptation of national laws,[11] and, with their exceptional conditions, formed a new and peculiar public subject, or subject of the public sphere. As already mentioned, this resulted, first of all, in a fundamental distinction being made between publishers on the one hand and intermediaries or distributors on the other (cf. pp. 68–69). Publishers or editorial staffs, who bear the (distribution and copyright) responsibility for their publications, are now confronted with brokers or intermediaries, who do not assume any liability for this intermediary activity, unless they specifically commission, edit, or modify the materials posted by third parties. Messaging services, for example, have the legal status of telephone lines, but systematically produce dynamic public realms, or rather, they produce something that circumvents the distinction between private and public communications. The free distribution of content of all kinds has become autonomous, so to speak. Thus, Facebook, for example, may now see itself as the largest supplier of "information" and a "massive publisher" that "publishes more in a day than most other publications have in the history of their whole existence."[12] Nonetheless, this publishing has now acquired a paradoxical status, being as effective as it is lacking in culpability: those who publish are not responsible, but those who are responsible for content are not publishing. This has created one of the conditions allowing opinion as such, opinion per se – free speech without liability, justification, or the need to give reasons – to become the standard measure of acts of expression in general (and, additionally, to trigger burlesque debates about whether the tens of millions of bots on the networks are also entitled to a fundamental right to freedom of expression).[13]

Secondly, the autonomy of this brokerage of online portals, websites, Internet services, platforms, and social media is also mirrored in the provision of self-imposed norms. Whereas one now operates – especially in Europe – with guidelines for reviewing platform activities (for example, to limit hate speech, fake news, or child pornography as in the German Network Enforcement Act [*Netzwerkdurchsetzungsgesetz*], which has been in force since January 2018),[14] the basic architecture remains untouched. As little as platforms and network services are responsible for circulating "information" and can at most be required to delete content after the fact, they are free under Section 230 to suppress, for example, "obscene, lewd, lascivious, filthy, excessively violent, harassing, or otherwise objectionable" material on their own initiative, according to their own criteria, and "in good faith," regardless of whether and how that material may in fact be "constitutionally protected"

[Section 230(c)(2)(A)]. Thus, they are not liable for the posted content or, conversely, for removing it for one reason or another (such as the sovereign blocking of Presidential accounts). By immunizing companies from legal prosecution, they should, in this way, be given leeway to introduce standards that can then be used to identify a possible range of "inappropriate" speech. But it is precisely the liability privilege under free speech that has allowed companies to now decide for themselves what free speech permits, and it thus raises the question of whether and how, for example, the First Amendment limits the reach of laws that grant private platforms the power to control what is expressed on them.

Taken together, both regulations – the exemption of intermediary carriers (i.e., their liability privileges) and the creation of autonomous normative enclaves – have created the conditions for those closed "ecosystems" that proclaim themselves as "global marketplaces" for free expression. Most importantly, this legal lacuna has attracted fresh investment capital to fund enterprises whose new business model is precisely to commercialize the protected space of the First Amendment itself, and that is: to distribute "free speech" and "information" in such scalable quantities (e.g., 6,000 tweets per second on Twitter or three million posts per minute on Facebook) that their legality or illegality, their "offensive" or "injurious" character, inevitably can no longer be adequately scrutinized or judged.[15] The liability privilege for so-called intermediaries has been the key driver of the expansion and exceptionalism of new media corporations, and has also created the special case of products whose market approval is not subject to any regulation or review. The unrestricted financing of the free speech market, protected by the First Amendment, has been supplemented by corporate structures that in turn guarantee investor protection for the capitalization of such markets.

Since the mid-1990s, jurisprudence and politics have thus favored the breeding of a hitherto unknown type of media company, which itself produces neither news nor information or other content, assumes no liability as a mere intermediary, and for this very reason presents itself as a self-confident protagonist of free expression of opinion, in a US sense of the phrase. Thirdly, this self-conception also includes a program with which the very media or intermediary practices of such companies present themselves as consistent "disintermediation." This is more than just the frequently celebrated dismissal of all gatekeepers and other guardians of thresholds, a group that has frequently included not only publishing houses, the press, publishers, editors, journalists, curators, libraries, and bookstores, but also educational institutions, retail stores in general, and political representatives.[16] This also goes hand-in-hand with the creation of illusions of immediacy, which are supposed to be reflected in direct communications with low access thresholds, in authenticity rituals, and in flexible self-governance, at the private level, in business transactions, and in political life. From the serendipity between individual sellers and customers to the hope of a liquid democracy, to publishing "self-service platforms," everywhere active and passive promises of participation are conveyed. One could recognize in them a privatization of all communication relationships and thus a digital reformation, a "digital Protestantism."[17] This may even be a kind of evangelical digital cult: the hoped-for "glad tidings" (in the gospel sense) are no longer filtered and distorted by intrinsically powerful functionaries or professional interpreters, or by overbearing institutions.

This is all the more remarkable, however, because nothing applies more precisely to the functioning of digital platforms and their variants than the observation that there has probably never been "more 'mediatedness' in the seemingly immediate."[18] For fourth, the proprietary markets thus created are, after all, characterized by the fact that they only begin to function through a technically speaking, highly sophisticated mediation process. This confirms the thesis that the activities of the channel precede all transmitted messages, all actions and passions of senders and receivers. Here, the preconditions for the intervention of the powers of control and thus for the profitable asymmetries in the information economy of platform companies have already been created on the technical level of transmissions and Internet protocols (cf. pp. 62–66). Given such preconditions, data transfer of this kind is supplemented by modes of operation that ensure, in the background and unnoticed, the obtainability, the availability, or perceptibility of the circulating digital artifacts.

Thus, the seemingly neutral transport of content in the transfer from user to user stands, by necessity, in contrast to selection processes that first transform platforms, search engines, and social media into promising businesses and offer different forms of hierarchization and filtering of datasets. Older search engines such as Alta Vista or Lycos operated lexically and ordered their search results according to the quantity of keywords found. By contrast, for example, PageRank, the winning algorithm that made Google (together with Google Analytics) the most successful search engine, ignores all semantic links and subscribes to a strictly economic procedure that reinforces existing evaluations with evaluations, and excitations with excitations. The assumption is that the relevance of content of any kind depends on the degree to which it is hypertextually linked or cited; query results are sorted according to the quantity and density with which websites are linked, with links to websites with dense linking being valued or ranked more highly. Agnostic to content, the linking coefficient becomes the measure of value. The claim "to organize the world's information and make it universally accessible and useful"[19] thus stands in contrast to a presentation process that sets up positive, self-reinforcing feedback loops, organizes the tableau of all the world's information according to immanent marketing strategies, and defines relevance criteria through accumulated majority-based decisions. The data upsurges thus generated are also fed back to advertisers along with prices in automated linguistic auctions for search terms, keywords, and catchphrases (AdWords). The ranking of search results is correlated with opportunities for value creation through strict information hierarchies, with advertising campaigns integrated into the logic of search results themselves. Thus, one is dealing with a machine-based editorial process that engages in a great deal of automatic decision-making and, with its recursive, quasi stock-market-like evaluation and voting dynamics, operates in a hidden but by no means neutral manner.[20]

Thus, a polling loop (*Abstimmungszirkel*) is established here that employs trend reinforcements of majority decisions via advertising transactions to arrive at economic weightings. At the other end of the spectrum of such selective operations is the production of informational monads that dictate the strict personalization of search results by means of ranking algorithms (e.g., by means of Google AdSense), but, above all, dictate the business policies of social media. The manifestos of the Facebook group, for example, wanted to leave no doubt about the fact that its self-image as the *voice of the people* ("giving people a voice," "giving everyone a voice") was to be combined with such mediating procedures as were capable of directing the sources of "news and public discourse" toward cultural, political, religious, and, last but not least, personal inclinations, preferences, and sensitivities of individual users and user communities. The generally proclaimed "approach" is to focus completely, in the spirit of the truth game "free speech," "less on banning disinformation" and removing false reports than on multiplying "additional perspectives and information." Conversely, "bad experiences" should be minimized, "different opinions" should be cherished, and the individual spaces of one's own experience should be protected and strengthened: "And just as it's a bad experience to see objectionable content, it's also a terrible experience to be told we can't share something we feel is important." And: it is "[o]ur job, our goal is to help people see the content that's going to be the most meaningful and interesting to them."[21] In much the same vein, Facebook's News Feed, through which a majority of people worldwide now get their news at least some of the time, has installed, along with the Edge Rank algorithm, a selection program in which – in strictly informational terms – the mere difference of changes or novelties has become the measure of what counts as information or news. (In other words, only data and events that make a difference count, from whatever addresses or websites they may come from with whatever content they hold, such as: "Bob is now dating Kate.") Algorithmic decisions are also made about who receives what notification from whom and with what priority. Pieces of information are aligned with identifiable, predictable user expectations. The existing and frequently used pathways in the contacts between users and other users or users and providers are thereby privileged in a way that actually deserves the title of feed, in the sense of feeding or fattening users. The idiosyncratic particularization of notifications through the reproduction and confirmation of existing patterns is in turn linked to the injection ("feeding in") of advertising and is the prerequisite for the business of microtargeting.[22] Here, too, then, positive feedback loops are set up, in which the stabilization of predictable user profiles simultaneously forms the individual targets for the more or less discreet attacks undertaken by the advertising industry.

It is therefore a very narrow and inappropriate interpretation, one that is oblivious to media and technology and thus anachronistic, to conceive of platform companies not as publishers but merely as neutral intermediaries of digital artifacts produced elsewhere. Instead, they must be approached as producers, moderators, curators, distributors, and gatekeepers of informational commodities that could only be fabricated and made profitable through extensive editorial interventions, albeit largely automated ones. The imperative to commodify nonrivalrous, nonscarce public goods has also directed the processes of editing, weighting, evaluating, and communicating about circulating information products; in other words, the specific way in which they are perceived and represented. This shapes the form of a new public subject, in which a legally structured irresponsibility is associated with the capitalization of all possible expressive events. The special case of companies and corporations has arisen, whose dominant or monopolistic position has come about precisely because they are not themselves responsible for the products they manufacture and distribute. A former US president put it this way: "I love Twitter .... It's like owning your own newspaper."[23]

On the one hand, in view of this information economy, reference has been made to the production of abstract knowledge and of a collective intelligence under capitalist conditions, with this "general intellect" being understood, with Marx, as a productive force that also controls "the conditions of the process of social life itself."[24] Under digital capitalism, the production of the social is itself a commercial-entrepreneurial project. On the other hand, it is probably not surprising that this truth game of the information economy has been repeatedly expressed in terms of mirroring and doubling, of reflection and re-reflection. These are terms that, in combination with the circumstances of "digitalization," "Internet," and "information," prompt a totality of world representation. According to this, search engines are a "virtual mirror of the world," Google a "mirror" of all world problems, while Facebook "is to reflect" the "current social norms" in its own system, and the Internet in general, like the market before it, represents all available "knowledge."[25] As little as such mirror metaphors are able to grasp the concrete mechanisms of information production (and have already steered some versions of Marxist ideology critique into theoretical dead ends), they are marked all the more by a desire to finally realize older philosophical dreams of the world book, world formulas, universal languages, and a *mathesis universalis*. Such dreams can equally be called rationalist or romantic. They range from Leibniz's attempts at a *characteristica universalis*, which sought to inscribe all things and beings with an unmistakable combination of signs, to the encyclopaedics of a Novalis, which understood itself in equally universal language as the representation of collected knowledge by means of metadata, as the "total function of the data and the facts."[26]

Let us assume that one can speak today of the general aggregation of world information being transformed into the representation of the world *as* information.[27] If this is the case, then under the conditions of information standards (cf. p. 32), Web 2.0, and platform capitalism, one must probably concede a special relation to reality that appeals to notions of representation precisely because it significantly undermines the difference between the item and its informational representation. Until recently, and based on the example of modern industrial capitalism, one sought to posit a general "reification" or "commodification" of labor and social relations by means of monetary function and the commodity economy, whose reality was distorted in "phantasmagorias" and "fetishisms," in the enchantments of commodities and the world of consumption. Such ideological distortions, however, are surpassed in the current finance and information regime by a hegemony of codes and informational concepts. Monetization has been overtaken by informatization. Therefore, it is no longer solely a matter of the production of an illusory social reality through the commodity form, through the production, distribution, and consumption of commercial goods. Rather, the production of the real itself is at stake: capitalism is rooted ontologically and is preparing to shape the structure of elementary relations of being. The associated schematism can probably be attributed less to the regions of ideological superstructure than to the basic structures of the most recent relations of production.

Martin Heidegger's persistent lament had already identified that with the "victory" of information concepts in cybernetics there also came about the domination of an overarching conception of the world, an inculcation into "uniformity," the neutralization and leveling of the event, of "that which comes into view" (*das Ereignis*). Moreover, this "victory" was also accompanied by the computational capture of the world as image and, at the latest by the end of the 1990s, was supplemented by the demand to refashion the world itself according to the image of the Internet.[28] In pursuing such issues, it seems logical to address the real in contemporary capitalism at the level of those information processes in which the representation of world has become indistinguishable from its management and exploitation.

It could be argued, for instance, that in the wake of the proliferation and capitalization of digital technologies, some software products have themselves assumed positions of a universal language. Moreover, object-oriented programming languages such as Java, C++, and their variants, in particular, operate with a specific logic for identifying, capturing, and mediating objects that has secured them a central place in contemporary information economies. They have also been assigned a vast or even universal field of application, ranging from everyday practices, via automated production, search engines, and social media, all the way to algorithmic finance and stock-market trading. They determine the order of things in postindustrial capitalism.

In a fundamental attempt to clarify the ontological status of information technology systems, Alexander Galloway was able to highlight the effective convergence of three domains: a mathematical formalization that is able to encode or represent the data structure of objects and object properties: for example, in terms of set or graph theory; software and programming languages that translate such formalizations into algorithmic machine instructions and prescriptions, thereby linking empirical practices with ontological profiling; and, finally, a mode of production whose entrepreneurial infrastructure provides for the production, distribution, and general utility or exploitation of information products.[29] Mathematical formalization is not self-sufficient; rather, via software, codes, and programming languages, it provides a specification of concepts and relations that can take effect "for an agent or a community of agents" and assert their ontological dimension by intervening practically and determinatively in a contingent, open, and malleable world.[30] At the heart of the information economy, then, is a representational scheme in which formalized and computable access to objects or events corresponds to the way "capitalism structures its world of business objects."[31] By recourse to the codifying power of formal "languages," the bridge between the information technologies of digital capitalism, on the one hand, and ontological categories, on the other, is built and consolidated. Here, the coincidence of ontology and capital ultimately lies in a capturing of objects, entities, events, actions, and their relations, wherein their representation cannot be separated from processes of evaluation and validation, and not least of all, from pricing. Data structure and the form of value have become convertible.

If the concept of a "capitalist realism" is thereby given a concise field of reference, it cannot refer exclusively to that "business ontology" with which competitive scenarios and competitive corporate models have been distributed across the flesh of society in recent decades and given the appearance of a "natural order" of the social.[32] Rather, it should refer to the fundamental mode of representation that constitutes the reality of the current information economy: In it, the designation or ascertainment of factual circumstances is directly linked to their informational version which, in turn, is linked to selective procedures and automatic evaluations of relevance. Finally, when all of this is taken together, it structures a reality continuum in which meanings and evaluations, that is, existential judgments, normalizing practices, selections, and evaluation procedures, flow into one another. Reality itself has taken on the character of an intrusive form of value. One could also say: "The real is not impossible; it is simply more and more artificial."[33]

This has also been described from different perspectives as a situation in which the circumstances of the world cannot be distinguished from their interpretations, phenomena cannot be distinguished from their effects, and facts cannot be distinguished from their production. The digital form of intuition (*Anschauungsform*) that is effective in this not only comprises an algorithmic sign structure in which interpreter and object coincide, meaning relations merge into designation relations, and interpretations are at the same time determinations.[34] Rather, this algorithmic sign structure has sometimes also been spoken of as representative of a current epistemological crisis, an empirical revolution, or a "crisis in knowledge."[35] Thus, one has tried to grasp the fundamental change to what is worth knowing – brought about by the Internet and digital technologies – with the transformation of knowledge of all kinds into inexhaustible volumes of data or "big data." The latter can then be worked through, sorted, weighted, and made available and readable according to the model of search engines and not least with the genius of Google algorithms. This transformation arises out of the history of statistics, which since the nineteenth century has been dedicated to the human science-based administration of large numbers and populations in the sense of a social physics. As a transformation of the world into information and thus the stabilization of a representative schema, it could only function under the condition that the world of events was strictly separated from the realm of their causes.[36] Similar to the way in which striking trends and cycles could be accounted for in the systematics of early social statistics solely by dispensing with consideration of individual intentions and motives, such statistical agnosticism now became a universal program.

On the one hand, this means that in the "age of petabytes" and cloud services, any intervention of explanations, questions of causality, justifications, and reflective subjects is dispensed with in order, by means of statistical algorithms, to get from data to metadata, to correlations, and to correlations of correlations, to previously unknown patterns or clusters in the flood of data. "Correlation is enough" and "correlation supersedes causation."[37] What is involved here is neither proof nor reasoning but establishing cross-connections. Here, too, a kind of information standard applies that corresponds with the older and clear-sighted expertise on a *postmodern condition*, at least in its imperative. The imperative of this condition is to translate knowledge into quantities of information and to disambiguate accordingly: any received forms of knowledge that cannot be translated in this way are necessarily excised and ignored.[38]

This "whole new way of understanding the world," on the other hand, is linked to an idiosyncratic methodological discourse that, in proclaiming a new science, also announces the "end of theory."[39] Traditional science, from this perspective, still struggles with complicated questions of method and associated hypotheses, with ambiguous semiotic processes, provisional modeling, possible explanations, and therefore the unpredictability of pathways and research trails, failed experiments, or disappointing falsifications. In contrast, the collection, aggregation, and arbitrary correlation of data: for example, between sandal wearers and taste in cinema, between preference for Harley-Davidsons and IQ, between the local distribution of chameleons and environmental factors, or between the gene sequences of different species,[40] simply provide evidentiary data that claim the title of "facts." The numbers speak for themselves, just as the facts have always done. These pieces of evidence justify themselves by their quick accessibility and general availability; they possess the merit that one combination of data cannot falsify another.

Moreover, in this shift, with which the present information economy defines itself as representing a privileged relation to the world, the way theory is conceptualized disqualifies not only the emphatic reference to uncertain knowledge, to the circumstances of the matter that have not yet been established, to disputed hypotheses and open procedural questions. Rather, through the end of theory and through a weakness for weak thinking, there is a hope to put an end, once and for all, to the discussion of epistemological fragilities and to hold out the prospect of an eternal peace in "the conflict of the faculties." In the pronouncements of digital capitalism, what is now called "knowledge" and actually means "information" has demonstratively broken away from the burdensome attachment to logics of reasoning or justification, to scientific communities, to their problematic boundaries, institutions, norms, and testing procedures. That is why arbitrary certainties have become even more certain, even if they contradict each other. Thus, insofar as the representational scheme of digital capitalism consists in bringing knowledge of any kind to the common denominator of information and Big Data, this does more than simply delegate the process of reality to an algorithmic processing with permanent votes and referenda. Especially recent disputes about the production, management, and exploitation of big data have in pointing to an end of theory also declared a systematic delegitimation of knowledge in general. In the midst of an informational explosion, an expansion of zones of ignorance has set in.

Against this background, it seems natural to call for a post-truth approach in the debate about the information economy and about the governing style of contemporary capitalism, that is, an approach that assumes a consistent devaluation of questions of truth and knowledge. This refers not only to a new and spreading trend of mendacity,[41] or to the circumstance that analyses of capitalism – from Karl Marx to Max Weber, from Werner Sombart to Albert O. Hirschman, from Walter Benjamin to Luc Boltanski and Ève Chiapello – have always made reference to the irrational core of capital-driven economic activity. Rather, the intent is also to point out that the production of ignorance and nonknowledge coincides with what capitalism itself calls for and is part and parcel of the field of "agnotology" in the history of science and discourse. Starting from studies on so-called junk sciences, on the staging of "Potemkin-like controversies," on the corporate-funded expert opinions casting doubt on climate change, the validity of evolutionary biology, or the risks of tobacco consumption,[42] questions about the deliberate or structural production of nonknowledge and about the economic resource of ignorance have particularly motivated recent studies on the history of (neo)liberalism in all its varieties. Liberalist programs to justify the capitalist economy have, since the first half of the twentieth century, invoked a resistance to negation and a certain immunity to falsification, and even in the postwar period these programs continued to resist empirical verifiability.[43] But apart from all this, the epistemic status of nonknowledge within this space of thought can be identified in two ways.

On the one hand, this involves the notorious assumption that economic processes, like all complex social relations, are fundamentally beyond the cognition of individual actors, experts, or sciences and are accessible only to the market qua cognitive subject. Especially the influential reflections of Friedrich Hayek had shown how the conception of the market as a price system equipped itself with information-theoretical and cybernetic assumptions and in this way elevated the market mechanism itself to a superior information processor (cf. pp. 25–26). However, this means more than just the emergence of a calculating entity that now acts in the place of other cognitive organs and claims, for instance, to be able to annul even the knowledge of the sciences in the dynamics of general market events. More crucially, it means that information itself has grown from a problematic to a transcendent quantity that cannot really be grasped and processed by anyone. And, while the scattered subjects are unconsciously haunted by "unknown unknowns" (to make use of Donald Rumsfeld's *bon mot*), only the market is able to sort the mass of all circulating information in such a way that an output of truth results from it.[44] Let it be noted in passing that this results in an extremely efficient fusion of informational (i.e., technical) and liberalistic (i.e., political) notions of truth. Insofar as it was only possible to form a cybernetic concept of information by subtracting its substantive and semantic aspects, the "truth" of information lies precisely not in the correctness of this or that factual reference, but solely in the fact that one guarantees the freedom of its transmission. The probabilistic "freedom of choice" in the technical transmission of news has, as Norbert Wiener noted, immediate political resonance in the liberal "freedom of speech or information."[45]

On the other hand, the nonknowledge of subjects acting on the market is not only necessary but desirable; it must be actively produced and conserved. Less a mere absence or insufficiency of economic knowledge, ignorance itself represents a productive force that guarantees that spontaneous patterns of order are produced at all in events on the market. According to this, a tendency toward equilibrium in markets, for instance, as Hayek noted in his canonical 1937 essay on "Economics and Knowledge," can be assumed only under the premise that all players remain equally ignorant, and the concern for evenly distributed blindness or ignorance alone keeps the coordinating power of market processes going. In this process, actors make no distinction between knowledge and belief, determinations and preferences, and everything works all the better the more actors' activities adapt to those circumstances about which they themselves have no knowledge.[46] With this liberal apologia for blind actors, one could still claim in 2015 that only an all-round, "symmetric ignorance" regarding risks and liquidity in financial markets will promote general welfare.[47] As a correlate of information, lack of knowledge has become constitutive and, as all possible experts in knowledge markets are nothing but paid apologists, one needs not more but less knowledge (or not less but more ignorance) to maintain the order-creating forces of the market.

Thus, starting from the liberal demand to install markets as a general evaluative agency of circulating information and relying on the productivity of nonknowledge, the truth game of contemporary capitalism is shaped by two converging developments. Premised upon digital technologies and promoted by the creation of legal exceptions via the First Amendment and the Communications Decency Act, along with international adaptations, an Internet exceptionalism has set in, starting in the US, which has led to the expansion and dominance of new kinds of media corporations. Their business model is characterized by an extremely productive contradiction that drives the dynamics of information capitalism. It consists in the fact that companies, which are not publishers in legal terms, supply the majority of a so-called public with informational goods, produce specific public sectors themselves, and derive their profit precisely from this: in 2017, two-thirds of US Americans received news from social networks.[48] Thus, such platforms or proprietary markets prove to be agents and transformers of a public space characterized by a systematic capitalization of free expression in which the production and distribution of information of any kind is strictly separated from binding categories such as liability, responsibility, or justification. Opinion as such (*das Meinungshafte*) has become the measure of value. At the same time, what is called digitalization in this context cannot be limited to individual sectors, fields of work, or social subsystems. Rather, it has organized vital processes in society together with associated regularities and, in addition, has claimed representational powers for itself that relate to a totality of world relations. The progressive transformation of the world into information has resulted in a production of realities guided by codes, programming languages, and software, in which the representation of things, events, and behaviors coincides with their evaluation, valorization, and economic utilization. This characterizes the truth game of a capitalist ontology. With the control and management, aggregation, and evaluation of large quantities of data, cumbersome procedures for the derivation or verification of the corresponding circumstances of the matter simply became obsolete. To put it bluntly: the logic applied to evaluate financial and information markets has become a paradigm for representing the world in general.

Excursus
Fable and Finance

The dynamics of contemporary finance, information, and platform capitalism cannot be grasped without the rise and consolidation of agnostic positions and agnotological procedures. Their spectrum ranges from (neo)liberal hostility to knowledge, via market-based valuation models and the value ghosts or referential illusions on the capital markets, to the equation of finance and opinion economy or to the systematic fusion of categories of being, meaning, and value. In the interplay between the financial industry, information capital, and opinion markets, the code of information, that is, the difference between information and non-information, has not only become a general standard of value that determines financial-economic business cycles as well as the excitement curves on platforms and social media. More importantly, it has also downgraded or blocked other ways of drawing distinctions. With the question "which data make or do not make a difference," a kind of "overallgorithm" installs itself, to whose functioning the various social, economic and political, private and professional, cultural and administrative communications are more or less directly related. The associated transformation of the public sphere and mass media has led to a zone of indifference in which the older separation of news, entertainment, and advertising no longer applies and has given way to a general denominator that could be called *infopinion.*[1] But even aside from this development, the truth game of the most recent form of capitalism is apparently characterized by a *pseudological* structure. Originating in psychiatry at the end of the nineteenth century, this term – *pseudologia fantastica* – is not, however, simply intended to cover "pathological lies" or "abnormal swindlers," as was the case at the time and in the clinical milieu.[2] Instead, what is at issue here is a nebulous mixture of simulation and dissimulation, at the center of which is the genre of fabulation or fabrication that is as effective as it is disinhibited. In the era of information standards and digital economy, the criterion of knowledge has been loosened, bracketed, or simply done away with.

With reference to the present and current financial and information capitalism, one has already pointed to manifold exemplary fields of application and forms of such fabrications: Be it so-called story stocks, that is, shares of companies which, as is often the case with recent IPOs, are characterized by a divergence between expected and actual earnings and thereby rely on more or less credible stories or product fables. (To take a random example from the recent annals of the US SEC: a company called Transition Systems, Inc., which went public with an "all-purpose generator," a machine for discovering "cancer, heart disease, and petroleum.")[3] Be it the creation of agencies specializing in inventing attractive data and legends for securities or corporations.[4] Be it the cycle of advertising and market value, in which marketing leads to brand awareness and this in turn leads to new value realities and price increases, documenting a unity "of romance and finance."[5] Be it the observation of rampant "bullshit," which divests itself of criteria of true and false, prescribes to the arbitrariness of opinions, and therefore recognizes no rules for stopping or limits to propagation.[6] Be it the boom of "truthiness," the objects of a neologism that has been circulating since 2005, and which, in the regime of current media technologies and information economies, refers to a point of indifference between belief and knowledge, to a performance of feelings of truth or truths of feelings.[7] Be it, finally, innovative industries or character masks, such as influencers, with which a successful marketing effort attempts to sell itself as an everyday way of life in such a way that it can be applied to a series of everyday ways of life.[8] All these manifestations and modes of expression involve a diversity of discursive species that is not exhausted in business cosmetics or fraud, in profitable nonsense or distortions, in humbug, mere lies, misrepresentations, or swindle. Beyond such episodic dimensions, however, it is right to suspect that these fabrications are indicative of a consequential framing of questions of truth and knowledge in the legitimation strategies of finance and information capitalism. It is also right to recognize in the economic genre of fabulation a particular variant from the history of truth-telling. In the context of the finance industry, digital capital, and opinion markets, its status and efficacy are characterized by the fact that it combines the production of credibility and trust with a consistent paralysis or overshadowing of scenarios of reasoning or explanation.

It is hardly surprising, however, that the analysis of such profitable truth games is less likely to come from those sciences that deal with the production and defense of economic regularities. Rather, those discourses come into play that inevitably observe, process, reflect upon, and examine the functions and strategies of fabulation and fabrication itself. Thus, arguably one of the most prominent and radical attempts of this kind was made as early as the mid-nineteenth century, a literary experiment that thrust itself straight into the context of the recently emerging and excessive finance capitalism of the United States. On April 1, 1857, almost simultaneously with the outbreak of one of the first global financial crises, a novel was published in New York that also had its narrative commence on April Fools' Day in the middle of the same century. Early in the morning on that day, the story goes, a steamboat leaves the port of St. Louis to begin its journey down the Mississippi River to New Orleans. Christened with the hopeful name of *Fidèle* – and thus endowed with the characteristics of the faithful, trustworthy, or believing – it gathers a cosmopolitan mix of nationals and foreigners of all kinds, a social microcosm whose hustle and bustle resembles that of exchange offices and business worlds, of "merchants on [the ex-]change" and, animated by a "Wall street spirit," leads into the "Tartarus" of young US capitalism: "Auctioneer or coiner, with equal ease, might somewhere here drive his trade."[9]

It may be no coincidence that the setting chosen in this way, namely the gateway to the West and the "cosmopolitan and confident tide" of the Mississippi, had already been a notorious subject and scene of fierce waves of speculation since the beginning of the eighteenth century. At one time, for example, the shares of the French Mississippi Company were supposed to finance the issuance of paper money by the Banque Royale in Paris to avert state bankruptcy following the death of Louis XIV. This bold financial-economic project, invented by the Scottish financial theorist and gambler John Law, began to flourish in 1717 but collapsed and perished in 1720. Moreover, after a second attempt to establish a US national bank on the part of President Andrew Jackson was aborted in 1836, a banking pluralism had set in, which led, especially in the western US, to a multiplication of banking institutions, a proliferation of barely regulated, so-called wildcat banks, and diverse currencies; by the 1860s, some 1,200 banks there had issued about 12,000 different sorts of private banknotes. Ultimately, as early as 1837, the associated uncontrolled expansion of credit contributed to a financial panic, the collapse of numerous private banks, and a prolonged economic crisis in the US, sparking widespread debates about the role of "trust" in American capital, monetary, and commercial transactions.[10]

Against this background, Herman Melville, in a novel entitled *The Confidence-Man: His Masquerade*, experimented with an astonishing interweaving of truth games, issues of trust, finance, and narrative aboard his capitalist ship of fools. This resulted in a distinctive narrative cycle that, in rhythmic reiteration, converts recounted stories into money, reports into banknotes, anecdotes into share certificates, and, in any case, narratives into payments, and vice versa. In this way it documents an intimate interconnectedness between the art of fabrication, narrative persuasion, and business transactions, and therefore might merit closer scrutiny. Thus, at one point in the novel it is stated: "In a low, half-suppressed tone, he began it. Judging from his auditor's expression, it seemed to be a tale of singular interest.... As the story went on, he [the auditor] drew from his wallet a banknote, but after a while,... changed it for another, probably of a somewhat larger amount" (23). This recurring synchronicity of financing and fabricating, of narrative and economic cycles, cannot be concluded in structural terms and is also marked by a series of internal narrators who continuously substitute for one another with their stories. They appear as "masquerades" of one and the same con(fidence) man, function as versions of the same motley figure, also called the "liberal" or "cosmopolitan" (157), and even draw the narrator himself into their bottomless game. When, for instance, one of these main characters or variants is distracted from the scene of the narrative, the narrator of the whole is not left unaffected. He is immediately carried away and falls back into the narrated: "At an interesting point of the narration, and at the moment when, with much curiosity, indeed, urgency, the narrator was being particularly questioned on that point, he was, as it happened, altogether diverted from both it and his story" (39).

The narrator and the narrator narrated about have become one here; when one takes into account the novel's narrative, the confusion of narrators and protagonists, and the multiplication of narrative instances – simultaneously one and many, single and multivoiced – it makes obsolete any reference to the reliability of a dependable narrator.[11] The coordinate according to which what is narrated in the novel could be authenticated or ratified is erased, opening a game of self-sustaining fabulation. Thus, throughout the novel, it is impossible to decide whether the multivoiced title character of *Confidence-Man* represents a veritable confidant or a pure fraud, or both at the same time. One must probably concede in complete bafflement that, in view of this narrative situation, neither the one nor the other can really be confirmed. At best, the narrator(s) can be understood as embodiments of "transaction[s]" (63) that follow the logic of a self-capitalizing form of speech. What speaks or fabricates here is identified as a character mask of capital.

This has several consequences and means, first of all, that all questions of substantiation, of legitimating and vouching for the events as narrated are thrust into the open. This happens immediately in one of the central scenes of authentication at the beginning of the novel. The appearance of a crippled black beggar on the ship deck has led not only to a "game of charity" and to profitable transactions somewhere between pitiful spectacle and charitable coin tosses, but at the same time to the suspicion that the cripple's "deformity" may have been "a sham, got up for financial purposes" (11). Alone the name of the black man, "Black Guinea" (9), refers to coinage or more precisely: to black, diabolic arts, or coin counterfeiting.[12] But apart from this, the demand for "documentary proof" attesting to the honest poverty of the beggar elicits his ambiguous reply: "haint none o'dem waloable papers" (12). Moreover, the urgent search for witnesses, vouchers, and guarantees for this very thing is answered only with the naming of those questionable figures who, like the man with a black ribbon, the one in a "gray coat" or the one with a "book" (13), will turn out to be the various avatars of the ominous Confidence-Man or Cosmopolitan. The search for references, in both the bureaucratic and semiotic sense, simply stumbles from one mask to another and finds neither a stopping point nor an original; it also includes the "poor ole darkie" (16) in the series of "confidence men" and thus in the vicious circle of referrals.

This pattern is confirmed again and again, with a similar case of circular reasoning at the end of the novel. There, it involves the authenticity of those privately issued banknotes that circulated with precarious backing and in a quasi-inflationary manner in the western US. In this specific case, it concerns a certain "three-dollar bill on the Vicksburgh Trust and Insurance Banking Company" (282), which is now to be checked against the characteristics of a "counterfeit detector" list that was regularly published at the time. However, as little as signifiers can be matched with references here ("if the bill is good, it must have in one corner ... the figure of a goose" – "I can't see this goose" – "and a famous goose it is" – "I don't see the goose" – a "beautiful goose" – "I don't see it" [282–283]), it remains unclear whether the counterfeit detector refers to an instrument for detecting counterfeits or, conversely, whether the detector itself is a counterfeit.[13] Thus, just as the question of a guarantee for the beggar's tale at the beginning cannot be distinguished from a wild goose chase (13) or a waste of effort, the "wild goose chase" (283) with regard to the authenticity of the banknotes at the end only identifies signifiers with blocked referentiality.

In all these and similar cases, appeals to the workings of an "improved judgment" (11) are not rewarded with any results. Together with the postings of narrators circling in an endless round of masquerades, "pretty" stories (106) are at best validated by means of further stories. For this very reason, however, the (narrated) narration in Melville's novel remains committed solely to the production of credibilities, convictions, or certainties with which investments are justified, loans induced, buyers inspired, and stocks touted. Indeed, the "word '*confidence*'" itself circulates in capital letters as the "countersign" (i.e., password) of this world (93). The aforementioned and narratively produced trust is thus theologically charged, in an almost Pauline sense: as "faith" it is based less on experience than on "inspiration" and is meant to survive the "fluctuations ... of the stock-exchange" (72). With its systematic intertwining of capital, credit, and questions of faith, the special character of this trust lies in the fact that the certainties associated with it elude any test or verifiability, any reality check. This leads to the heart of the truth games of the novel (as well as those of finance capital). In an exemplary conversation between a good-natured merchant and the broker or "stock agent" of the Black Rapids coal company (again a black or diabolical variant of the liberal cosmopolitan or confidence man), this is negotiated epistemologically, so to speak, and linked to the question of whether the "transfer-book" at hand for documenting profitable stock transactions was really deserving of trust and was not itself "bogus." This results in a lengthy conversation:

> "Dear me, you don't think of doing any business with me, do you? In my official capacity I have not been authenticated to you. This transfer-book now," holding it up so as to bring the lettering in sight, "how do you know that it may not be a bogus one? And I, being personally a stranger to you, how can you have confidence in me?"
>
> "Because," knowingly smiled the good merchant, "if you were other than I have confidence that you are, hardly would you challenge distrust in that way."
>
> "But you have not examined my book."
>
> "What need to, if already I believe that it is what it is lettered to be?"
>
> "But you had better. It might suggest doubts."
>
> "Doubts, may be, it might suggest, but not knowledge; for how, by examining the book, should I think I knew any more than I now think I do; since, if it be the true book, I think it so already; and since if it be otherwise, then I have never seen the true one, and don't know what that ought to look like."
>
> "Your logic I will not criticize, but your confidence I admire ..." (62)

Thus, just as it is the dispensing with verification that produces certainties, so distrust produces trust as much as trust itself. And perhaps, against the background of this small epistemic scene, the status of fabrication, the pseudo character of this world relation and the pseudological structure of the truth game connected to it can be grasped a bit more precisely. Thus, first of all, one is dealing with proliferating or inflationary strings of signs in which the signifieds slip away under the signifiers and corresponding seams and linkages do not hold. On the contrary, wherever the prospect is held out of corresponding connections or "quilting points,"[14] in order, for instance, to stitch together stories with their guarantees or "inscriptions" with "contents," that is, certain signifiers with certain signifieds, such a system of location and orientation is consistently blotted out and annulled. On the one hand, in the course of the novel, this fabrication or fabulation therefore results not in too few certainties, but in a melee of too many, all of which assert themselves as equally significant and equally groundless next to one another. On the other hand, this triggers cycles of recasting and reversals, in which, for example, opposing meanings such as trust and mistrust, philanthropy and malice, credibility and deceit, goodness and treachery, innocence and slyness take over from each other and represent one another, both abruptly and fully.

With its peculiar resistance to contradiction, the logic of this truth game thus does not merely fall prey to a modern principle of insufficient reason, which, with the "be it X or be it Y" of its narratives, commits itself to a diverging series of differing narratives of equal validity that never converge in a common reason, upon a common foundation. (Gilles Deleuze had already pointed out the proximity of Melville's narrative world to the "principle of insufficient reason" found in Musil's *Man Without Qualities*.)[15] Secondly, it is, however, much more likely to follow the principle that unassailable "knowledge" or certainty (with which it can be cogently equated) can only really be guaranteed by the disavowal or foreclosure of questions of reason. Here, "foreclosure" (*Verwerfung*) must probably be understood in a strict terminological sense and refer to such negations that, as in the example of the good merchant, do not take note of their object, and even more: quite fundamentally do not want to know anything about it and remove it as an "unknown unknown" from the reach of any possible power of judgment.[16] The absent or rejected referent of the "transfer book" is thus an object of speculation par excellence. In a similar way, and again uniting biblical and business credibilities, the portfolio of the stock agent has also, in fact, held out the prospect of "investing" in a "New Jerusalem." And it is an investment that appears trustworthy only as long as one refrains from checking the *terra firma* of this dignified building project on the banks of the Mississippi, which may in fact just be "water-lots" (55).

Accordingly, the trusting subject who subscribes to certainties, and thus represents the address and hope of all enterprising confidence men and brokers, cannot be characterized simply by a loss of reality or by a disturbed relation to it. What is suggested, instead, is a far-reaching partitioning of his or her sense of reality. On the one hand, credibilities and certainties are indistinguishable from irrealities. Thus, the narrator lets a conceited listener exclaim "How unreal all this is!" (206) in view of the narrated "antics" (206). On the other hand, every threatened reality check results in the triggering of uncomfortable "doubts." Real references trigger uneasiness. Here things work in the same way as with that trusting old man who, as it says in another story, "was so charmed" in the theater "with the character of a faithful wife, as there represented to the life," that he can no longer be dissuaded from the idea of such faithfulness. He thus marries a "beautiful girl from Tennessee," "yet such was his confidence" that he ignores all hints received regarding her infidelity. Once, however, on entering the marital bedroom, he comes upon a fleeing bedfellow of his wife: "'Begar [sic]!' cried he, 'now I *begin* to suspec [sic]'" (33–34). Plain certainty has been mirrored in pretended realities, while the passing reality's residue or referent can only be the object of deep skepticism. The realm of the real has been divided and provided with an uncrossable demarcation line. This characterizes the pseudological difference. Accordingly, real certainties on the one hand are contrasted with the recognition of uncertain realities on the other, whose existence is probably not really doubtful in normal cases, but rarely evident and unambiguous.[17] Therefore, one could also recognize the "realism" of Melville's novel in the fact that it recounts a disavowal of the real in the realities of the (finance) economy it accesses.

The truth games of the confidence man or his con games, this synecdoche of capitalist transactions,[18] thus elaborate a pseudological structure. In this way, they produce discursive effects in which one cannot separate fabricated certainties from proliferating signifiers, sliding signifieds, and a systematic rejection of reality checks, that is, from the production of unconscious nonknowledge.[19] For the subjects of these discourses, therefore, trust and suspicion lie indistinguishably within one another, and what produces persuasiveness cannot be distinguished from a "pantomime" (150) "specially" staged for its addressees. Such fables or certainties, however, should not be disqualified as mere lies or deceptions. Rather, they testify to the stabilization of a form of discourse in which the criterion and difference of fraud itself have been annulled. This is the point at which Melville's novel sought out the intersection of discursive economies with economic discourses and paid its tribute to the finance economy of his time. In the face of a financial system that is as erratic as it is expansive, he sketched out an implicit theory of fabulation in which capitalist business transactions lay claim to the rights of the irrational. It is a time when the word of two meanings "trust," that is, "fidelity and faith" (4), is starting to morph into a title for monopoly-like corporate structures. In this way, talk of trust, credibility, conviction, and certainty is beset by a power of the false that makes it easy to confound the messianic aspects of what is happening with diabolic ones.[20] Melville's capitalist ship of fools thus ends up heading, again framed in biblical or apocalyptic terms, toward a "darkness which ensued" (286), a darkness that may conceal a benevolent and trustworthy "creator" (281) but may also give cover to a diabolical principle of deception.

Thus, in the fabulous and fable-like business world of the novel, in this economic realm of the pseudo, there is no longer anything that provides cover for or guarantees the truth of reality. What predominates is the meaningful, but without meaning, and thus the force of a higher irrationalism, in whose milieu the real coincides with the counterfeit. In the observation of early stock-exchange transactions, that which was the most real was mixed with that which was most false (cf. p. 33). Similarly, this is also the connecting line that can be drawn from a literary exposition of the nineteenth century to the present interplay of finance capital, automated rating systems, and the information economy. What is at stake here concerns the way in which the representation of the world as information associates itself with the foreclosure of those onerous moments resulting from the protracted procedures of examination and arenas of exploration. The production of certainties and evidentia, in which simulations and dissimulations coincide, is the other side of a loss of symbolic efficiency, that is, the loss of a grounding or foundation in which all words and signifiers, as well as their subjects, might find a common mooring. Formulated in somewhat older terms, one might recognize in the cosmos of information a production of the real, in which the efficacy of an "evil spirit,"[21] a *genius malignus* or deceiver-god, cannot be excluded. In this truth game it is simply no longer certain whether something could exist that would not be absolutely deceptive or absolutely not deceptive.

6

The Cunning of Ressentiment-Driven Reason

Since the early modern period, the economization of governance has advanced from the emergence of a political economy to the management of populations and the imposition of market and competitive societies. It has also led to a financial regime in which the reproduction and accumulation of capital is combined with the diversification of elementary technologies of governance. However, the recent fusion of the finance and information economies has resulted not only in the occupation of social infrastructures, a refinement of the powers of control and the management of behavior, and a mutual strengthening of entrepreneurial and governmental practices. Rather, it is precisely the effectiveness of network architectures, platform enterprises, and digital corporations on the micro level that reveals the ways in which the evaluative principles of the finance economy determine the circulation and processing of information, and the expansion and hegemony of opinion markets. The circulation of information has become the paradigmatic form of capitalist economy. In this context, the stabilization and preservation of corresponding business formats cannot be separated from a mobilization of truth games. And, in these truth games, one construes market relations as general references to reality and, even as realities themselves, to the degree that they offer untapped opportunities for exploitation. Under contemporary information capitalism, relations to being and world are coded and represented from the perspective of their (economic) management.

In view of the fables and fictions connected with this, perspectives are again called for that grasp the history of the forms of capitalist economy not solely along the lines of rationalization processes. For this history must also be understood in terms of the resources and productive forces that ignorance, fantasies, and irrationalities bring to bear. In this context, it seems remarkable how even early modern appraisals of the social resonance of capitalist entrepreneurial culture drew particular attention to the emergence of new economies of affect. Thus, on the one hand, the model of the entrepreneurial or economic actor was presented as a small island of rationality from which one could organize a confusing world, as Robinson Crusoe once did, according to advantage and disadvantage, profit and loss. On the other hand, and in parallel, an anthropological reform took place, which transformed the traditional sociable and political animal, the familiar *zoon politikon*, into a dysfunctional and not very social being. Since the seventeenth century, an extensive literature on concepts such as "self-love" or "self-preservation" had documented that in the light of new social types one can at best speak of an "unsociable sociability" or a "nation of devils," as Kant did. For what had been envisioned as human substance since the Enlightenment was in a "depraved state" and referred to as a "[c]reature, subject to many vile inclinations."[1]

It was noted early on in this context that there was a relevant connection between affects and passions, on the one hand, and economic processes and market systems, on the other. The former deadly sins or primary vices – such as *avaritia*, *invidia*, or *luxuria* (i.e., avarice, envy, or lust) – are now given a positive turn, supported by the observation that it is not the moderate inclinations but rather the immoderate ones that prove to be truly inventive, cunning, creative, and productive. Moreover, it should be noted that all these various passions provoke and keep each other agitated, such that they ultimately balance each other out and compensate for each other's ill effects. Thus, one person's miserliness keeps another's wastefulness in check, and both together, with all of their tricks and wiles, contribute to the good of all. Thus, affects and passions, as described here by Bernard Mandeville, are conceived less as psychological traits and more as structures of social relations and communicative acts. What appears immoral, irregular, and reprehensible in the individual results in a dynamic and coherent order within the overall economic framework. Mandeville writes: A good politician has only to reckon with the worst in man. He does not proceed from virtues and average qualities, but from the extreme case of unbridled passions and considers them as reactants in their effect on each other when mixed – how they "melt away alike, and ... consume themselves by being beneficial to the several compositions they belong to."[2] Economic man comes into the world not merely with rational and computational talents, but as a particularly passionate subject, still capable of exchanging the old Christian vices for new and profitable assets.

The observation of a systemic and productive interconnection between affects and the economy or market processes ranges from the functionality of former indices of sin such as envy, avarice, and wastefulness to a more recent variant, which Karl Marx called the "abstract hedonism" of the capitalist.[3] By this he meant an uninhibited drive for enrichment that permeates the social field and follows the movement of capital: it cannot be reconciled with any concrete need or with any episodic satisfaction or fulfillment and, as a boundless, insatiable desire, documents the psychic absorption[4] of want (or lack) into the interior spaces of economic subjects. Parallel to this, since the second half of the nineteenth century, a similar affect and a related lack-in-being (*Seinsmangel*) have been discovered in a different conceptual formulation, in which disinhibited economic striving is intertwined with the legacy of the older catalog of vices. For the spectrum covered by what was now termed *ressentiment* was not only traced back, as in Nietzsche, to a long moral past or to a Judeo-Christian culture of self-poisoning. Instead, for the contemporary analysis of ressentiment, a general economic principle was invoked. Here, one sought to relate this principle directly to the epoch of expanding capital and finance economy in Europe, to emerging liberalism, to the structure of bourgeois society, to the dynamics of periods of rapid growth, and to modern economic man as subject. This applies, for example, to Kierkegaard's critical diagnosis of the times or to Werner Sombart's and Max Scheler's re-readings of Nietzsche's writings from the 1880s.

It also applies to Jean-Paul Sartre's use of Gustave Flaubert to exemplify his description of the self-enrichment regime in the Second Empire under Napoleon III as a culture of ressentiment. Clearly, such perspectives have themselves not always been free of ressentiment and, like Sombart's anti-Semitism or Scheler's world-war nationalism, recommend a critical interpretation of these ressentiment critiques themselves. Nonetheless, they still lay out a trail that points to an effective, reciprocal relationship between instances of ressentiment and capitalism.

In this context, one should first call to mind some elements that, since Nietzsche, have been essential for characterizing structures of ressentiment and have persisted across diverging analyses and standpoints. This includes, first, a peculiarly broken self-affirmation of the subject of ressentiment, which takes place only as the result of an unconditional "no" to an "outside," to an "other," to a "not-self," and thus derives from a negation. Second, this inversion of a negation into a negating self-affirmation is connected to a shift of forces, in which action is replaced by reaction and the latter by inhibition. This leads to a passive form of activity, to a forced or self-imposed block of action, and thus to a cultivation of powerlessness. The "re-" in ressentiment (French *se ressentir de qc.*: to sense the aftereffects or consequences of something) signals that blocked (re)actions have congealed into a permanent and unresolved state of mind. Third, this means that the objects and entities of the external world can become, in varying degrees, possible occasions for a felt grievance and injury, for the pain of being rejected. They can make themselves felt with an existential or life envy and with a burning sense of a lack-in-being, with memory serving as a self-reinforcing mechanism for such suffering. And this diminishment of being is not just linked to an inversion of the valorizing gaze, an inversion that itself becomes creative and produces values. It is also linked to a tendency to delegate, to an interest in turning over domains of activity, to a kind of punitivism that appeals to higher powers and instances for the harming or taming of others. Fourth and finally, a concretism is invoked, a preference for what are assumed to be immediately tangible embodiments, with which one makes attributions and assigns responsibility, sets one's own disadvantages against other people's advantages, identifies culprits, and even personalizes what may very well be due to "circumstances": "Someone must be to blame for the fact that I am in a bad way."[5] Causal reflexes and bits of evidence are privileged over real causal research; ressentiment cannot cope with the uncertainty of causes.

Thus, one can certainly call the individuals exhibiting ressentiment "profiteers par excellence" and term ressentiment itself a morality of the economic (or an economic moral principle) in general. But one can go further: ressentiment as a reflective affect, as a peculiar, "senti-mental" mixture of calculating reason and toxic sentiments, could enjoy a certain upswing or supremacy only under the condition that with it the claim to profits, advantages, gratuities, and compensations had been transformed from a mere thought or selective appetite into a "comprehensive system," into a general social and economic "mechanism."[6] With its structural elements, at any rate with negating self-affirmation, deferred impulse to act, envy of life, tendency to delegate, and addiction to apportioning blame, ressentiment has been credited, beyond all moral and religious-historical derivations, with making an essential contribution to the formation of a "capitalist spirit," and been declared a productive resource in the functioning of property-based, competitive societies.[7] This particular interlocking of affect economy and capitalism owes its existence to a number of factors that, according to Max Scheler and others, are particularly characteristic of the negative socialization found in liberal or liberalist conceptions of the market system. Let us consider ressentiment not as a subjective mood or mental state, but rather as a structure of relations and a mode of communication, taking it in its systemic and systematic dimension. It then becomes clear that its roots, its flashpoint, and its primary capital lie in a specific compulsion to compare and relate, in a reflex to valorize and evaluate, in a rampant desire to judge.

For this reason, Max Scheler, in particular, first related ressentiment to the normative order of liberalism, with reference to the liberal claim to legal equality or equality of rights. For in so doing, in the aftermath of the bourgeois revolutions, one claimed a right to recognition and leveling, with "the injured person always plac[ing] himself *on the same level* as his injurer."[8] In other words, one laid claim to a legal conversion of passivity and suffering and thus a right against the other, to intensified attributions of blame (such as the right, "*to attribute* to the bird of prey its predator status").[9] But, apart from these claims, special comparative routines took root, not least due to the notorious discrepancies between formal equality and actual material inequalities. Marx had already regarded the formal securing of equal rights as a prerequisite for the factual recourse to them, and thus as a prerequisite for the actual impact of concrete differences: for example, with respect to property, education, or employment. Therefore, just as the subjective rights of the private and "egoistic human being, separated from his fellow human being and from the community," are realized in bourgeois society in conjunction with a powerlessness in the political realm,[10] Scheler, too, contrasted formal equality with the "wide factual differences" in existing power and property relations. It is precisely the gap (or, more precisely, the functional connection) between equality of rights and the inequality of conditions, between legal promises of equality and actual incommensurabilities, that makes the permanently aroused and permanently disappointed desire for comparison and comparability a source of ressentiment, a source, at any rate, that springs not from these or those contingent circumstances and sensibilities, but from the "structure" of liberal economic society itself. Scheler thus even ventured toward conjecturing that "social ressentiment" could probably only be minimized by an overthrow of capitalist property relations, in a "democracy which ... tends toward equality of property." However, ressentiment cannot be accounted for by direct economic disadvantage alone. According to Scheler, "social ressentiment" does not simply result from inequality, but from specific combinations of inequalities and claims to equality. If there is no doubt that capitalist societies are structured by ressentiment, it is due to the way in which the interlocking of promises of participation and relations of production enable and direct an affective interpretation of power relations, the perception of divergences and competitions, and thus the efficacy of comparative mechanisms.[11] The issue, then, is the difficulty faced by an economic analysis that in fact cannot rely on firm evidence of a direct link between ressentiment and manifest economic disadvantages.

In this context, the systematic dimension of comparative consciousness and ressentiment comes to the fore precisely when they assert themselves as elementary principles of social intercourse in market and competitive constellations. On the one hand, the dynamic of ressentiment in the "system of competition" is nourished by permanent processes of evaluation and judgment, which correlate evaluations to devaluations and therefore come close to an "organic [i.e., structural] mendacity": One affirms in order to negate, and qualifies in order to disqualify.[12] Thus, it stands to reason to assume that the current atomization of competitive arenas and the distribution of micro-markets across the fabric of society have tapped into further sources of ressentiment-charged emotions. The evaluative form (*Wertungsform*) of ressentiment would be the moral-historical product of capitalist value creation; it would be an economic moral principle with the propensity to assume the heft of an objective spirit. In Kierkegaard's words, ressentiment manifests itself as a "negatively unifying principle," as the "negative unity of the negative mutual reciprocity [i.e., nonreciprocity] of individuals."[13]

On the other hand, the "competitive urge" is associated with the "inner boundlessness" of a drive that does not recognize any difference between what is desired and what is valued. Like Marx's abstract hedonism, it necessarily deceives itself about the lack-in-being disguised therein by appealing to concrete and competing interests. Basically, this economy of ressentiment is characterized by a circulating lack or shortage and the consequent production of scarcity, which is the basis of capitalist market systems. It refers to what has always been "snatched away": the other always has what no one has, every having means a not-having, every too much means too little, and every abundance means deprivation. Ressentiment suffers from the theft of what has never been possessed; it is afflicted by a covetous reluctance, by an inaccessible, suspected, and imputed abundance in the other that does not exist and that, for this very reason, enables one's own lack to be reflected in the phantasm of another's appetite or enjoyment.[14] In ressentiment, the abstractness of hedonism is thus linked with an equally abstract lust for retribution, which demands its fulfillment in this or that concrete case. All these elements give evidence of the economic productivity of a comparative consciousness that has congealed into ressentiment. As much as it manifests itself in the machinery of competition as a force for the creeping erosion or dissolution of principles of solidarity, it avoids the risks of open revolt and insurrection.[15] It may thus be concluded that it makes itself and its subjects useful instruments for the attainment and preservation of the system of market economy.

In several respects, then, a functional relationship between capitalism and ressentiment can be observed that encompasses, in equal measure, formal conditions, modes of social intercourse, subject forms, and judgment practices. Moreover, this *structural* connection between affect and economy has repeatedly been supplemented and reinforced by conspicuous *cyclical* movements. Thus, recent historical-statistical surveys have once again confirmed the assumption that precisely the dynamics of the finance and capital economy in almost all industrialized countries since the end of the nineteenth century have repeatedly been linked to significant political upheavals. In the context of a growing literature on the immediate political consequences of financial-economic turmoil, these surveys were able to demonstrate that financial and, in particular, banking crises (starting with the panics of the 1870s and continuing through the crashes in the interwar period up to the collapse of 2007 and 2008) have led not only to political polarization and to a fractionalization of parliaments and government action, but also to a strengthening of right-wing nationalist parties and positions, with an ethno-nationalist (*völkisch*) and xenophobic orientation. Their growth in representative elections has averaged up to thirty percent and, for the years after 2008, the emergence or marked growth of right-wing parties up to and including government participation has been documented for most industrialized countries. This finding seems all the more remarkable given that parties from the left of the spectrum did not benefit, or benefited only rarely and locally, and that, moreover, similar effects were not demonstrable in "normal" recessions and economic crises, in economic slumps without financial crashes. Financial crises, it was concluded, damage modern democracies and entail "politically disruptive" effects. One can, of course, point to possible explanatory relationships and in particular to the fact that episodes of financial crisis are probably perceived as "endogenous" and "avoidable," as the culpable behavior of political and economic actors, and that their consequences are often linked to fierce conflicts between creditors and debtors or to unpopular bailouts.[16] Even so, it still remains unclear in precisely what way the disasters of the finance and capital economy combine with such flagrant cyclical upswings of ressentiment.

A possible clue toward explaining these reciprocal relations between the finance economy, the occurrence of crises, and the evoked political responses may be provided by older analyses of critical theory. Take, for instance, Theodor W. Adorno's conjecture that the social preconditions for the latent existence of national, ethno-nationalist, or xenophobic ressentiments have persisted across various political regimes since the nineteenth century and can be found, not least, in the movements of capital concentration. Adorno spoke of the possibility that precisely those "strata of society that were clearly bourgeois in terms of their subjective class consciousness" see themselves subject to potential loss of class status and thus react with ressentiment.[17] This is bolstered by the observation that the tendencies toward concentration and accumulation in capitalism over the last century and a half have been accompanied by a periodic release of significant divergent forces, in the panics of the 1870s and in the interwar periods as well as since the 1990s. Together with the expansion of credit and debt economies, with speculative financial markets, and rising stock and real estate prices, they have repeatedly been reflected in rising returns on capital and in the increased shares of national incomes made up by large private fortunes and produced effects which in turn became noticeable in economic instabilities and in shifts in the balance of social and political power.[18] These findings may well correspond to the more general observation that the dynamics of capitalism have resulted in an "uninterrupted disturbance of all social conditions" and the continuous erosion or destruction of seemingly "idyllic relations."[19]

In this context of interplay between crisis events and finance capital, the mechanism of ressentiment follows a course that is as peculiar as it is exemplary. For example, the post-1870 financial panics were followed by an expansion and intensification of anti-Semitism, all the way to the emergence of anti-Semitic political parties. Here, we find an initial articulation of the cunning of ressentiment-driven reason as it consistently distracted from the immanent purposes of the economic system, and from the effectiveness of its apparatuses, infrastructures, and functional mechanisms. It found its need for the concretization of attribution, responsibility, and causation satisfied with the personification of the economic system in representatives of so-called high finance, ultimately targeting the figure of the "greedy" Jewish finance capitalist. (To this day, and in various guises, the attractive "greed" of overly greedy speculators continues to assume a comparable exculpatory function intellectually.)

On the one hand, such anti-Semitic, xenophobic, or racist means of addressing finance capital refer to a long social and political history in which the exclusion, persecution, and expulsion of Jews were combined with their privileged status in the field of money lending. Since the Middle Ages, this produced first the social figure of the Jewish usurer, then the Jewish state banker, and this was passed on, as it were, to the more recent denunciations of the money man.[20] On the other hand, from the earliest (e.g., Aristotelian) reflections on the quality of monetary transactions, like those of chrematistics, such transactions have been viewed not only as precariously nonproductive and nonnatural, but also as epitomizing the non-autochthonous and alien. According to Benveniste, in the Indo-European languages there is not even any evidence of a particular name or positive definition for commercial transactions. Thus, these forms of business apparently lie outside of all trades, outside of all practices and techniques, and also find no place in the activities defining a trifunctional society (which, according to Georges Dumézil and Georges Duby, is comprised of priesthood, peasantry, and warriorship).[21] And exactly the same holds for finance capital: persistently across a variety of standpoints and assessments, it has always marked the position of the unlocatable, the foreign, or the radically alien. For instance, in Herman Melville's novel, the *Confidence-Man* climbed aboard the capitalist ship of fools as a "stranger," or more precisely as "[a stranger] in the extremist sense of the word." And, even in Friedrich Hayek's work, the invocation of the figure of the *xenos* still serves as a justification for releasing capital and the capitalist from their ties to state territories and sovereign rights.[22]

It should be noted that Jewish entrepreneurs were long subject to confinement in the sphere of circulation and, in contrast to "indigenous" capitalists, only "at a late stage and with difficulty"[23] granted access to ownership of the means of production. And this enables the cunning of ressentiment to take the path of a logical regression: it extracts from the crisis-induced critique of international capitalism a critique of the sphere of circulation and brokerage, and from the critique of its representatives, finally, the anti-Semitic template. The topos of opposition between autochthonous and unbound, between productive and unproductive capital, which was sustained in the narratives of the most successful German national literature, such as Gustav Freytag's *Soll und Haben*, thereby found its racist cast; and with their dependence on the business cycles and structures of finance capital, with which they nonetheless conspired, the owners of larger capitals, just like the small savers of the Wilhelmine era (*Gründerzeit*), turned this constellation into a target that could be held socially and economically liable.[24] Against the internationalism of capital movements, nationalism was sought out as an organ for the collective representation of bourgeois interests, while mimetic desire or competitive mimicry, that is, one's own competition for appropriation and profit, was denounced. And it was denounced as the familiar in the alien, found in the picture of the parasitic enjoyment of Jewish financiers. This anti-Semitic figure thus fulfills all the conditions that a surrogate object can exhibit for incriminating one's economic system dependency and powerlessness, and thus as the embodiment of abstract retribution in ressentiment: the object must be sufficiently concrete, on the one hand, but not too tangible, on the other, in order not to be annihilated by its own reality; it must be located in history and be a conspicuous element of tradition; it must be able to be defined by stereotypes in order to remain recognizable and generalizable; and it should have characteristics in which ressentiment's denunciatory acts of judgment can be reflected.[25] Thus, by means of anti-Semitism, the cunning of ressentiment-driven reason dramatizes itself in the last third of the nineteenth century. The alliance between capital and race forged in this way, in conjunction with the exorcism of "unproductive" finance capital woven into anti-Semitism, turns out to be the conformist insurgency of ressentiment. Combined, these forces ultimately prove to be an efficient capitalist self-criticism, with which the economic system is able to ensure its survival in times of crisis. The system's conditions themselves remain unexamined.

Ressentiment can thus be understood as a basic structural and stabilizing affect of capitalism that undergoes special cycles under the contemporary finance economy and its crises. However, the management of the social by finance and information capital has provided this intertwining of affect communication and economic dynamics with a recent twist and intensification. Admittedly, the following examples are little more than disparate circumstantial evidence.

- For example, during the last inauguration of a Brazilian president, his supporters shouted "WhatsApp! WhatsApp! Facebook! Facebook!"
- The head of the Italian Lega accompanied some of his appearances with the slogan "Long live Facebook!"
- Mark Zuckerberg offered the Hindu nationalist president of India an exclusive forum on Facebook and, in election times, touted his direct communication style on social media and particularly on Facebook.
- Google's support for initiatives and organizations that oppose gun controls, climate protection, emissions limits, or advocate voter suppression and tax breaks for the tobacco industry has suggested talk of a "Googlization of the far right."
- In the United States, rabid wealth-promoting measures have been combined with the mobilization of racist and anti-democratic ressentiments.
- Employees of Facebook, Google, and Twitter were embedded in the 2016 Republican presidential campaign.
- The massacres of the Muslim minority in Myanmar were fueled by Facebook.
- The Alternative for Germany (AfD) has 87 percent of all shares of political parties in Germany on Facebook.
- Or, finally, false reports in social media spread six times as fast and a hundred times as frequently as verifiable news.[26]

Clearly, these are at best sporadic indications of the current entanglement of finance and information capitalism on the one hand, and the upswings of ressentiment on the other. Moreover, a direct, empirically verifiable connection between Internet communication and political polarization is controversial, to say the least.[27] Nevertheless, it is possible to identify a number of structural elements in the transactions of the opinion markets under current network conditions that promote a propensity to ressentiment.

The exact interrelationship between the business with clickbaits, clickstreams, and political trends may remain unclear. Nonetheless, a concise concept of the political has emerged from corporate headquarters that systematically reckons with the immediacy effects of network communication accompanying growing market power. Although it should probably be chalked up to the usual promotional noise when Facebook claims, for example, that since 2017, in the "most recent election campaigns around the world, from India and Indonesia to Europe and the USA," it was always the candidates "with the largest and most engaged following on Facebook" who won. This corporate self-praise, however, is endowed with a political agenda, and it has a clear direction. Put in older and more familiar terms, it holds out the prospect of a disempowering of society (and its mediating institutions) and an empowering of communities (along with their associated rituals of authenticity). Here we find hybrid genres of pronouncement, which, like Facebook's *Building Global Community* of February 2017, oscillate between advertising brochure, house memo, pastoral letter, and political pamphlet and are worth reading precisely due to this mix. In these pronouncements, forms of community in all the current colors of the spectrum are offered up for the production of a corporate community of users or produsers and for the "products" and "businesses" advertised with it, combining, moreover, traditional and projective forms with one another. They range from "friendships," "families," "church congregations," "sports teams," and neighborhoods to ethnic groups, "tribes," and "nations," to the oxymoron of a global community. They extend to all possible dimensions of a life-in-community and aim at a specific kind of *community governance*. In the face of a supposed "decline" of "local communities" or "local groups," this means a reterritorialization or settling of social structures in "our community," in the Facebook Community or Facebook Nation. In this way, a bundle of governmental tasks and services such as precaution and care, security, prevention, or defense against danger are to be assembled and appropriated ("social infrastructure to keep us safe from threats around the world"). But that is not all.

This communitarian rhetoric goes back to the history of the various forms of American populism, which started at the end of the nineteenth century and, from Reagan to the Tea Party movement, found a firm anchoring in radical economic liberalism or libertarianism in the US. Aside from this, though, it is about the technological realization of such "social infrastructures" that coordinate "communities, media, and governments" in such a way that they guarantee political empowerment or the potential for empowerment. In more precise terms, it involves the direct "connections" between "people" and "elected representatives," an immediatization between populations and executives, between people and engaged leaders, produced "with a click."[28]

Beyond all debates about the political substance of the various forms of populism of the left and the right, about authoritarian or radical democratic versions, exclusive and inclusive variants, or about culturalist, economic, formal, or substantive versions of the concept of populism,[29] a dimension can be discerned in these promises of political immediacy that perhaps deserves the title of structural populism. This is less about references to specific doctrines or ideologies than about power practices and the specific sorting of a political force field. If one assumes that talk of populist politics can only be justified with regard to a particular arrangement of communication strategies, then the "social fabric" invoked by social platforms is dependent on the medial preconditions of social and political mobilization.[30] For this reason, a certain degree of caution has been called for here. For example, in view of the disastrous polarizing tendencies in American politics during the last decade, there has been a call for a perspective that refers to the media "ecosystem" in its entire breadth and thus to the interaction of networks, social media, blogs, media companies, radio, and TV stations alike.[31] Conversely, it is precisely the economic and media operations of platform companies that give us occasion to consider the political implications of network technologies. Thus, the platform industry's claim to hegemony, as with Facebook, is apparently directed at organizing collective decision-making power apart from and alongside established political procedures. This is the fabrication of a special version of digital "neo-communities,"[32] whose supply scheme consists not least in facilitating seemingly authentic direct communications on the basis of highly selective technical mediation procedures. The complex media operations of the opinion brokers are designed to generate phobias against all mediating entities.

The political character of such techno-social infrastructures shows itself in four aspects. It is seen first in the phantasm of immediate access to the addresses of political power, which accordingly manifests itself in exclusive private relations and demands participation through acclamation; everyone is addressed and heard at the same time. It is seen secondly in an informalization of the transfer and exercise of political power, which is accomplished by cutting out mediating entities and, in particular, by stigmatizing the formal character of representative institutions as false or falsifying, be they elections or parliaments, "elites" or the press. It is seen thirdly through the activation of nonspecific social ensembles and entities such as "communities," "humanity," "people," "us," "[a] coming together," or "meaningful groups." They do not take on any representative form and at best make themselves noticeable through a conspicuous eventfulness in their collective movements and impulses. This is a "metapolitical fiction" (Hans Kelsen)[33] of indefinite and diffuse community forces, which can be activated and concentrated by different collective identities. Then, via the procedures of algorithmic tribalization, the variants of a supposedly "authentic popular will" or various "political peoples"[34] also find their address and their place. Fourthly and finally, the associated modes of reaction and rapid communications have a ballistic character, as it were; they are about *targeting*, about getting one's bearings, addressing, and hitting the target. In other words, they aim to perfect a communicative striking skill, which, with the use of news bullets or hashtag-bundled formations, probably possesses a prototype in the procedures of military enemy recognition: "Boom. I press it, … and, within two seconds, 'We have breaking news.'"[35] Populism in this structural sense would thus be understood as a set of communication strategies that do the following: provide the basis for the formation of particularist collectives; link the claim to authentic communication with the hope of an immediate, as it were, "low-cost" exercise of executive power; favor authoritarian forms of empowerment; and logistically orient themselves to the identification of clearly profiled target objects. Platforms and social media promise nothing less than an immediatization of political participation and action.

However, even with these socio-technical preconditions, a dynamic propensity for ressentiment is only brought about under digital capitalism by the privileging of those opinion markets that define the business model of platform companies and have been made possible by Internet exceptionalism. In this context, one should probably consider the interplay of two factors. Thus, in the reciprocal relationship between economic dynamics and social or political ones, the form of opinion and opinion as such hold a special systemic position. For the scaling and algorithmic processing of information as well as the procedures for managing data only function under the condition that explanation-resistant substrates are communicated.

Accordingly, one subtracts from modes of expression the burden of proof, from preferences their justification, and from decisions the pressure to legitimate them. The proximity to financial and stock markets also shapes this. Both financial industries and Internet or platform companies engage in data brokerage and pursue algorithmic market operations. But apart from this, they also share in common the establishment of feedback loops, automatic response cycles, and a machine-based evaluation of relevance.[36] Just as financial markets operate as opinion markets under the conditions of information technology (cf. pp. 34–38), opinion markets on the platforms are conversely structured according to a finance-economic evaluation logic. When random utterances are transformed into scalable information, only the substrate of opinion is retained from content of all kinds. In other words, the only thing retained is that form of evaluation that first makes possible the installation of profitable community feedback loops.[37] Opinion as such, the circulation of standpoints and points of view, has become the yardstick for all statements on the private information markets, and it is precisely this liberation from rules of liability and justification of all kinds that has also established a new and unconstrained relationship to facts. Indeed, one can locate the quality of the factual, as Lorraine Daston has done in a brief account of the history of science, in the ways in which facts function discursively. Here we see that these functions have been characterized since modern times precisely by the circumstance that facts present themselves singly, insularly, manifestly, and simply; but also independently of contexts, of explanatory frameworks, justifications, and theory formations.[38] And this allows them to enter into a special alliance with the circulation of opinions. Both the appeal to opinions and the invocation of facts call for a renunciation of reasons: opinions and facts operate with apparently concrete things, with pieces of evidence, and certainties. Even the frenetic pitch reached by exchanges about the materials circulating since 2016 under the rubric of "fake news" or "fake facts" is only possible under the conditions of such an opinion market, where facts are fetishized and there is an effective symbiosis of infopinions and assertions of fact. A satirical aphorism from the nineteenth century retains its validity in this context: "This is my opinion, and I share it with myself!"[39]

At the same time, the self-conception and mode of operation of proprietary opinion markets demand that all users on the platforms also function as produsers. They are thus both addressees and producers of statements, and work together on the dissemination and reproducibility of statements. The business interests in a capitalization of data and informational raw materials coincide directly with the sociopolitical processes that generate particularist communities. At their point of intersection, trend reinforcements and a logic of valorization come into force, in which ratings force ratings and sharing generates sharing. The political project of "strengthening" "social connections" and "communities," of affective and cognitive segregations,[40] thus follows the business plan of social media and, incidentally, fulfills an older liberal or liberalist dream: namely, to directly link the production of the social to the processes of capital reproduction.

So here, too, the peculiar dynamic applies: that precisely the greatest possible and global inclusion of users through the accumulation of network effects is linked to processes of particularization, which owe their existence to the adaptation to predictable cultural, religious, political, and normative user expectations and are reinforced by positive feedback. The universalization of information standards constitutes the precondition for the production of particularized forms of community. Thus, the diversity of algorithmic management among the different variants of Internet platforms can be located along a spectrum, whose selective work is stretched between general, self-reinforcing processes of coordination on the one hand, and systemic monadization on the other. In other words, it is stretched between the two outermost poles of an information machine, which as a whole engages in a peculiar and profit-oriented processing of mass phenomena and produces social infrastructures (cf. pp. 91–94). Here, collectivizing and individualizing processes are not simply opposed to each other; rather, the forms of a *general* majoritization are supplemented by *special* majoritizations that take place through the expansive inclusion of users. In so doing, they reproduce idiosyncratic user profiles by means of processes of "triadic closure." According to the latter, the quality of relationships, for instance, between A and B on the one hand and A and C on the other, makes it seem likely that the relationship between B and C is also of a similar quality. This makes it possible to address the relationship network A–B–C as a self-contained cluster.[41] On both sides of the relationship, algorithmic selections such as filtering, arborization, and hierarchization of data structures produce statistical formations and molar, homogenizing units. These formations and units follow an automatic evaluation of relevance and one might attest to them, following the concept of flexible normalism (Jürgen Link), a flexible conformism. This is about parallel generation and the coordination of general and particular regularities: individual profiles are also nothing more than machine-structured mass phenomena that produce the data-generated habitus of the "dividual."[42] So-called digitalization does more than just make regularities visible that had already existed in the social anyway. What really happens here is that the social becomes hypersocialized. The recording of patterns and of laws of imitation has been possible since the nineteenth century only under the condition of administrative practices, communications media, and mass media.[43] In the same way, digital technologies and the information economy have produced a specific form of the social today that is characterized by the organization of *disjunctive syntheses*. Here, a general dynamic of normalization coincides with manifold processes of monadization or particularization, and converging and diverging regularities simultaneously determine the arrangement of social event series, leading not to a decrease but to an increase in elements of indifference or of equal validity. It is, namely, precisely through the generation and reinforcement of conformities that social powers of divergence are stimulated.

This constellation, however, cannot simply be grasped as a "crisis of the general," conditioned by a new upswing of social, political, and cultural singularities in current forms of society.[44] It is much more about the way in which the relations between the processes of generalization and particularization are interconnected and have undergone a specific and critical turn under the dominance of finance and information capitalism. More recent considerations in democracy theory envision an open process that, starting from particular social identities, strives toward a universal horizon. Here, the self-seclusion of the particular is to be undermined just as rigorously as the permanent occupation of the universal by particular interests.[45] In contrast, however, to these considerations in democracy theory, an opposite movement is actually taking place under the logic of information capital. The generality of codes and information is thereby confronted by a process that culminates in self-contained social monads, and the universalization of information capital is guaranteed precisely by producing disconnected particularities. Thus, it is no longer a matter of how particular identities open up and pluralize democratically toward a universal horizon, but, conversely, of how globally effective capital movements bring about an "idiocratic" intensification of power relations[46] and reproduce themselves by anti-democratically producing divergent, competing, and conflicting particularities. Through the production of plural self-contained entities, pluralistic spaces of action are cut off and undermined.

Therefore, under a supposed immediatization of (political) communications, unfiltered and, as it were, ethereal relations between leader and follower (and the repudiation of mediating instances) are linked in the platform economy with a mobilization of collective forces. These collective forces are recognizable in immediate modes of response and in the absorption of potentials for excitation and movement. At the same time, the privileging of the form of the opinion in the operation of social media and platforms has led to more than just a foreclosure of zones of reflection and scenarios of reasoning, as well as to a quasi-ballistic form of rapid communication. It has also led to a dual and opposing tendency in which the universalization of information standards coincides with an efficient monadization of user communities. Alongside the generalized establishment of competitive venues and the dissolution of milieus of solidarity in contemporary market societies, the economic dynamics and business models of information capitalism have thus created specific conditions or architectures in which, with structural populism, ressentiment has become an integral part of the capitalist economy of affect. In it, it functions both as a product and as a productive force, and contributes, particularly with its corrosive political and social forces, to the stabilization of the economic system of finance capitalism.

Thus, the economy of ressentiment promotes the competitive system; it supplies the opinion markets and fuses with evaluative auto-mechanisms. It also generates restricted domains of experience, multiplies the number of segregated pseudo-communities, and privileges plebiscitarian, authoritarian figures. Moreover, it turns the anxiety caused by global markets, transnational interventionist forces, and economic dependencies into tangible denunciatory formulas that can then refer equally to, say, the border transgressions of migrants, European bureaucrats, greedy investors, or conspirators in the financial industry. The critique festering in ressentiment always takes policing as its method: it searches and suspects and seeks out surrogate objects that are concretely tangible and supposedly liable for the efficacy of abstract system processes, whereas critique should actually move in the opposite direction, advancing from tangible and concrete instances to the conditions of their production.

On the one hand, the cunning of ressentiment has thus provided an answer to the question of how the valorization of fragmentation, parcellation, diversity, and contingency benefits global finance and information capital in such a way that the latter can neither be understood nor attacked as a totalizing power.[47] It is precisely the centrifugal forces of separate worlds and communities that have obscured the view of the conformist production of the real. On the other hand, this has brought about the most recent radicalization of negative socialization, in which particularities are related to particularities, following a divisive principle and, as Kierkegaard would have said, coming together in the negative unity of negative reciprocity. The private–public alliances under the governance of the finance economy are supplemented by the production of authoritarian social structures along the lines of the information industry. Even if history has no endings and never reaches an utter impasse, it must be conceded that the hostility of all against all has become not only a successful business model, but has also created an extremely sustainable feeling of community. It is not impossible that it will provide the ferment for a new prewar era.*

* This last sentence was written in October 2020 (J.V.)

Notes

1 Monetative Power

1 Henry Kaufman, *The Road to Financial Reformation: Warnings, Consequences, Reforms*, Hoboken (NJ) 2009, 134; John Bellamy Foster and Robert W. McChesney, *The Endless Crisis: How Monopoly-Finance Capital Produces Stagnation and Upheaval from the USA to China*, New York 2012, 43; Bundeszentrale für politische Bildung, "Größere Finanzkrisen seit 1970," November 15, 2017 (https://www.bpb.de/lookup/zahlenundfakten/globalisierung/52625/finanzkrisenseit1970). [Translator's note: please note that all links to electronic sources, such as this one, unless otherwise noted, have been accessed by the translator in the second half of 2021. Most sources can be found with an author/title search if link proves inoperable.] While the frequency of financial crises was zero between 1945 and 1971, they occurred thereafter with a probability of 4%, i.e., with a probability of four crises per year relative to a sample of 100 countries; see Laurence Scialom, *La Fascination de l'ogre: Comment desserrer l'étau de la finance*. Paris 2019, 40–41.

2 Amitai Etzioni, *The Active Society*, New York and London 1968, quoted in Wolfgang Streeck, *Buying Time: The Delayed Crisis of Democratic Capitalism*, trans. Patrick Camiller, London and New York 2014, 13; and Philipp Lepenies, *The Power of a Single Number: A Political History of GDP*, New

York 2017, 144–145; John Kenneth Galbraith, *The Affluent Society*, Harmondsworth 1958; Ludwig Erhard, *Prosperity through Competition*, Auburn (AL) 2011.

3 Aaron Sahr, *Das Versprechen des Geldes: Eine Praxistheorie des Kredits*. Hamburg 2017, 14. Representative of the extensive literature on this subject, cf. A. L. Keith Acheson, John F. Chant, and Martin F. J. Prachowny (eds.), *Bretton Woods Revisited: Evaluations of the International Monetary Fund and the International Bank for Reconstruction and Development*, Toronto 1972; Barry Eichengreen, *Globalizing Capital: A History of the International Monetary System*, Princeton 1996, 132–182; idem, *Global Imbalances and the Lessons of Bretton Woods*, Cambridge 2007; Fred L. Block, *The Origins of International Economic Disorder: A Study of United States International Monetary Policy from World War II to the Present*, Berkeley 1977, 193–199; Richard Tilly, *Geld und Kredit in der Wirtschaftsgeschichte*, Stuttgart 2003, 186–194; Robert Brenner, *The Boom and the Bubble: The US in the World Economy*, London 2003, 7–30; Filipo Cesarano, *Money Theory and Bretton Woods: The Construction of an International Monetary Order*, Cambridge 2006.

4 Gérard Duménil and Dominique Lévy, *The Crisis of Neoliberalism*, Cambridge (MA) and London 2011, 60; Peter Gowan, "Crisis in the Heartland: Consequences of the New Wall Street System," *New Left Review* 55, January/February 2009, 24–25; Yanis Varoufakis, *The Global Minotaur: America, Europe and the Future of the World Economy*, London and New York 2011, 95–101; idem, *And the Weak Suffer What They Must? Europe's Crisis and America's Economic Future*, New York 2016, 68–74, 82; William Greider, *Secrets of the Temple: How the Federal Reserve Runs the Country*, New York 1987, 46–47, 75–123, 168–169, 404–411, 551–553; Greta R. Krippner, *Capitalizing on Crisis: The Political Origins of the Rise of Finance*, Harvard 2011, 103–104, 116–120.

5 International Monetary Fund, *External Evaluation of IMF Surveillance: Report by a Group of Independent Experts*, Washington 1999, 20; Susan Strange, *Mad Money: When Markets Outgrow Governments*, Ann Arbor 1998, 163–167.

6 Mark Blyth, *Austerity: The History of a Dangerous Idea*, Oxford and New York 2013, 161–162; Stephen D. Krasner,

"Compromising Westphalia," *International Security* 20/3 (Winter 1995/1996), 132.

7 Jonathan Joseph, *The Social and the Global: Social Theory, Governmentality and Global Policies*, Cambridge 2012, 95–96; John Micklethwait and Adrian Wooldridge, *A Future Perfect: The Essentials of Globalization*, New York 2000, 178–179.

8 Treaty on European Union (Maastricht, February 7, 1992) (https://www.cvce.eu/content/publication/2002/4/9/2c2f2b85-14bb-4488-9ded-13f3cd04de05/publishable_en.pdf).

9 Robert Mundell, one of the advisors to the European Commission, as paraphrased in Michael Hudson, *Killing the Host: How Financial Parasites and Debt Bondage Destroy the Global Economy*, New York 2014, 277.

10 The data cited here are from Aaron Sahr, *Das Versprechen des Geldes: Eine Praxistheorie des Kredits*, Hamburg 2017, 232–235, 245–246; Foster and McChesney, *Endless Crisis*, 17, 43; Duménil and Lévy, *Crisis of Neoliberalism*, 104–111; Gowan, "Crisis in the Heartland," 6–7, 24–26; Núria Almiron, *Journalism in Crisis: Corporate Media and Financialization*, New York 2010, 24–28; Scialom, *La Fascination de l'ogre*, 160–162; Harry Magdoff and Paul M. Sweezy, *Stagnation and the Financial Explosion*, 2nd edn., New York 2009, 20; Gerald F. Davis and Suntae Kim, "Financialization of the Economy," *Annual Review of Sociology* 41, 2015, 203–221; Paul Windolf, "Was ist Finanzmarkt-Kapitalismus?" *Kölner Zeitschrift für Soziologie und Sozialpsychologie* (Special Issue on *Finanzmarkt-Kapitalismus*, ed. Paul Windolf), 45/2005, 20–57; Krippner, *Capitalizing on Crisis*, 3–4, 27–57; Christian Marazzi, *Verbranntes Geld*, Zürich and Berlin 2011, 32.

11 Quoted in Sylvain Leder, "BlackRock in Paris: Der Finanzriese und Macrons Rentenreform," *Le Monde Diplomatique* (German edition), January 2020, 9.

12 Thomas Piketty, *Capital in the Twenty-First Century*, trans. Arthur Goldhammer, Cambridge (MA) and London 2017, 33–36 and passim.

13 Klaus Dörre, "Demokratie statt Kapitalismus oder: Enteignet den Zuckerberg!" in Hanna Ketterer and Karina Becker (eds.), *Was stimmt nicht mit der Demokratie? Eine Debatte mit Klaus Dörre, Nancy Fraser, Stephan Lessenich und Hartmut Rosa*, Frankfurt am Main 2019, 38; Thomas Piketty, *Capital and Ideology*, trans. Arthur Goldhammer, Cambridge (MA) and

London 2020, 34; Nicola Liebert, "Fataler Reichtum: Zuviel Geld in falschen Händen," *Le Monde Diplomatique* (German edition), August 2012, 1, 10–11. Cf. Jacob Hacker and Paul Pierson, *Winner-Take-All Politics: How Washington Made the Rich Richer – And Turned Its Back on the Middle Class*, New York, London, Toronto, and Sydney 2010, 15–16; Tony Judt, *Ill Fares the Land*, London 2010, 14.

14 "Viel Lohn für wenige," *Süddeutsche Zeitung*, July 5, 2019, 8; "Ein Boom für die Reichen," *Süddeutsche Zeitung*, July 10, 2019, 17; Till Baldenius, Sebastian Kohl, and Moritz Schularick, "Die neue Wohnungsfrage: Gewinner und Verlierer des deutschen Immobilienbooms," *Marcrofinance Lab*, University of Bonn, June 2019 (https://pure.mpg.de/rest/items/item_3070687_1/component/file_3070688/content); Ulrike Hermann, "Die wenigen Reichen besitzen fast alles," *die tageszeitung*, July 16, 2020, 3. A particularly dramatic redistribution was also guaranteed by land speculation: building land prices have risen by 2300% in Germany since the early 1960s, and by more than 39,000% in urban centers such as Munich since the 1950s; cf. Hans-Jochen Vogel, *Mehr Gerechtigkeit! Wir brauchen eine neue Bodenordnung – nur dann wird Wohnen auch wieder bezahlbar*, Freiburg 2019, 35.

15 David Leonhardt, "Why You Shouldn't Believe Those G.D.P. Numbers," *New York Times*, December 15, 2019 (https://www.nytimes.com/2019/12/15/opinion/gdp-america.html); on the genesis and problems involved in calculating G.D.P. as "the most powerful statistical figure in human history," cf. Lepenies, *The Power of a Single Number*, ix and passim.

16 Cf. the following exemplary studies and surveys: David Levi-Faur, "The Global Diffusion of Regulatory Capitalism," *Annals of the American Academy of Political and Social Science* (*AAAPSS*) 598/1 (2005), 12–32; Fabrizio Gilardi, "The Institutional Foundations of Regulatory Capitalism: The Diffusion of Independent Regulatory Agencies in Western Europe," *AAAPSS*, 598: 84–101.

17 Cf. John Braithwaite, *Regulatory Capitalism: How it Works, Ideas for Making it Work Better*, Cheltenham (UK) and Northampton (MA) 2008, 1–31; Anne-Marie Slaughter, *A New World Order: Government Networks and the Disaggregated State*, Princeton 2004, 36–64; Anastasia Nesvetailova and Carlos Belli, "Global Financial Governance: Taming Financial

Innovation," in Sophie Harman and David Williams (eds.), *Governing the World? Cases in Global Governance*, London and New York 2013, 46–61.

18 Karl Marx, "Economic and Philosophical Manuscripts," in idem, *Early Writings*, introd. Lucio Coletti, trans. Rodney Livingstone and Gregory Benton, London 1992. Cf. Gilles Deleuze and Félix Guattari, *A Thousand Plateaus*, trans. Brian Massumi, Minneapolis 1987, 453, 460–466. On the definition of "capitalist sovereignty," cf. Michael Hardt and Tony Negri, "Capitalist Sovereignty, or Administering the Global Society of Control," Chap. 3.6 in idem, *Empire*, Cambridge (MA) and London 2000, 325–350.

19 In the felicitous choice of terms by Aaron Sahr. See his *Keystroke-Kapitalismus: Ungleichheit auf Knopfdruck*, Hamburg 2017, 154 (an English translation is planned for 2022; see Bibliography). Cf. here Joseph Vogl, *The Ascendency of Finance*, Cambridge (UK) 2017, 93–131.

20 Yanis Varoufakis, *Adults in the Room: My Battle with the European and American Deep Establishment*, New York 2017, 231–233, 447 (quote); cf. idem, *And the Weak Suffer*, 397 n. 2; Michael Hudson, "Creation of the Troika: Its Pro-Bank, Anti-Labor Agenda," Chap. 21 in idem, *Killing the Host*, 254–264. The prerequisite for such interventions is Article 123 of the Treaty on the Functioning of the European Union, which prohibits the use of national central banks or the ECB to finance government spending. This has led to an "indirect monetarization" of sovereign debt and the dependence of euro states on private actors; cf. Aaron Sahr, Friedo Karth, Carolin Müller, "Staatliche Zahlungs(un)fähigkeit: Missverständnisse und Missverhältnisse monetärer Souveränität in Europa," *Soziopolis*, January 28, 2020 (https://www.soziopolis.de/staatliche-zahlungsunfaehigkeit.html).

21 Comments of the former German Minister of Finance Wolfgang Schäuble and economists from J. P. Morgan, quoted in Adam Tooze, *Crashed: How a Decade of Financial Crises Changed the World*, New York 2018, 522; Varoufakis, *Adults in the Room*, 236; Paul Mason, *PostCapitalism: A Guide to Our Future*, London 2015, xx.

22 Milton Friedman, *Capitalism and Freedom*, Chicago 1962, ix.

23 Florian Rödl, "EU im Notstandsmodus," *Blätter für deutsche und internationale Politik* 5/2012, 5–8. Cf. also Andreas Fisahn,

"Stellungnahme zur Anhörung des Haushaltsausschusses des Deutschen Bundestages am 7.5.2012 zum Fiskalvertrag u. a." (available by clicking on the link "Prof. Dr. Andreas Fisahn" at https://eurodemostuttgart.wordpress.com/2012/05/09/realsatire-deutscher-bundestag-ii-die-gutachten/); Heribert Prantl, "Das Finale nach dem Ende," *Süddeutsche Zeitung*, June 29, 2012, 2; Steffen Vogel, *Europas Revolution von oben: Sparpolitik und Demokratieabbau in der Eurokrise*, Hamburg 2013, 95–102; Ernst-Wolfgang Böckenförde, "Kennt die europäische Not kein Gebot?" *Neue Zürcher Zeitung*, June 21, 2010.

24 Ulrike Herrmann and Stefan Reinecke "Deutschland verhindert, mehr nicht, Interview mit Adam Tooze," *die tageszeitung*, April 21, 2020, 3; Gerald Braunberger, "Deutschland und Italien: das Wirtschaftswachstum," *Fazit – Frankfurter Allgemeine Wirtschaftsblog*, May 27, 2018 (https://blogs.faz.net/fazit/2018/05/27/deutschland-und-italien-das-wirtschaftswachstum-9957/).

25 Ulrike Sauer, "Nichts als leere Versprechen," *Süddeutsche Zeitung*, April 27, 2020, 17.

26 Herbert Giersch, "Beschäftigung, Stabilität, Wachstum – wer trägt die Verantwortung?" in Giersch (ed.), *Wie es zu schaffen ist: Agenda für die deutsche Wirtschaftspolitik*, Stuttgart 1983, 31.

27 Dieter Grimm, *Die Verfassung und die Politik: Einsprüche in Störfällen*, Munich 2001, 11–12; Marazzi, *Verbranntes Geld*, 85.

28 Charles E. Lindblom, "The Market as Prison," *Journal of Politics* 44, 1982, 324–336, here 332.

29 Tooze, *Crashed*, 14.

30 Tooze, *Crashed*, 15, 306, 461; Philip Mirowski, *Never Let a Serious Crisis Go to Waste: How Neoliberalism Survived the Financial Meltdown*, London and New York 2014, 350–351; Vogel, *Europas Revolution von oben*, 15–16; Capgemini, *World Wealth Report 2011*, June 22, 2011 (https://www.capgemini.com/resources/world-wealth-report-2011/).

31 Cf. Markus Demary and Thomas Schuster, *Die Neuordnung der Finanzmärkte: Stand der Finanzmarktregulierung fünf Jahre nach der Lehman-Pleite*, Cologne 2013; Adair Turner, *Between Debt and the Devil: Money, Credit, and Fixing Global Finance*, Princeton 2015, xii.

32 Alan Greenspan, quoted in Justin Fox, *The Myth of the Rational Market: A History of Risk, Reward, and Delusion on Wall Street*, New York 2009, xi–xii.
33 Quoted in Mirowski, *Never Let a Serious Crisis*, 189.
34 Martin Mayer, *The Fed: The Inside Story of How the World's Most Powerful Financial Institution Drives the Markets*, New York 2001, x–xi; Benjamin M. Friedman, "The Future of Monetary Policy: The Central Bank as an Army with Only a Signal Corps?" in NBER Paper Series, *National Bureau of Economic Research*, Working Paper 7429, November 1999, 28 (https://www.nber.org/papers/w7420).
35 Piet Clement, "Introduction," in Claudio Borio, Gianni Toniolo, and Piet Clement (eds.), *Past and Future of Central Bank Cooperation*, Cambridge 2008, 6; cf. Tooze, *Crashed*, 12–13.
36 Cf. the exemplary analysis of Hasan Cömert, *Central Banks and Financial Markets: The Declining Power of US Monetary Policy*, Cheltenham (UK) and Northampton (MA) 2013; Duménil and Lévy, *Crisis of Neoliberalism*, 195–203; Hudson, *Killing the Host*, 230–231.
37 Scialom, *La Fascination de l'ogre*, 62; Adair Turner, *Economics After the Crisis: Objectives and Means*, Cambridge (MA) and London 2012, 41; idem, *Between Debt and the Devil*, 125–130. Cf. Jan Willmroth, "Die Null wird stehen," *Süddeutsche Zeitung*, July 26, 2019, 15.
38 Gerhard Illing, *Zentralbanken im Griff der Finanzmärkte: Umfassende Regulierung als Voraussetzung für eine effiziente Geldpolitik*, Bonn 2011, 6–7; Scialom, *La Fascination de l'ogre*, 64; Turner, *Between Debt and the Devil*, 7, 128; Thierry Philipponnat, *Le Capital: De l'abondance à l'utilité*, Paris 2017, 16–27.
39 Quoted in Ingo Arzt, "Die Geister, die ich rief," *die tageszeitung*, July 30, 2019, 3.
40 E.g., Mason, *PostCapitalism*.

2 The Information Standard: On the Episteme of the Finance Economy

1 Almiron, *Journalism in Crisis*, 43–49; Peter Burke, *A Social History of Knowledge: From Gutenberg to Diderot*, Cambridge

(UK) 2000, 155–157; Dan Schiller, *Digital Depression: Information Technology and Economic Crisis*, Urbana (IL) and Chesham (UK) 2014, 43–56.

2 As stated by Nasdaq Chairman Frank Zarb in June 2000, quoted in Mark Ingebretsen, *Nasdaq: A History of the Market that Changed the World*, Roseville (CA) 2002, 2.

3 Ibid., 239, 303, and passim; Ramon Reichert, *Das Wissen der Börse: Medien und Praktiken des Finanzmarktes*, Bielefeld 2009, 123–124; Marina Mazzucato, *The Entrepreneurial State: Debunking Public vs. Private Sector Myths*, New York 2013, 57; William Lazonick and Marina Mazzucato, "The Risk–Reward Nexus in the Innovation–Inequality Relationship: Who Takes the Risks? Who Gets the Rewards? *Industrial and Corporate Change* 22/4 (2013), 1112; Geoffrey G. Parker, Marshall W. Van Alstyne, and Sangeet Paul Choudary, *Platform Revolution: How Networked Markets Are Transforming the Economy – And How to Make Them Work for You*, New York and London 2016, xi; Manuel Castells, *The Internet Galaxy: Reflections on the Internet, Business, and Society*, Oxford 2003, 82; John Cassidy, *Dot.con – How America Lost its Mind and Money in the Internet Era*, New York 2003, 295.

4 Reichert, *Das Wissen der Börse*, 98–100; Ingebretsen, *Nasdaq*, 140, 181–184; Almiron, *Journalism in Crisis*, 134; William Shawcross, *Murdoch: The Making of a Media Empire*, 2nd edn., New York 1997, 132–135; Cees J. Hamelink, *Finance and Information: A Study of Converging Interests*, Norwood (NJ) 1983, 44–45 and passim.

5 Ingebretsen, *Nasdaq*, viii.

6 Holger Lyre, quoted in Martin Donner, *Äther und Information: Die Apriori des Medialen im Zeitalter technischer Kommunikation*, Berlin 2017, 10; cf. Dan Schiller, *Digital Depression*, 4–35, 40–44; Ingebretsen, *Nasdaq*, 78; Lilly E. Kay, *Who Wrote the Book of Life: A History of the Genetic Code*, Stanford 2000, 19–30.

7 F. A. Hayek, "The Use of Knowledge in Society," *American Economic Review* 35/4, September 1945, 526, quoted in Philip Mirowski and Edward Nik-Khah, *The Knowledge We Have Lost in Information: The History of Information in Modern Economics*, Oxford 2017, 67.

8 Franz Böhm, "Rule of Law in a Market Economy," in Alan T. Peacock and Hans Willgerodt (eds.) *Germany's Social Market*

Economy: Origins and Evolution, New York 1989, 53, quoted in Quinn Slobodian, *Globalists: The End of Empire and the Birth of Neoliberalism*, Cambridge and London 2018, 233. On the boom of information concepts and the dogmatic changes in neoliberalism associated with it, cf. ibid., 224–240; Mirowsky and Nik-Khah, *The Knowledge We Have Lost in Information*, 31–44, 62–72, 73–100, 126–130 and passim.

9 Paul A. Samuelson, "A Few Remembrances of Friedrich von Hayek (1899–1992)," *Journal of Economic Behavior and Organization*, 69/1, 2009, 2; quoted in ibid., 63.

10 Eugene Fama and Merton H. Miller, *The Theory of Finance*, Hinsdale (IL) 1972, 335; cf. Yves Thépaut, "Le Concept d'information dans l'analyse économique contemporaine," *Hermès: La Revue* 44, 2006/1, 161–168. Cf. here and on the following: Joseph Vogl, *The Specter of Capital*, Stanford 2015, 67–80.

11 Louis Bachelier, "Théorie de la Spéculation," *Annales scientifiques de l'École Normale Supérieure*, 3/17, 1900, 21–86. This has been translated into English as "Theory of Speculation," Chap. 2 in *The Random Character of Stock Market Prices*, ed. Paul Cootner, Cambridge 1964, 17–79 (available at Internet Archive: https://archive.org/details/randomcharactero00coot/page/n4/mode/1up); cf. John Cassidy, *How Markets Fail: The Logic of Economic Calamities*, New York 2009, 86–90.

12 Norbert Wiener, *Cybernetics or Control and Communication in the Animal and the Machine*, reissue of the 1961 2nd edn., Cambridge (MA) 1985, 70.

13 Cf. Burton G. Malkiel, *A Random Walk Down Wall Street*, New York 2003, 196–197; Fama and Miller, *The Theory of Finance*, 339–340; Paul A. Samuelsen, "Proof that Properly Anticipated Prices Fluctuate Randomly" [1965], in *Collected Papers of Paul A. Samuelson*, vol. 3, Cambridge (MA) and London 1972, 782–790; Jürg Niehans, *A History of Economic Theory: Classic Contributions, 1729–1980*, Baltimore and London 1990, 441–442.

14 Cf. Donald MacKenzie, "Opening the Black Boxes of Global Finance," in Alexandros-Andreas Kyrtsis (ed.), *Financial Markets and Organizational Techologies: System Architectures, Practices and Risks in the Era of Deregulation*, London and New York 2010, 92–116, here: 96; Tobias Preis, *Ökonophysik: Die Physik des Finanzmarktes*, Wiesbaden 2011, 7–14.

15 On this and more generally on the models of Black and Scholes, and of Merton: Elena Esposito, "Trading Uncertainty," Chap. 10 in idem, *The Future of Futures: The Time of Money in Financing and Society*, trans. Elena Esposito with assistance of Andrew K. Whitehead, Cheltenham (UK) and Northampton (MA) 2011, 134–153; Nicholas Dunbar, *Inventing Money: The Story of Long-Term Capital Management and the Legends behind It*, Chichester 2000, passim; Donald MacKenzie, *An Engine, Not a Camera: How Financial Models Shape Markets*, Cambridge (MA) and London 2006, 119–178; Marieke de Goede, *Virtue, Fortune, and Faith: A Genealogy of Finance*, Minneapolis and London 2005, 125–132. The foundational publications here include Fisher Black and Myron Scholes, "The Pricing of Options and Corporate Liabilities," *Journal of Political Economy* 81, May/June 1973, 637–654; and Robert C. Merton, *Theory of Rational Option Pricing*, Cambridge 1971.

16 In this context, reference has been made not only to the calculations of Bachelier (1900), but also to the *Theorie der Prämiengeschäfte* (1908) by Vinzenz Bronzin, a Boltzmann student and political arithmetician; cf. Wolfgang Hafner and Heinz Zimmermann, "Ein vergessener genialer Wurf zur Bewertung von Optionen: Vinzenz Bronzin nahm die nobelpreiswürdige Black-Scholes-Formel vorweg," *Neue Züricher Zeitung, Fokus der Wirtschaft*, October 8/9, 2005, 29.

17 Robert C. Merton, *Continuous-Time Finance*, Cambridge (MA) 1990, 15.

18 Wiener, *Cybernetics*, 132; cf. H. Schnelle, "Information," in Joachim Ritter, Karlfried Gründer, and Gottfried Gabriel (eds.) *Historisches Wörterbuch der Philosophie*, Darmstadt 2007, vol. 4, 356.

19 F. A. Hayek, "Competition as a Discovery Procedure," trans. Marcellus S. Snow, *Quarterly Journal of Austrian Economics* 5/3 (Fall 2002), 9, 15.

20 MacKenzie, *An Engine, Not a Camera*, 20, 158, 174; Edward LiPuma and Benjamin Lee, *Financial Derivatives and the Globalization of Risk*, Durham and London 2004, 38, 60–61; Esposito, *Future of Futures*, 136, 203; Randy Martin, "The Twin Towers of Financialisation: Entanglements of Political and Cultural Economies," *The Global South* 3/1, Spring 2009, 119.

21 Benoit B. Mandelbrot and Richard L. Hudson, *The (Mis)Behaviour of Markets: A Fractal View of Risk, Ruin and Reward*, London 2008, 254. Cf. Alexandros-Andreas Kyrtsis, "Introduction: Financial Deregulation and Technological Change," in idem (ed.), *Financial Markets and Organizational Technologies*, 22.

22 Merton, *Continuous-Time Finance*, 470; cf. Reichert, *Das Wissen der Börse*, 113–114, 217.

23 "Remarks by Chairman Alan Greenspan," *Technology and Financial Services* (before the Journal of Financial Services Research and the American Enterprise Institute Conference, in Honor of Anna Schwartz, Washington, DC, on April 14, 2000) (https://www.federalreserve.gov/boarddocs/speeches/2000/20000414.htm). Quoted in Kyrtsis, "Introduction," 1.

24 Karl Marx, *Capital, Volume 1: A Critical Analysis of Capitalist Production*, trans. Samuel Moore and Edward Aveling, introd. Mark G. Spencer, Hertfordshire (UK) 2013, 205. [Translation modified – translator's note.]

25 Vega, Don Joseph de la, *Die Verwirrung der Verwirrungen: Vier Dialoge über die Börse in Amsterdam*, trans. and introd. Otto Pringsheim, Breslau 1919, 3, 38–93. [Translator's note: The original text was published in Spanish in 1688. It has been republished in Spanish as *Confusión de Confusiones*, Universidad Nacional de Cuyo, Mendoza (Argentina) 2013. A modest selection has been published in English as Jose de la Vega, *Confusion de Confusiones: Portions Descriptive of the Amsterdam Stock Exchange* (1688), select., trans., and introd. Hermann Kellenbenz, Boston 1957, 42 p. Though it gives the reader a good sense of the original, most of the material quoted here comes from the "Second Dialogue," which is highly abridged in the English translation. The full German translation of the original will be cited here and the translations into English are my own.]

26 Vega, *Verwirrung,* 79; cf. 43–44, 49, 65, 88, 136.

27 Ibid., 8, 41–42, 131, 154.

28 Sinan Aral, *The Hype Machine: How Social Media Disrupts Our Elections, Our Economy and Our Health – and How We Must Adapt*, London 2020, 28–30.

29 [Translator's note: The translation of this sentence, the rest of this paragraph, and the subsequent two paragraphs (ending at "doxological substrate") follows very closely the translation

provided in Joseph Vogl, *The Specter of Capital*, trans. Joachim Redner and Robert Savage, Stanford 2015, 113–115. I would like to express my indebtedness in the rendering of this passage to this fine translation.]

30 Immanuel Kant, *Critique of the Power of Judgment* (Cambridge Edition of the Works of Immanuel Kant), ed. Paul Guyer, transl. Paul Guyer and Eric Matthews, Cambridge 2000, §§ 6, 8, 22.

31 John Maynard Keynes, *The General Theory of Employment, Interest and Money*, New York 1936, 156; Robert Skidelsky, *Keynes: The Return of the Master*, New York 2009, 83, 93. Cf. André Orlean, *Le Pouvoir de la finance*, Paris 1999, 32–62; on the consistent replacement of "rational expectations equilibria" by "rational belief equilibria," cf. e.g., Mordecai Kurz, *Endogenous Uncertainty and Rational Belief Equilibrium: A Unified Theory of Market Volatility*, Stanford University, July 14, 1999 (http://www.stanford.edu/~mordecai/OnLinePdf/13.UnifiedView_1999.pdf).

32 Michel Aglietta and André Orléan, *La Violence de la monnaie* (1984), quoted in Luhmann, *Die Wirtschaft der Gesellschaft*, Frankfurt/M. 1988, 116–117.

33 The fact that a theological dimension – as praise to God – resonates in the concept of the "doxological" only reinforces its meaning, insofar as financial transactions are about branding and the stoking of attention; cf. Eric L. Santner, "The Rebranding of Sovereignty in the Age of Trump: Toward a Critique of Manatheism," in William Mazzarella, Eric L. Santner, and Aaron Schuster, *Sovereignty, Inc.: Three Inquiries in Politics and Enjoyment*, Chicago 2019, 25–29.

34 Gabriel Tarde, *Psychologie économique*, vol. 1, Paris 1902, 51 (http://classiques.uqac.ca/classiques/tarde_gabriel/psycho_economique_t1/psycho_economique_t1.pdf); cf. here Bruno Latour and Vincent Antonin Lépinay, "It Is Because the Economy Is Subjective that It Is Quantifiable," Part I of idem, *The Science of Passionate Interests: An Introduction to Gabriel Tarde's Economic Anthropology*, Chicago 2009, 7–32.

35 In the words of the economist, Gary Gorton, cited in Cassidy, *How Markets Fail*, 308.

36 [Translator's note: "*das Meinungshafte*" is rendered here and throughout as "opinion as such," which the author later defines as opinion freed of "liability, justification, or the need to give reasons."]

37 Milton Friedman, "Should There Be an Independent Monetary Authority?" in *The Essence of Friedman*, ed. K. K. Leube, Stanford 1987, 443; idem, "The Economics of Free Speech," in ibid., 9–17.

38 Elena Esposito, "Information," in Claudio Baraldi, Giancarlo Corsi, and Elena Esposito, *Unlocking Luhmann: A Keyword Introduction to Systems Theory*, trans. Katherine Walker, Bielefeld 2021, 109–110; Niklas Luhmann, *Social Systems* [1984], trans. John Bednarz, Jr., with Dirk Baecker, Stanford 1995, 95, 122; idem, *The Reality of the Mass Media*, trans. Kathleen Cross, Stanford 2000, 17–19, 53–54; idem, *Die Wirtschaft der Gesellschaft*, 18–19; Donald M. MacKay, "In Search of Basic Symbols," in Claus Pias (ed.), *Cybernetics/Kybernetik: The Macy-Conferences 1946–1953*, vol. 1: *Transactions/Protokolle*, Zürich and Berlin 2003, 480–482; idem, "Appendix I: The Nomenclature of Information Theory," in ibid., 511–512. Cf. Kay, *Who Wrote the Book of Life*, 20–21; Stephan Schäffler, *Mathematik der Information: Theorie und Anwendungen der Shannon-Wiener Information*, Heidelberg, Berlin, and New York 2015, 11; David G. Luenberger, *Information Science*, Princeton and Oxford 2006, 10.

39 Luhmann, *Wirtschaft der Gesellschaft*, 19.

40 Sahr, *Das Versprechen des Geldes*, 266–267.

41 Castells, *The Internet Galaxy*, 85–86; Carlota Perez, *Technological Revolutions and Financial Capital: The Dynamics of Bubbles and Golden Ages*, Cheltenham (UK) and Northampton (MA) 2002, 71–73.

42 Christopher Ingraham, "One Chart Shows How the Stock Market Is Completely Decoupled from the Labor Market," *Washington Post*, May 9, 2020.

43 From Robert Musil, *The Man Without Qualities*, trans. Sophie Wilkins and ed. Burton Pike, London 2011, 231 [translation modified – translator's note]. On the relationship between knowledge, uncertainty, and the processes of irreduction, cf. Bruno Latour, *An Inquiry into Modes of Existence: An Anthropology of the Moderns*, trans. Catherine Porter, Cambridge (MA) 2013, 32–35; Ludwig Wittgenstein, *Über Gewißheit/On Certainty*, ed. G. E. M. Anscombe and H. G. von Wright, New York 1972, nos. 109–110. On "solutionism" as a feature of digital capitalism, cf. Oliver Nachtwey and

Timo Seidl, "Die Ethik der Solution und der Geist des digitalen Kapitalismus," *IFS Working Paper 11*, Institut für Sozialforschung, Frankfurt am Main, October 2017, 21; and a first systematic discussion of knowledge concepts in economics, in particular on the processuality of knowledge, is found in Frank H. Knight, "'What Is Truth' in Economics?" *Journal of Political Economy* 48/1, February 1940, 1–32, esp. 13–14.

3 Platforms

1 Philipponnat, *Le Capital*, 18–19; Scialom, *La Fascination de l'ogre*, 62–64.
2 Priceline.com Prospectus, March 18, 1999, 1–21 (available at the US Securities and Exchange Commission website: https://www.sec.gov/Archives/edgar/data/1075531/0001047469-99-012711.txt), quoted in John Cassidy, *Dot.con*, 5 (the presentation here of Priceline's IPO owes much to this study).
3 Ibid., 2–5, 8, 216–219, 307; Ingebretsen, *Nasdaq*, 220, 235.
4 Mary Meeker and Chris DePuy, *The Internet Report, Morgan Stanley Global Technology Group*, New York 1996, 1–1; cf. also further remarks by the prominent analyst, Mary Meeker, and the Head of the Department for Investment Banking at Morgan Stanley, Joseph Perella, quoted in Cassidy, *Dot.con*, 216, 218. Cf. Dirk Baecker, *4.0 oder Die Lücke, die der Rechner lässt*, Berlin 2018, 111.
5 Nick Srnicek, *Platform Capitalism*, Cambridge 2017, 20–21; Matthew Crain, "Financial Markets and Online Advertising: Reevaluating the Dotcom Investment Bubble," *Information, Communication and Society* 17/3, 2014, 374; Philipp Staab, *Digitaler Kapitalismus: Markt und Herrschaft in der Ökonomie der Unknappheit*, Berlin 2019, 18–19.
6 On the origins and privatization of the Internet, cf. Cassidy, *Dot.con*, 9–24; Robert W. McChesney, *Digital Disconnect: How Capitalism Is Turning the Internet Against Democracy*, New York and London 2013, 98–109. One of the most recent examples of such funeral orations and swan songs: Geert Lovink, *Sad by Design: On Platform Nihilism*, London 2019.
7 Mazzucato, *Entrepreneurial State*, 6, 29, 99–119, 182 and passim.

8 Staab, *Digitaler Kapitalismus*, 104, 109–111, 170, 245; Thomas Ammann, *Die Machtprobe: Wie Social Media unsere Demokratie verändern*, Hamburg 2020, 179–180; Forum on Information and Democracy, *Working Group on Infodemics: Policy Framework*, November 2020 (https://informationdemocracy.org/wp-content/uploads/2020/11/ForumID_Report-on-infodemics_101120.pdf).

9 Cf. Parker et al., *Platform Revolution*, 5, 274–275; on the filiation between the finance and Internet economies, cf. Staab, *Digitaler Kaptalismus*, 82–149.

10 Cf. Srnicek, *Platform Capitalism*, 75–76.

11 Cassidy, *Dot.con*, 146.

12 Srnicek, *Platform Capitalism*, 45–47; Parker et al., *Platform Revolution*, 20; McChesney, *Digital Disconnect*, 132. On the celebration of exponential curves and the power law (as the law of the universe per se), cf. Peter Thiel and Blake Masters, *Zero to One: Notes on Startups or How to Build the Future*, New York 2014, 82–92.

13 Parker et al., *Platform Revolution*, 18–20; McChesney, *Digital Disconnect*, 131–133; David Singh Grewal, *Network Power: The Social Dynamics of Globalization*, New Haven (CT) and London 2008, 17–18; Justus Haucap and Torben Stühmeier, "Competition and antitrust in Internet markets," in Johannes M. Bauer and Michael Latzer (eds.), *Handbook on the Economics of the Internet*, Cheltenham (UK) and Northampton (MA) 2016, 186.

14 Srnicek, *Platform Capitalism*, 45, 59, 86; McChesney, *Digital Disconnect*, 131; Patrizia Mazepa and Vincent Mosco, "A Political Economy Approach to the Internet," in Bauer et al. (eds.), *Handbook on the Economics of the Internet*, 164–165.

15 Remarks from the (former) Editor-in-Chief of *Wired*, Chris Anderson, and the founder of Pay-Pal, Peter Thiel, as quoted in McChesney, *Digital Disconnect*, 141–142; Nachtwey and Seidel, "Die Ethik der Solution"; cf. Parker et al., *Platform Revolution*, 79; Staab, *Digitaler Kapitalismus*, 23–27.

16 Thiel and Masters, *Zero to One*, 25, 53.

17 [Translator's note: Wirecard fraudulently inflated their reported revenue in order to attract investors and increase their share price. For more detail, see the coverage in the *New York Times* at https://www.nytimes.com/2020/06/26/business/wirecard-collapse-markus-braun.html.]

18 Srnicek, *Platform Capitalism*, 75–76, 87; Martin Kenney and John Zysman, "The Rise of the Platform Economy," *Issues in Science and Technology* 32/3, Spring 2016, 13; Crain, "Financial markets and online advertising," 373–377; Cassidy, *Dot.con*, 164; Staab, *Digitaler Kapitalismus*, 132–136. On Uber's losses, see: "Wie Uber täglich 10 Millionen Euro Verlust einfährt," *Orange by Handelsblatt*, June 5, 2019 (https://orange.handelsblatt.com/artikel/61372).

19 Following a term coined by Stephen Hymer, cited in Foster and McChesney, *Endless Crisis*, 116.

20 William Lazonick, *Sustainable Prosperity in the New Economy? Business Organization and High-Tech Employment in the United States*, Kalamazoo 2009, 258–259; Mazzucato, *Entrepreneurial State*, 32; Gérard Duménil and Dominique Lévy, *The Crisis of Neoliberalism*, Cambridge (MA) and London 2011, 63–64.

21 Srnicek, *Platform Capitalism*, 30–32.

22 Dina Scornos and Niels Bammens, "International Corporate Taxation of Digital Platforms," in Bram Devolder (ed.), *The Platform Economy: Unravelling the Legal Status of Online Intermediaries*, Cambridge (UK), Antwerp, and Chicago 2019, 327–331.

23 Srnicek, *Platform Capitalism*, 33.

24 Shoshanna Zuboff, "Big Other: Surveillance Capitalism and the Prospects of an Information Civilization," *Journal of Information Technology* 30, 2015, 80; Srnicek, *Platform Capitalism*, 4; Parker et al., *Platform Revolution*, 32; Pepe Egger, "Außer Kontrolle," *Der Freitag*, April 30, 2020, 6. Facebook did, in fact, offer $1 billion, financed with stock, to buy Instagram; because of a short-term drop in Facebook's stock price, the effective purchase price ended up being only $715 million.

25 Kenney and Zysman, "The Rise of the Platform Economy," 67; Srnicek, *Platform Capitalism*, 77–80; Mazzucato, *Entrepreneurial State*, 183–186; Paul Schoukens, Alberto Barrio, and Saskia Montebovi, "Social Protection of Non-Standard Workers: The Case of Platform Work," in Devolder (ed.), *Platform Economy*, 227–258; Colin Crouch, *Will the Gig Economy Prevail?* Cambridge (UK) 2019, 36–42, 74–90. The most recent example of this is the so-called "juicers," mini-jobbers who collect and recharge ("juice") the electric scooters

left lying around (cf. Lukas Waschbüsch, "Saftig ausgepresst," *die tageszeitung*, July 9, 2019, 21).

26 Benjamin H. Bratton, *The Stack: On Software and Sovereignty*, Cambridge (MA) 2015, 48.

27 Srnicek, *Platform Capitalism*, 122.

28 Axel Bruns, *Blogs, Wikipedia, Second Life, and Beyond: From Production to Produsage*, New York 2008, 21; cf. Tiziana Terranova, "Free Labor: Producing Culture for the Digital Economy," *Social Text* 18/2 (Summer 2000), 33–58; Brian A. Brown and Anabel Quan-Haase, "'A Worker's Inquiry 2.0': An Ethnographic Method for the Study of Produsage in Social Media Contexts," in Christian Fuchs and Vincent Mosco (eds.), *Marx in the Age of Digital Capitalism*, Leiden 2016, 447–448.

29 In accordance with the famous formulations of Marx and Engels, in Karl Marx and Frederick Engels, *The German Ideology*, in idem, *Marx/Engels Collected Works (MECW)*, London and New York 1975ff., Vol. 5, 47.

30 Shoshana Zuboff, *The Age of Surveillance Capitalism: The Fight for a Human Future at the New Frontier of Power*, New York 2019, 130–132.

31 Bruns, *Blogs, Wikipedia*, 173–175.

32 Marx, *Capital*, 174, 177; cf. Srnicek, *Platform Capitalism*, 40, 56, 133.

33 Zuboff, *Surveillance Capitalism*, 128–138; Christian Fuchs, "Labor in Informational Capitalism and on the Internet," *The Information Society* 26, 2010, 179–196; Yochai Benkler, *The Wealth of Networks: How Social Production Transforms Markets and Freedom*, New Haven 2006, 34–35; Daniel Greene and Daniel Joseph, "The Digital Spatial Fix," *tripleC* 13/2, 2015, 231–234.

34 Gary Becker, "A Theory of the Allocation of Time," *Economic Journal* 75/299, 1965, 493, 513.

35 Dan Schiller, *How to Think About Information*, Urbana (IL) and Chicago 2007, xiv.

36 Hannah Arendt, *The Origins of Totalitarianism*, New York and London 1973, 147–150. [Translation slightly modified – translator's note.]

37 Cf. Klaus Dörre, "Landnahme und die Grenzen kapitalistischer Dynamik: Eine Ideenskizze," *Berliner Debatte INITIAL* 22/4, 2011, 56–72 (https://www.linksnet.de/artikel/27742); idem,

"Demokratie statt Kapitalismus oder: Enteignet Zuckerberg," in Hanna Ketterer and Karina Becker (eds.), *Was stimmt nicht mit der Demokratie?* Berlin 2019, 21–51.

38 Bratton, *The Stack*, 82–83.

39 Mattias Ekman, "The Relevance of Marx' Theory of Primitive Accumulation for Media and Communication Research," in Fuchs and Mosco (eds.), *Marx in the Age of Digital Capitalism*, 124–125; Zuboff, *Surveillance Capitalism*, 99–101, 138–155.

40 Srnicek, *Platform Capitalism*, 4–5; Staab, *Digitaler Kapitalismus*, 88–89.

41 Michel Foucault, *The Birth of Biopolitics: Lectures at the Collège de France, 1978–1979*, ed. Michel Senellart, trans. Graham Burchell, New York 2008, 118.

42 Gilles Deleuze, "Postscript on the Societies of Control," *October*, 59 (Winter, 1992), 3–7 (www.jstor.org/stable/77 8828).

4 Control Power

1 Staab, *Digitaler Kapitalismus*, 223; cf. 27–52, 150–225, 340–344.

2 Ibid., 176–178; Dominique Cardon, *À quoi rêvent les algorithms: Nos vies à l'heure des big data*, Paris 2015, 16–19; Bratton, *Stack*, 43. On the increasing discomfort of so-called competition watchdogs, cf., for instance, Björn Finke, "EZ-Kommission wirft Amazon unfaire Tricks vor," *Süddeutsche Zeitung*, November 11, 2020, 19.

3 Staab, *Digitaler Kapitalismus*, 135.

4 The considerations made here were largely adopted from Alex Galloway, "Protocol, or, How Control Exists After Decentralization," *Rethinking Marxism* 13/3–4, 2001, 81–88 (https://www.tandfonline.com/doi/abs/10.1080/08935690110 1241758); Galloway, *Protocol: How Controls Exists After Decentralization*, Cambridge (MA) and London 2006, 1–53; Alexander Galloway and Eugene Thacker, "Protocol, Control, and Networks," *Grey Room*, 17 (Fall, 2004), 6–29 (https:// direct.mit.edu/grey/article/doi/10.1162/1526381042464572 /10432/Protocol-Control-and-Networks). Cf. Bratton, *Stack*, 61–63; Wendy Hui Kyong Chung, *Control Freedom: Power and Paranoia in the Age of Fiber Optics*, Cambridge (MA) and

London 2006, 66–76; on the relationship between communication and control in cybernetics and in Norbert Wiener, cf. Kay, *Who Wrote the Book of Life*, 90–91.

5 Bruno Latour, "Centres of Calculation," Chap. 6 in idem, *Science in Action: How to Follow Scientists and Engineers through Society*, Cambridge (MA) 1987, 223, 227.

6 Vincent Mosco, *The Digital Sublime: Myth, Power, and Cyberspace*, Boston 2004, 162–164; Bratton, *Stack*, 24, 206–208.

7 On the concept of abstract machines, cf. Deleuze and Guattari, *Thousand Plateaus*, 510–514; Gilles Deleuze, *Foucault*, Minneapolis and London 1988, 34–41.

8 Galloway, *Protocol*, 8, 246; cf. Robert Simanowski and Ramón Reichert, *Sozialmaschine Facebook: Dialog über das politisch Unverbindliche*, Berlin 2020, 54–55.

9 Zuboff, *Age of Surveillance Capitalism*, 115–119 and passim.

10 Egger, "Außer Kontrolle," 6–7; Félix Tréguer, "Wenn die Polizei Fieber misst," *Le Monde Diplomatique* (German edition), May 2020, 7.

11 Christopher Zara, "The Most Important Law in Tech Has a Problem," *Wired*, March 1, 2017 (https://www.wired.com/2017/01/the-most-important-law-in-tech-has-a-problem/); cf. also Zuboff, *Surveillance Capitalism*, 101–122; Mazzucato, *Entrepreneurial State*, 186–187.

12 Bobbie Johnson, "Privacy No Longer a Social Norm, Says Facebook Founder," *Guardian*, 01.11.2010 (https://www.theguardian.com/technology/2010/jan/11/facebook-privacy).

13 Zuboff, quoted in Srnicek, *Platform Capitalism*, 101; cf. Dirk Helbig, Bruno S. Frey, Gerd Gigerenzer et al., "Das Digital-Manifest," *Spektrum*, December 17, 2015, 12 (https://www.spektrum.de/news/wie-algorithmen-und-big-data-unsere-zukunft-bestimmen/1375933).

14 Mike McConnell, "Mike McConnell on How to Win the Cyber-War We Are Losing," *Washington Post*, February 28, 2010 (https://www.washingtonpost.com/wp-dyn/content/article/2010/02/25/AR2010022502493.html). Quoted in Zuboff, *Surveillance Capitalism*, 119–120. The reflections made here draw from Zuboff's study; see also Christopher Wylie, *Mindf*ck: Inside Cambridge Analytica's Plot to Break the World*, London 2020, 112–113. On the cooperation between the state and the private sector, on the monopolization of

European data on US servers, and on the controversy around the so-called Safe Harbour Agreement, cf. Ammann, *Die Machtprobe*, 186–189.

15 According to the remarks of the CEO of Google, Larry Page, in 2013, quoted in Zuboff, *Surveillance Capitalism*, 105. On the way in which modern law produces and privileges capital, cf. Katharina Pistor, *The Code of Capital: How the Law Creates Wealth and Inequality*, Princeton 2019.

16 Slobodian, *Globalists*, 345–353 (especially on the economic law initiatives made by Jan Tumlir in the GATT negotiations); Commission on Global Governance, *Our Global Neighborhood*, New York 1995, 95, quoted in Joseph, *Social and the Global*, 89–90; Bruce R. Scott, *Capitalism: Its Origins and Evolution as a System of Governance*, New York et al. 2011, 518–519.

17 Nils Jansen and Ralf Michaels, "Beyond the State? Rethinking Private Law" (Introduction to the special symposium issue of the same name), *American Journal of Comparative Law* 56/3, Summer 2008, 527–539. Cf. Vogl, *Ascendency of Finance*, 148–151.

18 Andrew L. Shapiro, *The Control Revolution: How the Internet Is Putting Individuals in Charge and Changing the World We Know*, New York 1999; Lawrence Lessing, *Code: And Other Laws of Cyberspace*, New York 1999. On the struggle between the legal and digital code, cf. Pistor, "A New Code," Chap. 8 in *Code of Capital*, 183–204.

19 Cf. Regina Ogorek, *Richterkönig oder Subsumtionsautomat? Zur Justiztheorie im 19. Jahrhundert*, Frankfurt am Main 1986; Sabine Gless and Wolfgang Wohlers, "Subsumtionsautomat 2.0: Künstliche Intelligenz statt menschlicher Richter?" in Martin Böse, Kay H. Schumann, and Friedrich Toepel (eds.), *Festschrift für Urs Kindhäuser zum 70. Geburtstag*, Baden-Baden 2019, 147–165.

20 The felicitously chosen term "polis of solution" comes from Evgeny Morozov; on this, cf. Nachtwey and Seidl, "Die Ethik der Solution," 19–21.

21 Tom Slee, *What's Yours is Mine: Against the Sharing Economy*, New York and London 2015, 8, quoted in ibid., 22; cf. Dirk Helbig, "The Birth of a Digital God," in idem (ed.), *Towards Digital Enlightenment*, Cham (CH), 103. On the generation of machinic surplus value (following Marx) by

means of information, cf. Gilles Deleuze and Félix Guattari, *Anti-Oedipus*, trans. Robert Hurley, Mark Seem, and Helen R. Lane, Minneapolis 1983, 226–228, 232–237; Matteo Pasquinelli, "Italian Operaismo and the Information Machine," *Theory, Culture and Society* 32/3, May 2015, 56–57.

22 Staab, *Digitaler Kapitalismus*, 260–266; Vogl, *Ascendency of Finance*, 70–71.

23 Anna-Verena Nosthoff and Felix Maschewski, *Die Gesellschaft der Wearables: Digitale Verführung und soziale Kontrolle*, Berlin 2019, 67–72; cf. Bratton, *Stack*, 7; Aral, *Hype Machine*, x–xi; Andrian Kreye, "Nutzlose App," *Süddeutsche Zeitung*, November 30, 2020, 4. On the rapid rise in sales of the notorious Internet companies since the spring of 2020, cf. "Tech-Konzerne profitieren," *Süddeutsche Zeitung*, October 31/November 1, 2020, 24.

24 Staab, *Digitaler Kapitalismus*, 188–189; Norbert Häring, "Wer steckt hinter der Libra Association und was ist das Ziel von Libra?" *publikum.net*, December 18, 2019 (https://publikum.net/wer-steckt-hinter-der-libra-association-und-was-ist-das-ziel-von-libra/).

25 Thiel and Masters, *Zero to One*, 17.

26 Norbert Häring, "Wie die USA ihre Dollar-Weltwährung ins Zeitalter von Libra retten wollen," *Handelsblatt*, May 9, 2020 (https://www.handelsblatt.com/politik/international/kryptowaehrungen-wie-die-usa-ihre-dollar-weltwaehrung-ins-zeitalter-von-libra-retten-wollen/25813190.html?ticket=ST-3228297-FnOSMecO2aMq6S1utO21-cas01.example.org); Dorothea Schäfer, "Facebook-Währung Libra: Nur ein genialer Marketingtrick?" *DIW Wochenbericht* 86/37, 2019, 688 (https://www.diw.de/de/diw_01.c.678097.de/publikationen/wochenberichte/2019_37_5/facebook-waehrung_libra__nur_ein_genialer_marketing-trick__kommentar.html).

27 Henry S. Simons, "Rules versus Authorities in Monetary Policy," *Journal of Political Economy* 44/1, 1936, 4–8, 17, 22–25; cf. here: Thorvald Grung Moe, "Control of Finance as a Prerequisite for Successful Monetary Policy: A Reinterpretation of Henry Simons's 'Rules versus Authorities in Monetary Policy,'" in *Levy Economics Institute Working Paper Collection*, Levy Economics Institute of Bard College, Working Paper No. 713, April 2012 (http://www.levyinstitute.org/pubs/wp_713.pdf).

28 Friedrich Hayek, *Denationalisation of Money: The Argument Refined. Analysis of the Theory and Practice of Concurrent Currencies* (1976), 3rd edn., London 1990, 23, 28, 48 (quote), 100 ff. On the first discussion of free banking, cf. the dissertation of a Hayek student: Vera C. Smith, *The Rationale of Central Banking and the Free Banking Alternative* [1936], Indianapolis 1990.

29 In Catherine Malabou's kind paraphrase of the Declaration of Currency Independence (https://medium.com/@currencyindependence/declaration-of-currency-independence-b404296bf03b), which, in turn, took the American Declaration of Independence as its template: Catherine Malabou, "Cryptocurrencies: Anarchist Turn or Strengthening of Surveillance Capitalism? From Bitcoin to Libra," trans. Robert Boncardo, *Australian Humanities Review* 66, May 2020, 45 (http://australianhumanitiesreview.org/2020/05/31/issue-66-may-2020/); for a critical examination of these promises of freedom, cf. Stefan Münker, "Freiheit, die in Ketten liegt: Zur Philosophie der *blockchain*," *Zeitschrift für Medien und Kulturforschung* 10/2 (2019), 117–126.

30 Libra Association Members, "An Introduction to Libra," in *White Paper: From the Libra Association Members*, June 18, 2019, 1–4 (available at https://www.scribd.com/document/413733914/LibraWhitePaper-en-US). [This is the original version of the Libra White Paper – translator's note.]

31 In the words of Volker Wieland, a member of the German Council of Economic Experts (Sachverständigenrat zur Begutachtung der gesamtwirtschaftlichen Entwicklung), quoted in Alexander Hagelüken, *Das Ende des Geldes, wie wir es kennen: Der Angriff auf Zinsen, Bargeld und Staatswährungen*, Munich 2020, 155.

32 Libra Association Members, "An Introduction to Libra," 1; cf. Daniel Tischer, "Cutting the network? Facebook's Libra currency as a problem of organization," *Finance and Society* 6/1, 2020, 19–33 (in more recent versions of Libra documents, the previously frequent references to investors and investments have been thinned out and toned down; cf. ibid., 30).

33 Libra Association Members, "An Introduction to Libra," 18.

34 Christian Catalini, Oliver Gratry, J. Mark Hou, Sunita Parasuraman, Nils Wernerfelt, "The Libra Reserve," August 2019, 2. (https://mitsloan.mit.edu/shared/ods/documents?Pub

licationDocumentID=5860); cf. here Volker Brühl, "Libra – A Differentiated View on Facebook's Virtual Currency Project," *Intereconomics* 55/1, January/February 2020, 60–61 (https://www.intereconomics.eu/contents/year/2020/number/1/article/libra-a-differentiated-view-on-facebook-s-virtual-currency-project.html); Stefan Eichler and Marcel Thum, "Libra – Totengräberin für gescheiterte Währungen, Herausforderung für gute Regulierung," *ifo Schnelldienst* 72/17, September 12, 2019, 20; Andreas Hanl, "Währungswettbewerber Facebook: Ökonomische Implikationen der Corporate Cryptocurrency Libra," *MAGKS Joint Discussion Paper Series in Economics* 30, 2019, 8–10 (http://hdl.handle.net/10419/213471); Christian Hofmann, "The Changing Concept of Money: A Threat to the Monetary System or an Opportunity for the Financial Sector?" *European Business Organization Law Review* 21, 2020, 55.

35 Yves Mersch, "Money and Private Currencies: Reflections on Libra," in *Building Bridges: Central Banking Law in an Interconnected World*. ECB Legal Conference 2019, European Central Bank, December 2019, 16 (https://www.ecb.europa.eu/pub/pdf/other/ecb.ecblegalconferenceproceedings201912~9325c45957.en.pdf); Lars Hornuf, "Libra: Eine Währung, die die Welt (nicht) braucht?" *ifo Schnelldienst* 72/17, September 12, 2019, 10.

36 Libra Association Members, "An Introduction to Libra," 4; Tischer, "Cutting the Network?" 27.

37 Libra Association Members, "An Introduction to Libra," 14; Libra Association, *Libra White Paper. Version 2.0*, 25; Julian Grigo and Patrick Hansen, "Digitalwährungen stehen vor dem Durchbruch," *ifo Schnelldienst* 72/17, September 12, 2019, 8; Ramaa Vasudevan, "Libra and Facebook's Money Illusion," *Challenge*, 63, 1 (2020), 22 (https://doi.org/10.1080/05775132.2019.1684662); Markus K. Brunnermeier, Harold James, and Jean-Pierre Landau, "The Digitalization of Money," *National Bureau of Economic Research (NBER) Working Papers Series*. Working Paper 26300, 11–16 (https://www.nber.org/papers/w26300); Häring, "Wer steckt hinter der Libra Association," 9.

38 As Nick Szabo, one of the early protagonists of cryptocurrency, announced in 1994: "Smart contracts will replace, and even protect against, lawyers, politicians, and violent enforcement in many business and social interactions. They will also be

used to design lucrative new free-market institutions." Szabo, "Smart Contracts," 1994 (https://web.archive.org/web/20011102030833/http://szabo.best.vwh.net:80/smart.contracts.html). Quoted in Oliver Leistert, "The Blockchain as a Modulator of Existence," *MoneyLab*, February 7, 2018 (https://networkcultures.org/moneylab/2018/02/07/the-blockchain-as-a-modulator-of-existence/); cf. here and in the following: Leistert, "Kontrolle ist gut, Vertrauen ist besser, Bezahlung am besten: Zur Souveränität von Blockchain," *Zeitschrift für Medien- und Kulturforschung* 10/2, 2019, 155–170 (https://ikkm-weimar.de/site/assets/files/8580/zmk_2-2019_schwerpunkt.pdf). Cf. Pistor, *Code of Capital*, 187–191.

39 In the words of Joachim Wuermeling, the member of the German Federal Bundesbank's Executive Board responsible for banking supervision, in an interview with Alexander Hagelüken and Markus Zydra: "Libra steht völlig quer zu allem," *Süddeutsche Zeitung*, November 5, 2019, 19. On the debate on Libra's format, cf., for instance, Louis Abraham and Dominique Guégan, "The Other Side of the Coin Risks of the Libra Blockchain," *Working Papers 30*, Department of Economics, Ca' Foscari University of Venice, 2019; Mersch, "Money and Private Currencies"; Maik Schmeling, "What Is Libra? Understanding Facebook's Currency," *SAFE Policy Letter*, No. 76, Goethe University Frankfurt, 2019 (http://hdl.handle.net/10419/204501).

40 Izabella Kaminska, "Alphaville's Libra Cheat Sheet," *FTalphaville*, June 18, 2019 (https://www.ft.com/content/be3b7636-a9df-3672-a324-e85762057a4d), quoted in Vasudevan, "Libra and Facebook's Money Illusion," 12. On the limits of previous control mechanisms, cf. Mersch, "Money and Private Currencies," 17–18; Hornuf, "Libra," 11; Schmeling, "What Is Libra?" 7–8; Tischer, "Cutting the network?" 21.

41 Brunnermeier, James, and Landau, "The Digitalization of Money," 2.

42 Ibid., 15, 19–22.

43 Mark Zuckerberg in "Hearing before the United States House of Representatives Committee on Financial Services," October 23, 2019 (https://financialservices.house.gov/uploadedfiles/hhrg-116-ba00-wstate-zuckerbergm-20191023.pdf), 1, quoted in Alan Cassidy and Claus Hulverscheidt, "Was habt ihr denn?" *Süddeutsche Zeitung*, October 24, 2019, 17; Häring, "Wie die

USA ihre Dollar-Weltwährung"; cf. Libra White Paper. Version 2.0, 2, 11, 25; Hagelüken, *Das Ende des Geldes*, 170.

44 Fernand Braudel, *Afterthoughts on Material Civilization and Capitalism*, Baltimore 1977, 64. On the online state, cf. Hanl, "Währungswettbewerber Facebook," 16; Hofmann, "Changing Concept of Money," 55–57; Mersch, "Money and Private Currencies," 16; Schmeling, "What Is Libra?" 3. And on renaming Libra Diem, cf. "Aus Libra wird Diem," *Spiegel Netzwelt*, October 2, 2020.

5 Truth Games

1 Bratton, *Stack*, 7–9, 14, 31–32; Reijer Hendrikse and Rodrigo Fernandez, "Offshore Finance: How Capital Rules the World," in Nick Buxton and Deborah Eade (eds.) *State of Power 2019: Finance*, n.p. 2019, 33–35 (https://www.tni.org/files/publication-downloads/state_of_power_2019_-_finance_-_full_draft.pdf).

2 Slobodian, *Globalists*, 9–28, 336–337; Foucault, *Birth of Biopolitics*, 188–190; Hendrikse and Fernandez, "Offshore Finance," 30.

3 Friedrich Hayek, *Road to Serfdom*, 204, quoted in Mirowski, *Never Let a Serious Crisis*, 79.

4 Milton Friedman, *Capitalism and Freedom* [1962], Chicago and London 2002, 3, 16–17, 23, 51–55; Friedman, "Should There Be an Independent Monetary Authority?" in idem, *Essence of Friedman*, 443; idem, "The Economics of Free Speech," in ibid., 9–17.

5 Herbert I. Schiller, *Information and the Crisis Economy*, Oxford and New York 1986, 37; *First National Bank of Boston v. Bellotti*, 435 US 765 (1978) at 766 (https://supreme.justia.com/cases/federal/us/435/765/).

6 *Citizens United v. Federal Election Commission*, 558 U.S. 310 (2010) (https://www.fec.gov/resources/legal-resources/litigation/cu_sc08_opinion.pdf), 19; cf. Wendy Brown, "Law and Legal Reason," Chap. 5 in idem, *Undoing the Demos: Neoliberalism's Stealth Revolution*, New York 2015, 151–174.

7 For instance, from Nicholas Negroponte; cf. Mosco, *Digital Sublime*, 73.

8 Electronic Frontier Foundation, "CDA 230: The Most

Important Law Protecting Internet Speech" (https://www.eff.org/issues/cda230).

9 *Communications Decency Act*, 47 U.S. Code § 230: Protection for private blocking and screening of offensive material (1996), Subsections (c)(1) and (b)(2) as well as (a)(4) (https://www.law.cornell.edu/uscode/text/47/230); cf. Jeff Kosseff, *The Twenty-Six Words That Created the Internet*, Ithaca and London 2019, 57–76; Christopher Zara, "The Most Important Law in Tech Has a Problem," *Wired*, March 1, 2017 (https://www.wired.com/2017/01/the-most-important-law-in-tech-has-a-problem/); Zuboff, *Surveillance Capitalism*, 110–111.

10 *Directive 2000/31/EC of the European Parliament and of the Council of 8 June 2000 on certain legal aspects of information society services, in particular electronic commerce, in the Internal Market* ("Directive on electronic commerce") (https://eur-lex.europa.eu/legal-content/EN/TXT/HTML/?uri=CELEX:32000L0031&from=EN). Cf. Articles 12–14 in this directive, which define the nonliability of Internet services; on the similarities and differences between US and European legislation or jurisprudence, which relate primarily to the relative weight given to freedom of speech vs. privacy, cf. Kosseff, *Twenty-Six Words*, 149–163; Kenneth Propp, "The Emerging EU Regulatory Landscape for Digital Platform Liability," *Atlantic Council*, October 22, 2019 (https://www.atlanticcouncil.org/blogs/new-atlanticist/the-emerging-eu-regulatory-landscape-for-digital-platform-liability/); Daphne Keller, "Internet Platforms: Observations on Speech, Danger, and Money," *Hoover Working Group on National Security, Technology, and Law*, Aegis Series Paper No. 1807, June 13, 2018, 11–15 (https://www.hoover.org/research/internet-platforms-observations-speech-danger-and-money).

11 See, for example, the German *Teledienstgesetz* (Teleservices Act) of July 22, 1997 (Section 3: Responsibility), which was superseded in February 2007 by the *Elektronischer-Geschäftsverkehr-Vereinheitlichungsgesetz* (Electronic Commerce Standardization Act) (Section 3: Responsibility). Teleservices Act: Gesetz über die Nutzung von Telediensten (*Teledienstgesetz – TDG*), July 22, 1997 (Art. 1 in Gesetz zur Regelung der Rahmenbedingungen für Informations- und Kommunikationsdienste-Gesetz [*Informations- und Kommunikationsdienste-Gesetz – IuKDG*]) (https://www

.lehrer.uni-karlsruhe.de/~za186/MMB/recht/gesetz.htm); Electronic Commerce Standardization Act: Gesetz zur Vereinheitlichung von Vorschriften über bestimmte elektronische Informations- und Kommunikationsdienste (*Elektronischer-Geschäftsverkehr-Vereinheitlichungsgesetz – ElGVG*), February 26, 2007 (https://www.buzer.de/s1.htm?g=TDG+1997&f=1).

12 Mark Zuckerberg, in an interview with Andy Kessler: Andy Kessler, "WSJ: Weekend Interview with Facebook's Mark Zuckerberg," March 24, 2007 (https://www.andykessler.com/andy_kessler/2007/03/wsj_weekend_int.html), quoted in Nicole S. Cohen, "The Valorization of Surveillance: Towards a Political Economy of Facebook," *Democratic Communiqué* 22, No. 1, Spring 2008, 13–14. Cf. Forum on Information and Democracy, *Working Group on Infodemics*, 87–88.

13 Adrian Lobe, "Der redet nur Blech, doch das darf er," *Süddeutsche Zeitung*, August 18, 2020, 11.

14 Since June 2020, a reform of Section 230 has been under discussion in the US, in the form of a Platform Accountability and Consumer Transparency (PACT) bill aimed at transparency in content moderation and complaint mechanisms; cf. Forum on Information and Democracy, *Working Group on Infodemics*, 39. The sharpest initiative to date was envisioned by the EU at the end of November 2020 with a Data Governance Act: the establishment of independent organizations that would act as noncommercial trustees in the transport and bundling of data flows in Europe and thus break the monopolies of US corporations (see Holger Beckmann, "Europas Angriff auf Google & Co.," *tagesschau.de*, November 25, 2020 (https://www.tagesschau.de/ausland/eu-datenschutz-115.html).

15 Kosseff, *Twenty-Six Words*, 139–140; Matt Reynolds, "The strange story of Section 230, the obscure law that created our flawed, broken internet," *Wired*, March 24, 2019, 5–6 (https://www.wired.co.uk/article/section-230-communications-decency-act). On the legal discussion of free speech on the Internet, especially in the US, cf. Keller, *Internet Platforms*.

16 Shapiro, *Control Revolution*, 53–59; Parker et al., *Platform Revolution*, 7–8.

17 Evgeny Morozov, *To Save Everything, Click Here: The Folly of Technological Solutionism*, New York 2013, 165–166.

18 Baecker, *4.0*, 18.

19 The pillars of Google Search (https://www.google.com/search/howsearchworks/our-approach/).

20 Cardon, *À quoi rêvent les algorithms*, 24–29; Eric Goldman, "Search Engine Bias and the Demise of Search Engine Utopianism," *Yale Journal of Law and Technology* 8, 2006, 188–200; A. Diaz, "Through the Google Goggles: Sociopolitical Bias in Search Engine Design," in Amanda Spink and Michael Zimmer (eds.), *Web Search: Multidisciplinary Perspectives*, Berlin and Heidelberg 2008, 11–34; Hal R. Varian, "The Economics of Internet Search," in Johannes M. Bauer and Michael Latzer (eds.), *Handbook on the Economics of the Internet*, Northampton 2016, 385–394.

21 Quotes from Mark Zuckerberg in idem, "Building Global Community," February 16, 2017, 7–11 (https://www.facebook.com/notes/mark-zuckerberg/building-global-community/10154544292806634/), and in Olivia Solon, "Facebook's Fake News: Mark Zuckerberg Rejects 'Crazy Idea' That It Swayed Voters," *Guardian*, November 11, 2016 (https://www.theguardian.com/technology/2016/nov/10/facebook-fake-news-us-election-mark-zuckerberg-donald-trump), as quoted in Ammann, *Die Machtprobe*, 207; cf. also the "community standards" of Facebook: https://transparency.fb.com/policies/community-standards/?from=https%3A%2F%2Fwww.facebook.com%2Fcommunitystandards. On the nonneutrality of the selections made by search machines, cf. Goldman, *Search Engine Bias*.

22 Cardon, *À quoi rêvent les algorithms*, 66–71; Cohen, "Valorization of Surveillance," 12–13; Cathy O'Neil, *Weapons of Math Destruction: How Big Data Increases Inequality and Threatens Democracy*, New York 2016, 179–185; Zuboff, *Surveillance Capitalism*, 458–461; Brian Morrissey, "Facebook Gives New Face to Online Ads," *Brandweek* 47/35, October 2, 2006.

23 Tweet from Donald Trump, cited in Ammann, *Die Machtprobe*, 241.

24 Karl Marx, *Grundrisse: Foundations of the Critique of Political Economy (Rough Draft)*, trans. with foreword Martin Nicolaus, London 1973, 706; Cohen, "Valorization of Surveillance," 13; Paolo Virno, *A Grammar of the Multitude: For an Analysis of Contemporary Forms of Life*, Cambridge (MA) and London 2010, 101–102 ("Thesis 3").

25 In the words of former Google executive Marissa Mayer, the

Google executive chairman Eric Schmidt, and Facebook's Zuckerberg, quoted in Morozov, *To Save Everything*, 144–145; and David Weinberger, *Too Big to Know: Rethinking Knowledge Now that the Facts Aren't the Facts, Experts Are Everywhere, and the Smartest Person in the Room Is the Room*, New York 2011, xiii.

26 Novalis, *Notes for a Romantic Encyclopaedia: Das Allgemeine Brouillon* (SUNY series, Intersections: Philosophy and Critical Theory), trans., ed., and introd. David W. Wood, Albany (NY) 2011, 30.

27 Bratton, *Stack*, 8.

28 Cf. Martin Heidegger, "The Provenance of Art and the Destination of Thought" [1967], trans. Dimitrios Latsis (reviewed and amended by Ullrich Haase), *Journal of the British Society for Phenomenology* 44/2 (2013), 119–128 (https://doi.org/10.1080/00071773.2013.11006794); on the Internet as image of the world, cf. Kevin Kelly, *New Rules for the New Economy* (1998), cited in Thomas Frank, *One Market under God: Extreme Capitalism, Market Populism, and the End of Economic Democracy*, London 2001, 345.

29 Alexander R. Galloway, "The Poverty of Philosophy: Realism and Post-Fordism," *Critical Inquiry* 39, Winter 2013, 352; cf. here also Lucas D. Introna, "Algorithms, Governance, and Governmentality: On Governing Academic Writing," *Science, Technology, and Human Values* 41/1, 2016, 27.

30 Thomas R. Gruber, "A Translation Approach to Portable Ontology Specifications," *Knowledge Acquisition*, 5/2 1993, 199–220, quoted in Adrian Mackenzie, *Cutting Code: Software and Sociality*, New York, Washington DC, and Bern 2006, 5–6.

31 Galloway, "Poverty of Philosophy," 352.

32 Mark Fisher, *Capitalist Realism: Is There No Alternative?* Winchester 2009, 17.

33 Deleuze and Guattari, *Anti-Oedipus*, 66.

34 Cf. Michel Betancourt, *The Critique of Digital Capitalism: An Analysis of the Political Economy of Digital Culture and Technology*, New York 2015 (http://library.oapen.org/handle/20.500.12657/25499), 160, 180; Cardon, *À quoi rêvent les algorithms*, 43; Frieder Nake, "Das algorithmische Zeichen," in W. Bauknecht, W. Brauer, and Th. Mück (eds.), *Informatik 2001: Tagungsband der GI/OCG Jahrestagung 2001*, vol. 2, Konstanz (DE) 2001, 736–742.

35 Weinberger, *Too Big to Know*, x.

36 Chris Anderson, "The End of Theory: The Data Deluge Makes the Scientific Method Obsolete," *Wired*, June 23, 2008, 5 (https://www.wired.com/2008/06/pb-theory/); Alex Pentland, *Social Physics: How Good Ideas Spread – Lessons from a New Science*, New York 2004.

37 Anderson, "End of Theory," 5.

38 Jean-François Lyotard, *The Postmodern Condition: A Report on Knowledge*, trans. Geoff Bennington and Brian Massumi, Minneapolis 1984, 4.

39 Anderson, "End of Theory," 5; cf. also Armin Nassehi, *Muster: Theorie der digitalen Gesellschaft*, Munich 2019, 80–82.

40 Examples from Anderson, "End of Theory," 5; Weinberger, *Too Big to Know*, 33, 194f.; and Ammann, *Die Machtprobe*, 201.

41 Tooze, *Crashed*, 22.

42 Cf., for instance, Robert N. Procter and Londa Schiebinger (eds.), *Agnotology: The Making and Unmaking of Ignorance*, Stanford 2008; Mirowski, *Never Let a Serious Crisis*, 226–237; Susan Jacoby, *The Age of American Unreason in a Culture of Lies*, 2nd edn., New York 2018, 221–243.

43 Cf. Ludwig von Mises, *Liberalism: The Classical Tradition* [1927], trans. Ralph Raico, Irvington-on-Hudson (NY) 1997, 9: "The fact that there is want and misery would not constitute an argument against liberalism even if the world today followed a liberal policy. It would always be an open question whether still more want and misery might not prevail if other policies had been followed." Hayek, "Competition," 10: The "validity of the theory of competition can never be empirically verified for those cases in which it is of interest."

44 Mirowski, *Never Let a Serious Crisis*, 81; Mirowski and Nik-Khah, *Knowledge We Have Lost*, 7, 70–72; William Davies and Linsey McGoey, "Rationalities of Ignorance: On Financial Crisis and the Ambivalence of Neoliberal Epistemology," *Economy and Society*, 41/1, February 2, 2012, 70 (https://doi.org/10.1080/03 085147.2011.637331).

45 As quoted in Ronald E. Day, *The Modern Invention of Information: Discourse, History, and Power*, Carbondale (IL) 2008, 42–48; William Aspray, "The Scientific Conceptualization of Information: A Survey," *Annals of the History of Computing* 7/2, April 1985, 123.

46 Friedrich August von Hayek, "Economics and Knowledge," *Economica*, New Series 4/13, February 1937, 33–54; cf. here Slobodian, *Globalists*, 82f.

47 Tri Vi Dang, Gary Gorton, and Bengt Holmström, "Ignorance, Debt and Financial Crises," Columbia University, April 2015, 1, 4, 38 (http://www.columbia.edu/~td2332/Paper_Ignorance.pdf); here: Mirowski and Nik-Khah, *Knowledge We Have Lost*, 33. See also Slobodian, *Globalists*, 228; Mirowski, *Never Let a Serious Crisis*, 78, 214–215, 224–226; Colin Crouch, *The Knowledge Corrupters: Hidden Consequences of the Financial Takeover of Public Life*, Cambridge (UK) 2016, 2–3.

48 Elisa Shearer and Jeffrey Gottfried, "News Use Across Social Media Platforms 2017," in *Pew Research Center*, September 7, 2017 (https://www.pewresearch.org/journalism/2017/09/07/news-use-across-social-media-platforms-2017/).

Excursus: Fable and Finance

1 Baecker, *4.0.*, 196–197 (which includes a reference to Peter Glaser, "Der Überallgorithmus: Sind Programmiersprachen die neuen Weltsprachen?" *Neue Zürcher Zeitung*, February 16, 2016, 37). The coining of the term "infopinion" – denoting a systematic indifference between information and opinion – is attributed to David Weinberger.

2 Cf. Anton Delbrück, *Die pathologische Lüge und die psychisch abnormen Schwindler: Eine Untersuchung über den allmählichen Übergang eines normalen psychischen Vorgangs in ein pathologisches Symptom – Für Ärzte und Juristen*, Stuttgart 1891, 124.

3 Ingebretsen, *Nasdaq*, 58–59, 63–64.

4 Aral, *Hype Machine*, 26–28.

5 Crain, "Financial Markets and Online Advertising," 374, 376, 379; Cassidy, *Dot.con*, 81.

6 Harry G. Frankfurt, *Bullshit*, Frankfurt am Main 2006.

7 Cf. Janine Wedel, *Shadow Elite: How the World's New Power Brokers Undermine Democracy, Government, and the Free Markets*, New York 2009, 23–45.

8 Wolfgang Ullrich, "Ganz ohne Einflussangst: Zur Karriere der Influencer," *POP. Kultur und Kritik* 12, Spring 2018, 45–49 (https://www.uni-muenster.de/Ejournals/index.php/pop/article

/view/2365/2250); Sebastian Löwe, "Social Media Oktober," *PopZeitschrift*, October 22, 2018 (https://pop-zeitschrift.de/2018/10/22/social-media-oktober-von-sebastian-loewe/).

9 Herman Melville, *The Confidence-Man: His Masquerade*, ed. Elizabeth S. Foster, New York 1954, 7, 45, 81. (In the following, page references in the text refer to this publication.)

10 Michel Imbert, "The Confidence-Man d'Herman Melville ou le discrédit des signes: du papiermonnaie aux Saintes Ècritures," *Social Science Information* 30/2, June 1, 1991, 305–322 (https://journals.sagepub.com/doi/pdf/10.1177/053901891030002007); Matt Seybold, "The Political Economy of *The Confidence-Man*," *Leviathan* 21/3, October 2019, 51–59.

11 Christopher W. Sten, "The Dialogue of Crisis in The Confidence-Man: Melville's 'New Novel,'" *Studies in the Novel* 6/2, Summer 1974, 165–185; Alexandra Vasa and Philippe Roepstorff-Robiano, "Börsen, Spekulations- und Inflationsroman," in Joseph Vogl and Burkhardt Wolf (eds.), *Handbuch Literatur und Ökonomie*, Berlin and Boston 2019, 578. Whereas the "cosmopolitan" dominates the second half of the novel, he surfaces in the first half in the following guises: as a deaf-mute, a man with crepe, "Black Guinea," a man in a gray coat, a man with a big book, an herb doctor, and a representative of the Philosophical Intelligence Office.

12 John W. Shroeder, "Sources and Symbols for Melville's Confidence-Man," *PMLA* 66/4, 1951, 371; Wolfgang Pircher, "Die Inszenierung von Vertrauen: Zur Theatralität des Geldes," in Ralf Bohn and Heiner Wilharm (eds.), *Inszenierung und Ereignis*, Bielefeld 2015, 200.

13 Imbert, "Confidence-Man," 308.

14 Jacques Lacan, *The Seminar, Book III: The Psychoses*, ed. Jacques-Alain Miller, trans. Russell Grigg, New York and London 1997, 268.

15 Gilles Deleuze, "Bartleby; or, The Formula," in idem, *Deleuze: Essays Critical and Clinical*, trans. Daniel W. Smith and Michael A. Greco, London 1998, 10, 16 (n. 15).

16 Lacan, *Psychoses*, 149–150; cf. Lars Distelhorst, *Kritik des Postfaktischen: Der Kapitalismus und seine Spätfolgen*, Paderborn 2019, 179.

17 Lacan, *Psychoses*, 74–76. Lacan offers the complementary episode of the jealous individual, who, precisely as a "normal subject," rejects certainty: "There is the famous story of the

jealous husband who pursues his wife to the door of the very bedroom in which she has locked herself with someone else. This contrasts sufficiently with the fact that the delusional exempts himself from any real references" (ibid., 76).

18 Seybold, "Political Economy of *The Confidence-Man*," 52.

19 Similar forms of argumentation, also making recourse to Jacques Lacan, led to the diagnosis of the "psychotic structure" of such discourses; cf. Distelhorst, *Kritik des Postfaktischen*, 170–183.

20 John G. Cawelti, "Some Notes on the Structure of *The Confidence-Man*," *American Literature* 29/3, November 1957, 285; Imbert, "Confidence-Man," 319. Cf. also here and on the following: Lacan, *Psychoses*, 64–65.

21 Cf. Latour, *Inquiry into Modes of Existence*, 93 (with indirect reference to Descartes); on the loss of symbolic efficiency, see Slavoj Žižek, *The Ticklish Subject: The Absent Centre of Political Ontology*, London and New York 2009, 322–334.

6 The Cunning of Ressentiment-Driven Reason

1 Immanuel Kant, "Idea for a Universal History from a Cosmopolitan Point of View," in Lewis White Beck (ed.), *On History: Immanuel Kant*, Indianapolis and New York, 1963, 15; Immanuel Kant, "Perpetual Peace," in ibid., 112; Samuel Pufendorf, *The Whole Duty of Man, According to the Law of Nature*, trans. Andrew Tooke [1691], ed. Ian Hunter and David Saunders, Indianapolis 2003, 21. Cf. Joseph Vogl, *Kalkül und Leidenschaft: Poetik des ökonomischen Menschen*, 3rd edn., Zürich and Berlin 2008, 41–44.

2 Bernard Mandeville, *The Fable of the Bees: Or, Private Vices, Public Benefits*, ed. Frederick B. Kaye, Oxford 1924, 106–112.

3 Marx, *Grundrisse*, 222.

4 [*Einverseelung*. Walter Kaufmann renders this term of art of Nietzsche's with one of his own: "inpsychation"; Friedrich Nietzsche, "On the Genealogy of Morals," trans. Walter Kaufmann and R. J. Hollingdale, in Walter Kaufmann (ed.) *On the Genealogy of Morals and Ecce Homo*, New York 1989, 57 – translator's note.]

5 Nietzsche, "Genealogy of Morals," 36–37, 127; Friedrich Nietzsche, "Twilight of the Idols or How to Philosophize with

a Hammer," trans. R. J. Hollingdale, in idem, *Twilight of the Idols and the Anti-Christ*, London and New York 1990, 50–51; Max Scheler, *Ressentiment*, ed. Lewis A. Coser, trans. William W. Holdheim, New York 1961, 43–49; Jean-Paul Sartre, "Father and Son: F. Resentment," in *The Family Idiot: Gustave Flaubert, 1821–1857*, vol. 1, trans. Carol Cosman, Chicago 1981, 386–409. Cf. Gilles Deleuze, *Nietzsche and Philosophy*, trans. Hugh Tomlinson, New York 2006, 111–119; Reinhard Olschanski, *Ressentiment: Über die Vergiftung des europäischen Geistes*, Paderborn 2015, 15–50.

6 Deleuze, *Nietzsche*, 119.

7 Werner Sombart, *The Quintessence of Capitalism: A Study of the History and Psychology of the Modern Business Man* [1913], ed. Bryan S. Turner, trans. M. Epstein, London and New York 1998, 340–341; Scheler, *Ressentiment*, 52–54. However, from the eighteenth century onwards, ressentiment had already taken on the character of a feeling of impotent pain, combined with thoughts of revenge (Peter Probst, "Ressentiment," in Joachim Ritter, Karlfried Gründer, and Gottfried Gabriel [eds.] *Historisches Wörterbuch der Philosophie*, Darmstadt 2007, vol. 8, 921). From the time of Adam Smith and against the background of emerging market models, it had led, as "resentment," to an economy of merit, in which sympathies with acts of reward and punishment are accounted for equally as response patterns of resentment (Adam Smith, *The Theory of Moral Sentiments*, ed. Ryan Patrick Hanley, London 2009, 79–129; cf. Ashraf H. A. Rushdy, *After Injury: A Historical Anatomy of Forgiveness, Resentment, and Apology*, Oxford 2018, 124–125).

8 Scheler, *Ressentiment*, 49. [Translation slightly modified – translator's note.]

9 Nietzsche, "Genealogy," 45. On this and on the critique of liberal legal equality, cf. Christoph Menke, *Critique of Rights*, Cambridge (UK) and Medford (MA) 2020, 249–253.

10 Karl Marx, "On the Jewish Question" (pp. 211–241), in idem, *Karl Marx, Early Writings*, introd. Lucio Coletti, trans. Rodney Livingstone and Gregor Benton, London and New York 1992, 230 [Translation modified – translator's note]; cf. Menke, *Critique*, 1–5.

11 Scheler, *Ressentiment*, 50; cf. Patrick Lang, "Max Scheler's Analysis of Ressentiment in Modern Democracies," in

Bernardino Fantini, Dolores Martín Moruno, and Javier Moscoso (eds.), *On Resentment: Past and Present*, Newcastle 2013, 64; Uffa Jensen, *Zornpolitik*, Berlin 2017, 37–38. On the lack of evidence of a link between ressentiment and economic disadvantage, see Philip Manow, *Die politische Ökonomie des Populismus*, Berlin 2018, 13; Jan-Werner Müller, *Was ist Populismus? Ein Essay*, Berlin 2016, 33; Karin Priester, *Rechter und linker Populismus: Annäherung an ein Chamäleon*, Frankfurt am Main 2012, 17–18; Tooze, *Crashed: How a Decade of Financial Crises Changed the World*, New York 2018, 576.

12 Scheler, *Ressentiment*, 52–58, 77–78, 141–142; Jean-Paul Sartre, *The Family Idiot: Gustave Flaubert, 1821–1857*, vol. 5, trans. Carol Cosman, Chicago 1993, 224–225; Olschanski, *Ressentiment*, 18–19.

13 Sören Kierkegaard, *Two Ages: The Age of Revolution and the Present Age – A Literary Review*, ed. and trans., with introd. Howard V. Hong and Edna H. Hong, Princeton 1978, 81, 84. Kierkegaard employs the Danish term *misundelse*, which has been rendered in German as "Neid" (envy) and in English as envy or ressentiment. As "ethical envy" (ibid., 82) it displays a close structural affinity with the concept of ressentiment in Nietzsche and Scheler: connected to a "reflection-game" of comparing and "leveling" (ibid., 86); here, cf. Rushdy, *After Injury*, 146–170. On the "form of evaluation" of ressentiment in Scheler, cf. Lang, "Max Scheler's Analysis of Ressentiment," 66; and on the "neurotization" of the objective spirit by ressentiment: Sartre, *The Family Idiot*, vol. 5. [In the original French and in the German translation this volume is entitled "Objective and Subjective Neurosis" (and is "Part Four" of Sartre's work) – translator's note.]

14 Jacques Lacan, *La Logique du fantasme: Séminaire 1966–1967*, Paris 2004 (session of May 31, 1967); cf. Slavoij Žižek, "Enjoy Your Nation as Yourself! Der andere und das Böse – vom Begehren des ethnischen Dings," in Joseph Vogl (ed.), *Gemeinschaften: Positionen zu einer Philosophie des Politischen*, Frankfurt am Main 1994, 145; Samo Tomšič, *The Capitalist Unconscious: Marx and Lacan*, London and New York 2015, 67–69.

15 Sartre, *The Family Idiot*, vol. 1, 386–388; similarly, Kierkegaard, *Two Ages*, 69–70.

16 Manuel Funke, Moritz Schularick, and Christoph Trebesch, "Going to Extremes: Politics after Financial Crises, 1870–2014," *European Economic Review* 88, 2016, 227–260, esp. 227–229; Manuel Funke and Christoph Trebesch, "Financial Crises and the Populist Right," *ifo DICE Report* 15/4, December 2017, 6–9.

17 Theodor W. Adorno, *Aspects of the New Right-Wing Extremism*, trans. Wieland Hoban, Cambridge (UK) 2020, 2.

18 Cf. Thomas Piketty, *Capital in the Twenty-First Century*, trans. Arthur Goldhammer, Cambridge (MA) and London 2017.

19 Karl Marx and Friedrich Engels, *The Communist Manifesto*, trans. Samuel Moore, London and New York 1985, 82–83.

20 Hannah Arendt, *The Origins of Totalitarianism*, New York and London 1973, 11–41; cf. Gerhard Hanloser, *Krise und Antisemitismus: Eine Geschichte in drei Stationen von der Gründerzeit über die Weltwirtschaftskrise bis heute*, Münster 2003, 39–62.

21 Joseph Vogl, *The Specter of Capital*, trans. Joachim Redner and Robert Savage, Stanford 2015, 90–92.

22 Herman Melville, *The Confidence-Man: His Masquerade*, ed. Elizabeth S. Foster, New York 1954, 1; Hayek, quoted in Reijer Hendrikse and Rodrigo Fernandez, "Offshore Finance: How Capital Rules the World," in Nick Buxton and Deborah Eade (eds.) *State of Power 2019: Finance*, n.p. 2019, 24–36, here 29 (https://www.tni.org/files/publication-downloads/state_of_power_2019_-_finance_-_full_draft.pdf).

23 Max Horkheimer and Theodor W. Adorno, *Dialectic of Enlightenment: Philosophical Fragments*, ed. Gunzelin Schmid Noerr, trans. Edmund Jephcott, Stanford 2002, 143.

24 Arendt, *Origins of Totalitarianism*, 39, 148.

25 Theodor W. Adorno, "Studies in the Authoritarian Personality," in *Gesammelte Schriften*, ed. V. R. Tiedemann, Darmstadt 1998, vol. 9/1, *Soziologische Schriften II, Erste Hälfte*, 269; cf. Bernd Sommer, *Prekarisierung und Ressentiment: Soziale Unsicherheit und rechtsextreme Einstellungen in Deutschland*, Wiesbaden 2010, 250–258.

26 Cf. Evgeny Morozov, "Bizarre Freundschaften: Die neuen Rechten und Big Tech," *Süddeutsche Zeitung*, January 21, 2019, 11; "Tränen in der Facebook-Zentrale," *Spiegel Netzwelt*, September 28, 2015 (https://www.manager-magazin.de/unternehmen/personalien/indiens-regierungschef-trifft-mark-zucke

rberg-a-1055024.html). "Facebook CEO Mark Zuckerberg Hails PM Narendra Modi for Connecting with Masses via Facebook," *NDTV*, February 17, 2017 (https://www.ndtv.com/india-news/facebook-ceo-mark-zuckerberg-hails-pm-narendra-modi-for-connecting-with-masses-via-facebook-1660719); Shoshanna Zuboff, *The Age of Surveillance Capitalism: The Fight for a Human Future at the New Frontier of Power*, New York 2019, 126; Yochai Benkler, Robert Faris, and Hal Roberts, *Network Propaganda: Manipulation, Disinformation, and Radicalization in American Politics*, Oxford 2018, 272; Jacob S. Hacker and Paul Pierson, *Let Them Eat Tweets: How the Right Rules in an Age of Extreme Inequality*, New York 2020; Maik Fielitz and Holger Marcks, *Digitaler Faschismus: Die sozialen Medien als Motor des Rechtsextremismus*, Berlin 2020, 121; Roger McNamee in an interview with Jannis Brühl in "Die Aussteiger," *Süddeutsche Zeitung*, September 15, 2020, 9; Sinan Aral, *The Hype Machine: How Social Media Disrupts Our Elections, Our Economy and Our Health – and How We Must Adapt*, London 2020, 47.

27 Benkler et al., *Network Propaganda*, 269–288.

28 Mark Zuckerberg, *Building Global Community*, February 16, 2017, 1–10 (https://www.facebook.com/notes/mark-zuckerberg/building-global-community/10154544292806634/); cf. "Facebook CEO Mark Zuckerberg Hails PM Narendra Modi"; Forum on Information and Democracy, *Working Group on Infodemics: Policy Framework*, November 2020, 68 (https://informationdemocracy.org/wp-content/uploads/2020/11/ForumID_Report-on-infodemics_101120.pdf). On the relationship of liberalism, populism, and concepts of community in the United States, cf. Priester, *Rechter und linker Populismus*, 193–195.

29 Cf. ibid., passim; Müller, *Was ist Populismus*; Manow, *Politische Ökonomie*.

30 Zuckerberg, *Building Global Community*, 3; Herfried Münkler, *Populismus in Deutschland: Eine Geschichte seiner Mentalitäten, Mythen und Symbole*, London 2012 [eBook], 8.

31 Benkler et al., *Network Propaganda*, 13–14.

32 Cf. Andreas Reckwitz, *The Society of Singularities*, trans. Valentine A. Pakis, Cambridge 2020, 188–194.

33 Quoted in Müller, *Was ist Populismus*, 58.

34 Ibid., 56–57.

35 According to a remark by the last US president: "How Trump

Reshaped the Presidency in Over 11000 Tweets," in the *New York Times*, November 2, 2019 (https://nyti.ms/32aaAbV). For this reason, demands for the introduction of frictions, delays, and interruptions in network communication seem extremely plausible; cf. Forum on Information and Democracy, 76.

36 Michael Latzer, Katharina Hollnbuchner, Natascha Just, and Florian Saurwein, "The Economics of Algorithmic Selection on the Internet," in Johannes M. Bauer and Michael Latzer (eds.), *Handbook on the Economics of the Internet*, Cheltenham et al. 2016, 395–425.

37 Geoffrey G. Parker, Marshall W. Van Alstyne, and Sangeet Paul Choudary, *Platform Revolution: How Networked Markets Are Transforming the Economy – And How to Make Them Work for You*, New York and London 2016, 10–11.

38 Lorraine Daston and Michelangelo Ferraro, "Perché i Fatti Sono Brevi?" *Quaderni Storici*, 36/108 (2001), 745–770.

39 "C'est mon opinion, et je la partage." Coined by Henri Monnier's philistine character Joseph Prudhomme, it is quoted here from a translator's note made by Traugott König in her German translation of Sartre's *Idiot of the Family* [*Idiot der Familie: Gustave Flaubert, 1821–1857*, vol. 1, Reinbek 1977, 620].

40 Zuckerberg, *Building Global Community*, 4; Forum on Information and Democracy, 68.

41 Aral, *The Hype Machine*, 65–67.

42 Deleuze, "Postscript on the Societies of Control," *October*, 59, 1992, 5 (www.jstor.org/stable/778828). On the concept of molar, see Gilles Deleuze and Félix Guattari, *A Thousand Plateaus: Capitalism and Schizophrenia*, trans. Brian Massumi, Minneapolis 1987, 213–218.

43 Gabriel Tarde, *The Laws of Imitation* (1890), trans. Elsie Clews Parsons, New York 1903. On the thesis that digitalization simply makes social regularities visible "without having invented them," cf. Armin Nassehi, *Muster: Theorie der digitalen Gesellschaft*, Munich 2019, 44.

44 Cf. Reckwitz, "Conclusion: The Crisis of the General?" in idem, *Society of Singularities*, 310–319; Zoran Terzić, *Idiocracy: Thinking and Acting in the Age of the Idiot*, trans. Michael Turnbull, Zürich (distrib. University of Chicago Press) (in press).

45 Ernesto Laclau, "Universalism, Particularism and the Question

of Identity," Chap. 2 in idem, *Emancipation(s)*, London 2007, 20–35.

46 "Idiocy as Political Paradigm," Terzić, *Idiocracy* (in press). Perhaps the term "plutocratic populism" would also be appropriate, insofar as mechanisms of tribalization are linked to strategies of enrichment (cf. Hacker and Pierson, *Let Them Eat Tweets*, 5 and passim).

47 Jodi Dean, *Publicity's Secret: How Technoculture Capitalizes on Democracy*, Cornell 2002, 8.

Bibliography

1 Books and articles

Anonymous. "Ein Boom für die Reichen," *Süddeutsche Zeitung*, July 10, 2019, 17.

Anonymous. "Facebook CEO Mark Zuckerberg Hails PM Narendra Modi for Connecting with Masses via Facebook," *NDTV*, February 17, 2017 (https://www.ndtv.com/india-news/facebook-ceo-mark-zuckerberg-hails-pm-narendra-modi-for-connecting-with-masses-via-facebook-1660719).

Anonymous. "Tech-Konzerne profitieren," *Süddeutsche Zeitung*, October 31/ November 1, 2020, 24.

Anonymous. "Tränen in der Facebook-Zentrale," *Spiegel Netzwelt*, September 28, 2015 (https://www.spiegel.de/netzwelt/netzpolitik/facebook-fragestunde-mit-indiens-regierungschef-modi-endet-mit-traenen-a-1055000.html).

Anonymous. "Viel Lohn für wenige," *Süddeutsche Zeitung*, July 5, 2019, 8.

Anonymous. "Wie Uber täglich 10 Millionen Euro Verlust einfährt," *Orange by Handelsblatt*, June 5, 2019 (https://orange.handelsblatt.com/artikel/61372).

Abraham, Louis and Dominique Guégan. "The Other Side of the Coin: Risks of the Libra Blockchain," University Ca' Foscari of Venice, Dept. of Economics Research Paper Series No. 30/WP/2019. (https://ssrn.com/abstract=3474237, http://dx.doi.org/10.2139/ssrn.3474237).

Acheson, A. L. Keith, John F. Chant, and Martin F. J. Prachowny (eds.). *Bretton Woods Revisited: Evaluations of the International Monetary Fund and the International Bank for Reconstruction and Development*, Toronto 1972.

Adorno, Theodor W. *Aspects of the New Right-Wing Extremism*, trans. Wieland Hoban, Cambridge (UK) 2020.

—. "Studies in the Authoritarian Personality," in idem, *Gesammelte Schriften*, ed. R. Tiedemann, Vol. 9/1, Soziologische Schriften II, Darmstadt 1998.

Almiron, Núria. *Journalism in Crisis: Corporate Media and Financialization*, New York 2010.

Ammann, Thomas. *Die Machtprobe: Wie Social Media unsere Demokratie verändern*, Hamburg 2020.

Anderson, Chris. "The End of Theory: The Data Deluge Makes the Scientific Method Obsolete," *Wired*, June 23, 2008 (https://www.wired.com/2008/06/pb-theory/).

Aral, Sinan. *The Hype Machine: How Social Media Disrupts Our Elections, Our Economy and Our Health – and How We Must Adapt*, London 2020.

Arendt, Hannah. *The Origins of Totalitarianism*, New York and London 1973.

Arzt, Ingo. "Die Geister, die ich rief," *die tageszeitung*, July 30, 2019, 3.

Aspray, William. "The Scientific Conceptualization of Information: A Survey," *Annals of the History of Computing* 7/2 (1985), 117–145.

Bachelier, Louis. "Théorie de la Spéculation," *Annales scientifiques de l'École Normale Supérieure*, Series 3, Vol. 17 (1900), 21–86. Translated into English as "Theory of Speculation," Chap. 2 in Paul Cootner (ed.) *The Random Character of Stock Market Prices*, Cambridge 1964, 17–79 (available at Internet Archive: https://archive.org/details/randomcharactero00coot/page/n4/mode/1up).

Baecker, Dirk. *4.0 oder Die Lücke, die der Rechner lässt*, Berlin 2018.

Baldenius, Till, Sebastian Kohl, and Moritz Schularick. "Die neue Wohnungsfrage: Gewinner und Verlierer des deutschen Immobilienbooms," Macrofinance Lab, University of Bonn, June 2019 (https://pure.mpg.de/rest/items/item_3070687_1/component/file_3070688/content).

Becker, Gary. "A Theory of the Allocation of Time," *Economic Journal* 75/299 (1965), 493–517.

Beckmann, Holger. "Europas Angriff auf Google & Co.," *tagesschau.de*, November 25, 2020 (https://www.tagesschau.de/ausland/eu-datenschutz-115.html).

Benkler, Yochai. *The Wealth of Networks: How Social Production Transforms Markets and Freedom*, New Haven 2006.

Benkler, Yochai, Robert Faris, and Hal Roberts. *Network Propaganda: Manipulation, Disinformation, and Radicalization in American Politics*, Oxford 2018.

Betancourt, Michael. *The Critique of Digital Capitalism: An Analysis of the Political Economy of Digital Culture and Technology*, New York 2015 (http://library.oapen.org/handle/20.500.12657/25499).

Black, Fischer and Myron Scholes. "The Pricing of Options and Corporate Liabilities," *Journal of Political Economy* 81/3 (1973), 637–654.

Block, Fred L. *The Origins of International Economic Disorder: A Study of United States International Monetary Policy from World War II to the Present*, Berkeley, Los Angeles, and London 1977.

Blyth, Mark. *Austerity: The History of a Dangerous Idea*, Oxford and New York 2013.

Böckenförde, Ernst-Wolfgang. "Kennt die europäische Not kein Gebot?" *Neue Zürcher Zeitung*, June 21, 2010.

Böhm, Franz. "Rule of Law in a Market Economy," in Alan T. Peacock and Hans Willgerodt (eds.) *Germany's Social Market Economy: Origins and Evolution*, New York 1989.

Braithwaite, John. *Regulatory Capitalism: How It Works, Ideas for Making It Work Better*, Cheltenham (UK) and Northampton (MA) 2008.

Bratton, Benjamin H. *The Stack: On Software and Sovereignty*, Cambridge (MA) 2015.

Braudel, Fernand. *Afterthoughts on Material Civilization and Capitalism*, Baltimore 1977.

Braunberger, Gerald. "Deutschland und Italien: das Wirtschaftswachstum," *Fazit, Frankfurter Allgemeine Wirtschaftsblog*, May 27, 2018 (https://blogs.faz.net/fazit/2018/05/27/deutschland-und-italien-das-wirtschaftswachstum-9957/).

Brenner, Robert. *The Boom and the Bubble: The US in the World Economy*, London 2003.

Brown, Brian A. and Anabel Quan-Haase. "'A Worker's Inquiry

2.0': An Ethnographic Method for the Study of Produsage in Social Media Contexts," in Christian Fuchs and Vincent Mosco (eds.), *Marx in the Age of Digital Capitalism*, Leiden 2016, 447–481.

Brown, Wendy. "Law and Legal Reason," Chap. 5 in idem, *Undoing the Demos: Neoliberalism's Stealth Revolution*, New York 2015, 151–174.

Brühl, Jannis. "Schauen Sie sich um: Alle spielen verrückt" (Interview with Tristan Harris and Roger McNamee), *Süddeutsche Zeitung*, September 14, 2020, 9.

Brühl, Volker. "Libra: A Differentiated View on Facebook's Virtual Currency Project," *Intereconomics* 55/1 (2020), 54–61 (https://www.intereconomics.eu/contents/year/2020/number/1/article/libra-a-differentiated-view-on-facebook-s-virtual-currency-project.html).

Brunnermeier, Markus K., Harold James, and Jean-Pierre Landau, "The Digitalization of Money," *National Bureau of Economic Research (NBER) Working Papers Series*. Working Paper 26300 (https://www.nber.org/system/files/working_papers/w26300/w26300.pdf).

Bruns, Axel. *Blogs, Wikipedia, Second Life, and Beyond: From Production to Produsage*, New York 2008.

Burke, Peter. *A Social History of Knowledge: From Gutenberg to Diderot*, Cambridge (UK) 2000.

Cardon, Dominique. *À quoi rêvent les algorithms: Nos vies à l'heure des* big data, Paris 2015.

Cassidy, Alan and Claus Hulverscheidt. "Was habt ihr denn?" *Süddeutsche Zeitung*, October 24, 2019, 17.

Cassidy, John. *Dot.con: How America Lost Its Mind and Money in the Internet Era*, New York 2003.

—. *How Markets Fail: The Logic of Economic Calamities*, New York 2009.

Castells, Manuel. *The Internet Galaxy: Reflections on the Internet, Business, and Society*, Oxford 2003.

Catalini, Christian, Oliver Gratry, J. Mark Hou, Sunita Parasuraman, and Nils Wernerfelt. "The Libra Reserve," August 2019 (https://mitsloan.mit.edu/shared/ods/documents?PublicationDocumentID=5860).

Cawelti, John G. "Some Notes on the Structure of The Confidence-Man," *American Literature* 29/3 (1957), 278–288.

Cesarano, Filipo. *Money Theory and Bretton Woods: The*

Construction of an International Monetary Order, Cambridge 2006.

Chung, Wendy Hui Kyong. *Control and Freedom: Power and Paranoia in the Age of Fiber Optics*, Cambridge (MA) 2005.

Clement, Piet. "Introduction," in Claudio Borio, Gianni Toniolo, and Piet Clement (eds.), *Past and Future of Central Bank Cooperation*, Cambridge 2008.

Cohen, Nicole S. "The Valorization of Surveillance: Towards a Political Economy of Facebook," *Democratic Communiqué* 22/1 (2008), 13–14.

Cömert, Hasan. *Central Banks and Financial Markets: The Declining Power of US Monetary Policy*, Cheltenham (UK) and Northampton (MA) 2013.

Crain, Matthew. "Financial Markets and Online Advertising: Reevaluating the Dotcom Investment Bubble," *Information, Communication and Society* 17/3 (2014), 371–384.

Crouch, Colin. *The Knowledge Corrupters: Hidden Consequences of the Financial Takeover of Public Life*, Cambridge (UK) 2016.

—. *Will the Gig Economy Prevail?* Cambridge (UK) 2019.

Dang, Tri Vi, Gary Gorton, and Bengt Holmström. "Ignorance, Debt and Financial Crises," Columbia University, April 2015 (http://www.columbia.edu/~td2332/Paper_Ignorance.pdf).

Daston, Lorraine and Michelangelo Ferraro. "Perché i Fatti Sono Brevi?" *Quaderni Storici*, 36/108 (2001), 745–770.

Davies, William and Linsey McGoey. "Rationalities of Ignorance: On Financial Crisis and the Ambivalence of Neo-liberal Epistemology," *Economy and Society* 41/1 (2012), 64–83 (https://doi.org/10.1080/03085147.2011.637331).

Davis, Gerald F. and Suntae Kim, "Financialization of the Economy," *Annual Review of Sociology* 41 (2015), 203–221.

Day, Ronald E. *The Modern Invention of Information: Discourse, History, and Power*, Carbondale (IL) 2008.

Dean, Jodi. *Publicity's Secret: How Technoculture Capitalizes on Democracy*, Ithaca and London 2002.

Delbrück, Anton. *Die pathologische Lüge und die psychisch abnormen Schwindler: Eine Untersuchung über den allmählichen Übergang eines normalen psychischen Vorgangs in ein pathologisches Symptom. Für Ärzte und Juristen*, Stuttgart 1891.

Deleuze, Gilles. "Bartleby; or, The Formula," in idem, *Essays Critical and Clinical*, trans. Daniel W. Smith and Michael A. Greco, London 1998, 68–90.

—. *Foucault*, trans. Seán Hand, Minneapolis 1988.
—. *Nietzsche and Philosophy*, trans. Hugh Tomlinson, London 1983.
—. "Postscript on the Societies of Control," *October*, 59 (Winter, 1992), 3–7 (www.jstor.org/stable/778828).
Deleuze, Gilles and Félix Guattari. *Anti-Oedipus*, trans. Robert Hurley, Mark Seem, and Helen R. Lane, Minneapolis 1983.
—. *A Thousand Plateaus*, trans. Brian Massumi, Minneapolis 1987.
De Goede, Marieke. *Virtue, Fortune, and Faith: A Genealogy of Finance*, Minneapolis and London 2005.
Demary, Markus and Thomas Schuster. *Die Neuordnung der Finanzmärkte: Stand der Finanzmarktregulierung fünf Jahre nach der Lehman-Pleite*, Cologne 2013.
Diaz, A. "Through the Google Goggles: Sociopolitical Bias in Search Engine Design," in Amanda Spink and Michael Zimmer (eds.), *Web Search: Multidisciplinary Perspectives*, Berlin and Heidelberg 2008, 11–34.
Distelhorst, Lars. *Kritik des Postfaktischen: Der Kapitalismus und seine Spätfolgen*, Paderborn 2019.
Donner, Martin. *Äther und Information: Die Apriori des Medialen in Zeitalter technischer Kommunikation*, Berlin 2017.
Dörre, Klaus. "Demokratie statt Kapitalismus oder: Enteignet den Zuckerberg!" in Hanna Ketterer and Karina Becker (eds.), *Was stimmt nicht mit der Demokratie? Eine Debatte mit Klaus Dörre, Nancy Fraser, Stephan Lessenich und Hartmut Rosa*, Frankfurt am Main 2019, 21–51.
Dörre, Klaus. "Landnahme und die Grenzen kapitalistischer Dynamik: Eine Ideenskizze," *Berliner Debatte INITIAL* 22/4 (2011), 56–72.
Duménil, Gérard and Dominique Lévy. *The Crisis of Neoliberalism*, Cambridge (MA) and London 2011.
Dunbar, Nicholas. *Inventing Money: The Story of Long-Term Capital Management and the Legends behind it*, Chichester (UK), New York, Weinheim (DE) et al. 2000.
Egger, Pepe. "Außer Kontrolle," *Der Freitag*, April 30, 2020, 6.
Eichengreen, Barry. *Global Imbalances and the Lessons of Bretton Woods*, Cambridge (MA) 2007.
—. *Globalizing Capital: A History of the International Monetary System*, Princeton 1996.
Eichler, Stefan and Marcel Thum. "Libra: Totengräberin für

gescheiterte Währungen, Herausforderung für gute Regulierung," *ifo Schnelldienst* 72/17, September 12, 2019, 20.

Ekman, Mattias. "The Relevance of Marx's Theory of Primitive Accumulation for Media and Communication Research," in Christian Fuchs and Vincent Mosco (eds.), *Marx in the Age of Digital Capitalism*, Leiden 2016, 105–132.

Erhard, Ludwig. *Prosperity through Competition* [1957], Auburn (AL) 2011.

Esposito, Elena. *The Future of Futures: The Time of Money in Financing and Society*, trans. Elena Esposito with assistance of Andrew K. Whitehead, Cheltenham (UK) and Northampton (MA) 2011.

—. "Information," in Claudio Baraldi, Giancarlo Corsi, and Elena Esposito, *Unlocking Luhmann: A Keyword Introduction to Systems Theory*, trans. Katherine Walker, Bielefeld 2021.

Fama, Eugene and Merton H. Miller. *The Theory of Finance*, Hinsdale (IL) 1972.

Fielitz, Maik and Holger Marcks. *Digitaler Faschismus: Die sozialen Medien als Motor des Rechtsextremismus*, Berlin 2020.

Finke, Björn. "EZ-Kommission wirft Amazon unfaire Tricks vor," *Süddeutsche Zeitung*, November 11, 2020, 19.

Fisahn, Andreas. "Stellungnahme zur Anhörung des Haushaltsausschusses des Deutschen Bundestages am 7.5.2012 zum Fiskalvertrag u. a." (available by clicking on the link "Prof. Dr. Andreas Fisahn" at https://eurodemostuttgart.wordpress.com/2012/05/09/realsatire-deutscher-bundestag-ii-die-gutachten/).

Fisher, Mark. *Capitalist Realism: Is There No Alternative?* Winchester (UK) 2009.

Foster, John Bellamy and Robert W. McChesney. *The Endless Crisis: How Monopoly-Finance Capital Produces Stagnation and Upheaval from the USA to China*, New York 2012.

Foucault, Michel. *The Birth of Biopolitics: Lectures at the Collège de France, 1978–1979*, ed. Michel Senellart, trans. Graham Burchell, New York 2008.

Fox, Justin. *The Myth of the Rational Market: A History of Risk, Reward, and Delusion on Wall Street*, New York 2009.

Frank, Thomas. *One Market under God: Extreme Capitalism, Market Populism, and the End of Economic Democracy*, London 2001.

Frankfurt, Harry G. *On Bullshit*, Princeton 2005.

Friedman, Benjamin M. "The Future of Monetary Policy: The Central Bank as an Army with Only a Signal Corps?" *National Bureau of Economic Research (NBER) Working Papers Series*. Working Paper 7420, 1999, 1–28 (https://www.nber.org/system/files/working_papers/w7420/w7420.pdf).

Friedman, Milton. *Capitalism and Freedom* [1962], Chicago and London 2002.

—. *The Essence of Friedman*, ed. Kurt R. Leube, Stanford 1987.

Fuchs, Christian. "Labor in Informational Capitalism and on the Internet," *The Information Society* 26 (2010), 179–196.

Funke, Manuel, Moritz Schularick, and Christoph Trebesch. "Going to Extremes: Politics after Financial Crises, 1870–2014," *European Economic Review* 88 (2016), 227–260.

Funke, Manuel and Christoph Trebesch. "Financial Crises and the Populist Right," *ifo DICE Report* 15/4 (2017), 6–9.

Galbraith, John Kenneth. *The Affluent Society*, Harmondsworth 1958.

Galloway, Alexander R. *Protocol: How Control Exists after Decentralization*, Cambridge (MA) and London 2004.

——. "Protocol, or, How Control Exists after Decentralization," *Rethinking Marxism* 13/3–4 (2001), 81–88.

——. "The Poverty of Philosophy: Realism and Post-Fordism," *Critical Inquiry* 39 (2013), 347–366.

Galloway, Alexander R. and Eugene Thacker. "Protocol, Control, and Networks," *Grey Room*, 17 (Fall, 2004), 6–29 (https://direct.mit.edu/grey/article/doi/10.1162/1526381042464572/10432/Protocol-Control-and-Networks).

Giersch, Herbert. "Beschäftigung, Stabilität, Wachstum: wer trägt die Verantwortung?" in Giersch (ed.), *Wie es zu schaffen ist: Agenda für die deutsche Wirtschaftspolitik*, Stuttgart 1983, 21–33.

Gilardi, Fabrizio. "The Institutional Foundations of Regulatory Capitalism: The Diffusion of Independent Regulatory Agencies in Western Europe," *Annals of the American Academy of Political and Social Science* 598/1 (2005), 84–101.

Glaser, Peter. "Der Überallgorithmus: Sind Programmiersprachen die neuen Weltsprachen?" *Neue Zürcher Zeitung*, February 16, 2016, 37.

Gless, Sabine and Wolfgang Wohlers. "Subsumtionsautomat 2.0: Künstliche Intelligenz statt menschlicher Richter?" in Martin Böse, Kay H. Schumann, and Friedrich Toepel (eds.), *Festschrift für Urs Kindhäuser zum 70. Geburtstag*, Baden-Baden 2019, 147–165.

Goldman, Eric. "Search Engine Bias and the Demise of Search Engine Utopianism," *Yale Journal of Law and Technology* 8 (2006), 188–200.

Gowan, Peter. "Crisis in the Heartland: Consequences of the New Wall Street System," *New Left Review* 55 (2009), 5–29.

Greene, Daniel and Daniel Joseph. "The Digital Spatial Fix," *tripleC* 13/2 (2015), 223–247.

Greider, William. *Secrets of the Temple: How the Federal Reserve Runs the Country*, New York 1989.

Grewal, David Singh. *Network Power: The Social Dynamics of Globalization*, New Haven (CT) and London 2008.

Grigo, Julian and Patrick Hansen. "Digitalwährungen stehen vor dem Durchbruch," *ifo Schnelldienst* 72/17 (2019), 6–12.

Grimm, Dieter. *Die Verfassung und die Politik: Einsprüche in Störfällen*, Munich 2001.

Hacker, Jacob S. and Paul Pierson. *Let Them Eat Tweets: How the Right Rules in an Age of Extreme Inequality*, New York 2020.

—. *Winner-Take-All Politics: How Washington Made the Rich Richer – And Turned Its Back on the Middle Class*, New York, London, Toronto, and Sydney 2010.

Hafner, Wolfgang and Heinz Zimmermann. "Ein vergessener genialer Wurf zur Bewertung von Optionen: Vinzenz Bronzin nahm die nobelpreiswürdige Black-Scholes-Formel vorweg," *Neue Züricher Zeitung*, Fokus der Wirtschaft, October 8/9, 2005, 29.

Hagelüken, Alexander. *Das Ende des Geldes, wie wir es kennen: Der Angriff auf Zinsen, Bargeld und Staatswährungen*, Munich 2020.

Hagelüken, Alexander and Markus Zydra. "Libra steht völlig quer zu allem," (Interview with Joachim Wuermeling), *Süddeutsche Zeitung*, November 5, 2019, 19.

Hamelink, Cees J. *Finance and Information: A Study of Converging Interests*, Norwood (NJ) 1983.

Hanl, Andreas. "Währungswettbewerber Facebook: Ökonomische Implikationen der Corporate Cryptocurrency Libra," *MAGKS Joint Discussion Paper Series in Economics* 30 (2019), Philipps-University Marburg, School of Business and Economics, Marburg (https://www.econstor.eu/handle/10419/213471).

Hanloser, Gerhard. *Krise und Antisemitismus: Eine Geschichte in drei Stationen von der Gründerzeit über die Weltwirtschaftskrise bis heute*, Münster 2003.

Hardt, Michael and Tony Negri. *Empire*, Cambridge (MA) and London 2000.

Häring, Norbert. "Wer steckt hinter der Libra Association und was ist das Ziel von Libra?" *publikum.net*, December 18, 2019 (https://publikum.net/wer-steckt-hinter-der-libra-association-und-was-ist-das-ziel-von-libra/).

—. "Wie die USA ihre Dollar-Weltwährung ins Zeitalter von Libra retten wollen," *Handelsblatt*, May 9, 2020 (https://www.handelsblatt.com/politik/international/kryptowaehrungen-wie-die-usa-ihre-dollar-weltwaehrung-ins-zeitalter-von-libra-retten-wollen/25813190.html?ticket=ST-3223158-ULZ-1SUmztty34sgimvVt-ap4).

Haucap, Justus and Torben Stühmeier. "Competition and antitrust in Internet markets," in Johannes M. Bauer and Michael Latzer (eds.), *Handbook on the Economics of the Internet*, Cheltenham (UK) and Northampton (MA) 2016, 183–210.

Hayek, Friedrich August von. "Competition as a Discovery Procedure," trans. Marcellus S. Snow, *Quarterly Journal of Austrian Economics* 5/3 (Fall 2002), 9–23.

—. *Denationalisation of Money: The Argument Refined. Analysis of the Theory and Practice of Concurrent Currencies*, London 1990.

—. "Economics and Knowledge," *Economica*, *n.s.* 4/13 (1937), 33–54.

—. *The Road to Serfdom*, Chicago 1944.

—. "The Use of Knowledge in Society," *American Economic Review* 35/4, September 1945, 519–530.

Heidegger, Martin. "The Provenance of Art and the Destination of Thought" [1967], trans. Dimitrios Latsis (translation reviewed and amended by Ullrich Haase), *Journal of the British Society for Phenomenology* 44/2 (2013), 119–128 (https://doi.org/10.1080/00071773.2013.11006794).

Helbing, Dirk. "The Birth of a Digital God," in idem (ed.), *Towards Digital Enlightenment*, Cham (CH) 2019, 103–106.

Helbing, Dirk, Bruno S. Frey, Gerd Gigerenzer et al.: "Das Digital-Manifest," *Spektrum*, December 17, 2015, 12 (https://www.spektrum.de/news/wie-algorithmen-und-big-data-unsere-zukunft-bestimmen/1375933).

Hendrikse, Reijer and Rodrigo Fernandez. "Offshore Finance:

How Capital Rules the World," in Nick Buxton and Deborah Eade (eds.) *State of Power 2019: Finance*, n.p. 2019, 24–36. (https://www.tni.org/files/publication-downloads/state_of_power_2019_-_finance_-_full_draft.pdf).

Herrmann, Ulrike. "Die wenigen Reichen besitzen fast alles," *die tageszeitung*, July 16, 2020, 3.

Herrmann, Ulrike and Stefan Reinecke. "Deutschland verhindert, mehr nicht, Interview mit Adam Tooze," *die tageszeitung*, April 21, 2020, 3.

Hofmann, Christian. "The Changing Concept of Money: A Threat to the Monetary System or an Opportunity for the Financial Sector?" *European Business Organization Law Review* 21/2 (2020), 37–68.

Horkheimer, Max and Theodor W. Adorno. *Dialectic of Enlightenment: Philosophical Fragments*, ed. Gunzelin Schmid Noerr, trans. Edmund Jephcott, Stanford 2002.

Hornuf, Lars. "Libra: Eine Währung, die die Welt (nicht) braucht?" *ifo Schnelldienst* 72/17, September 12, 2019, 10.

Hudson, Michael. *Killing the Host: How Financial Parasites and Debt Bondage Destroy the Global Economy*, New York 2014.

Illing, Gerhard. *Zentralbanken im Griff der Finanzmärkte: Umfassende Regulierung als Voraussetzung für eine effiziente Geldpolitik*, Bonn 2011.

Imbert, Michel. "The Confidence-Man d'Herman Melville ou le discrédit des signes: du papier-monnaie aux Saintes Ècritures," *Social Science Information* 30/2, June 1, 1991, 305–322 (https://journals.sagepub.com/doi/pdf/10.1177/053901891030002007).

Ingebretsen, Mark. *Nasdaq: A History of the Market that Changed the World*, Roseville (CA) 2002.

Ingraham, Christopher. "One Chart Shows How the Stock Market Is Completely Decoupled from the Labor Market," *Washington Post*, May 9, 2020.

Introna, Lucas D. "Algorithms, Governance, and Governmentality: On Governing Academic Writing," *Science, Technology, and Human Values* 41/1 (2016), 17–49.

Jacoby, Susan. *The Age of American Unreason in a Culture of Lies*, 2nd edn., New York 2008.

Jansen, Nils and Ralf Michaels. "Beyond the State? Rethinking Private Law: Introduction to the Issue" (Special Symposium Issue: Beyond the State: Rethinking Private Law), *American Journal of Comparative Law* 56/3 (2008), 527–539.

Jensen, Uffa. *Zornpolitik*, Berlin 2017.

Johnson, Bobbie. "Privacy No Longer a Social Norm, Says Facebook Founder," *Guardian*, January 11, 2010 (https://www.theguardian.com/technology/2010/jan/11/facebook-privacy).

Joseph, Jonathan. *The Social and the Global: Social Theory, Governmentality and Global Policies*, Cambridge 2012.

Judt, Tony. *Ill Fares the Land: A Treatise on Our Present Discontents*, New York 2010.

Kaminska, Izabella, "Alphaville's Libra Cheat Sheet," *FTalphaville*, June 18, 2019 (https://www.ft.com/content/be3b7636-a9df-3672-a324-e85762057a4d).

Kant, Immanuel. *Critique of the Power of Judgment* (Cambridge Edition of the Works of Immanuel Kant), ed. Paul Guyer, trans. Paul Guyer and Eric Matthews, Cambridge 2000.

——. "Idea for a Universal History from a Cosmopolitan Point of View (1784)," in Lewis White Beck (ed.) *On History: Immanuel Kant*, trans. Lewis White Beck, Robert E. Anchor, and Emil L. Fackenheim, Indianapolis and New York 1963, 11–26.

——. "Perpetual Peace (1795)," in ibid., 85–135.

Kaufman, Henry. *The Road to Financial Reformation*, Hoboken (NJ) 2009.

Kay, Lily E. *Who Wrote the Book of Life: A History of the Genetic Code*, Stanford 2000.

Keller, Daphne. "Internet Platforms: Observations on Speech, Danger, and Money," *Hoover Working Group on National Security, Technology, and Law*, Aegis Series Paper No. 1807, June 13, 2018, 11–15 (https://www.hoover.org/research/internet-platforms-observations-speech-danger-and-money).

Kenney, Martin and John Zysman. "The Rise of the Platform Economy," *Issues in Science and Technology* 32/3 (2016), 61–69.

Keynes, John Maynard. *The General Theory of Employment, Interest and Money*, New York 1936.

Kierkegaard, Sören. *Two Ages: The Age of Revolution and the Present Age – A Literary Review* [1846], ed., trans., with introd. Howard V. Hong and Edna H. Hong, Princeton 2009 [1978].

Knight, Frank H. "'What Is Truth' in Economics?" *Journal of Political Economy* 48/1 (1940), 1–32.

Kosseff, Jeff. *The Twenty-Six Words That Created the Internet*, Ithaca and London 2019.

Krasner, Stephen D. "Compromising Westphalia," *International Security* 20/3 (1995/1996), 115–151.

Kreye, Andrian. "Nutzlose App," *Süddeutsche Zeitung* 30, November 2020, 4.

Krippner, Greta R. *Capitalizing on Crisis: The Political Origins of the Rise of Finance*, Cambridge (MA) 2011.

Kurz, Mordecai. "Endogenous Uncertainty and Rational Belief Equilibrium: A Unified Theory of Market Volatility," Stanford University, July 14, 1999 (http://www.stanford.edu/~mordecai/OnLinePdf/13.UnifiedView_1999.pdf).

Kyrtsis, Alexandros-Andreas. "Introduction: Financial Deregulation and Technological Change," in idem (ed.), *Financial Markets and Organizational Technologies: System Architectures, Practices and Risks in the Era of Deregulation*, London and New York 2010, 1–28.

Lacan, Jacques. *La Logique du fantasme: Séminaire 1966–1967*, Paris 2004. [An English translation is found on the Lacanian Works website, curated by Julia Evans: idem, *Seminar XIV: The Logic of Phantasy, 1966–1967: Begins 16th November 1966*, trans. Cormac Gallagher (http://www.lacanianworks.net/?p=1455)].

—. *The Seminar, Book III: The Psychoses*, ed. Jacques-Alain Miller, trans. Russell Grigg, New York and London 1997.

Laclau, Ernesto. "Universalism, Particularism and the Question of Identity," Chap. 2 in idem, *Emancipation(s)*, London 2007, 20–35.

Lang, Patrick. "Max Scheler's Analysis of Ressentiment in Modern Democracies," in Bernardino Fantini, Dolores Martín Moruno, and Javier Moscoso (eds.), *On Resentment: Past and Present*, Newcastle (UK) 2013.

Latour, Bruno. *An Inquiry into Modes of Existence: An Anthropology of the Moderns*, trans. Catherine Porter, Cambridge (MA) 2013.

—. "Centres of Calculation," Chap. 6 in idem, *Science in Action: How to Follow Scientists and Engineers through Society*, Cambridge (MA) 1987, 215–257.

Latour, Bruno and Vincent Antonin Lépinay. *The Science of Passionate Interests: An Introduction to Gabriel Tarde's Economic Anthropology*, Chicago 2009.

Latzer, Michael, Katharina Hollnbuchner, Natascha Just, and Florian Saurwein. "The Economics of Algorithmic Selection on the Internet," in Johannes M. Bauer and Michael Latzer (eds.), *Handbook on the Economics of the Internet*, Cheltenham (UK) and Northampton (MA) 2016, 395–425.

Lazonick, William. *Sustainable Prosperity in the New Economy? Business Organization and High-Tech Employment in the United States*, Kalamazoo (MI) 2009.

Lazonick, William and Marina Mazzucato. "The Risk–Reward Nexus in the Innovation–Inequality Relationship: Who Takes the Risks? Who Gets the Rewards?" *Industrial and Corporate Change* 22/4 (2013), 1093–1128.

Leder, Sylvain. "BlackRock, la finance au chevet des retraités français," *Le Monde Diplomatique*, January 2020, 16–17.

Leistert, Oliver. "The Blockchain as a Modulator of Existence," *MoneyLab*, February 7, 2018 (https://networkcultures.org/moneylab/2018/02/07/the-block- chain-as-a-modulator-of-existence/).

—. "Kontrolle ist gut, Vertrauen ist besser, Bezahlung am besten: Zur Souveränität von Blockchain," *Zeitschrift für Medien- und Kulturforschung* 10/2 (2019), 155–170.

Leonhardt, David. "Why You Shouldn't Believe Those G. D. P. Numbers," *New York Times*, November 15, 2019 (https://www.nytimes.com/2019/12/15/opinion/gdp-america.html).

Lepenies, Philipp. *The Power of a Single Number: A Political History of GDP*, New York 2017.

Lessing, Lawrence. *Code: And Other Laws of Cyberspace*, New York 1999.

Levi-Faur, David. "The Global Diffusion of Regulatory Capitalism," *Annals of the American Academy of Political and Social Science* 598/1 (2005), 12–32.

Liebert, Nicola. "Fataler Reichtum: Zuviel Geld in falschen Händen," *Le Monde Diplomatique* (German edition), August 2012, 1, 10–11.

Lindblom, Charles E. "The Market as Prison," *Journal of Politics* 44 (1982), 324–336.

LiPuma, Edward and Benjamin Lee. *Financial Derivatives and the Globalization of Risk*, Durham and London 2004.

Lobe, Adrian. "Der redet nur Blech, doch das darf er," *Süddeutsche Zeitung*, August 18, 2020, 11.

Lovink, Geert. *Sad by Design: On Platform Nihilism*, London 2019.

Löwe, Sebastian. "Social Media Oktober," *Pop-Zeitschrift*, October 22, 2018 (https://pop-zeitschrift.de/2018/10/22/social-media-oktober-von-sebastian-loewe/).

Luenberger, David G. *Information Science*, Princeton and Oxford 2006.

Luhmann, Niklas. *Social Systems* [1984], trans. John Bednarz, Jr., with Dirk Baecker, Stanford 1995.

—. *Die Wirtschaft der Gesellschaft*, Frankfurt am Main 1988.

Luhmann, Niklas. *The Reality of the Mass Media*, trans. Kathleen Cross, Stanford 2000.

Lyotard, Jean-François. *The Postmodern Condition: A Report on Knowledge* [1979], trans. Geoff Bennington and Brian Massumi, Minneapolis 1984.

McChesney, Robert W. *Digital Disconnect: How Capitalism Is Turning the Internet Against Democracy*, New York and London 2013.

MacKay, Donald M. "Appendix I: The Nomenclature of Information Theory (incl. Explanatory Glossary and Alphabetical Index of Terms)," in Claus Pias (ed.), *Cybernetics / Kybernetik. The Macy-Conferences 1946–1953*, Vol. 1: *Transactions / Protokolle*, Zürich and Berlin 2003, 511–523.

—. "In Search of Basic Symbols," in ibid., 480–509.

Mackenzie, Adrian. *Cutting Code: Software and Sociality*, New York, Washington DC, and Bern 2006.

MacKenzie, Donald. *An Engine, Not a Camera: How Financial Models Shape Markets*, Cambridge (MA) and London 2006.

—. "Opening the Black Boxes of Global Finance," in Alexandros-Andreas Kyrtsis (ed.), *Financial Markets and Organizational Technologies: System Architectures, Practices and Risks in the Era of Deregulation*, New York 2010, 92–116.

Magdoff, Harry and Paul M. Sweezy. *Stagnation and the Financial Explosion*, New York 2009.

Malabou, Catherine. "Cryptocurrencies: Anarchist Turn or Strengthening of Surveillance Capitalism? From Bitcoin to Libra," trans. Robert Boncardo, *Australian Humanities Review* 66, May 2020 (http://australianhumanitiesreview.org/2020/05/31/issue-66-may-2020/).

Malkiel, Burton G. *A Random Walk Down Wall Street*, New York 2003.

Mandelbrot, Benoit B. and Richard L. Hudson. *The (Mis)Behaviour of Markets: A Fractal View of Risk, Ruin and Reward*, London 2008.

Mandeville, Bernard, *The Fable of the Bees: or, Private Vices, Public Benefits*, ed. Frederick B. Kaye, Oxford 1924.

Manow, Philip. *Die politische Ökonomie des Populismus*, Berlin 2018.

Marazzi, Christian. *Verbranntes Geld*, Zürich and Berlin 2011.

Martin, Randy. "The Twin Towers of Financialisation: Entanglements of Political and Cultural Economies," *The Global South* 3/1 (2009), 108–125.

Marx, Karl. *Capital, Volume 1: A Critical Analysis of Capitalist Production*, trans. Samuel Moore and Edward Aveling, introd. Mark G. Spencer, Hertfordshire (UK) 2013.

—. "Economic and Philosophical Manuscripts," in idem, *Early Writings*, introd. Lucio Coletti, trans. Rodney Livingstone and Gregory Benton, London 1992, 279–400.

—. *Grundrisse: Foundations of the Critique of Political Economy (Rough Draft)*, trans. with foreword Martin Nicolaus, London 1973.

—. "On the Jewish Question," in idem, *Early Writings*, introd. Lucio Coletti, trans. Rodney Livingstone and Gregor Benton, London and New York 1992, 211–241.

Marx, Karl and Friedrich Engels, *The Communist Manifesto*, trans. Samuel Moore, London and New York 1985.

—. *The German Ideology*, in idem, *Marx/Engels Collected Works (MECW)*, London and New York 1975ff., Vol. 5.

Mason, Paul. *PostCapitalism: A Guide to Our Future*, London 2015.

Mayer, Martin. *The Fed: The Inside Story of How the World's Most Powerful Financial Institution Drives the Markets*, New York 2001.

Mazepa, Patrizia and Vincent Mosco. "A Political Economy Approach to the Internet," in Johannes M. Bauer and Michael Latzer Bauer (eds.), *Handbook on the Economics of the Internet*, Cheltenham (UK) and Northampton (MA) 2016, 163–183.

Mazzucato, Marina. *The Entrepreneurial State: Debunking Public vs. Private Sector Myths*, New York 2013.

Meeker, Mary and Chris DePuy. *The Internet Report, Morgan Stanley Global Technology Group*, New York 1996.

Melville, Herman. *The Confidence-Man: His Masquerade*, ed. Elizabeth S. Foster, New York 1954.

Menke, Christoph. *Critique of Rights*, trans. Christopher Turner, Cambridge (UK) and Medford (MA) 2020.

Mersch, Yves. "Money and Private Currencies: Reflections on Libra," in *Building Bridges: Central Banking Law in an Interconnected World*. ECB Legal Conference 2019, European

Central Bank, December 2019, 13–20 (https://www.ecb.europa.eu/press/key/date/2019/html/ecb.sp190902~aedded9219.en.html).

Merton, Robert C. *Continuous-Time Finance*, Cambridge (MA) 1990.

—. *Theory of Rational Option Pricing*, Cambridge (MA) 1971.

Micklethwait, John and Adrian Wooldridge. *A Future Perfect: The Essentials of Globalization*, New York 2000.

Mirowski, Philip. *Never Let a Serious Crisis Go to Waste: How Neoliberalism Survived the Financial Meltdown*, London and New York 2014.

Mirowski, Philip and Edward Nik-Khah. *The Knowledge We Have Lost in Information: The History of Information in Modern Economics*, Oxford 2017.

Mises, Ludwig von. *Liberalism: The Classical Tradition* [1927], trans. Ralph Raico, Irvington-on-Hudson (NY) 1997.

Moe, Thorvald Grung. "Control of Finance as a Prerequisite for Successful Monetary Policy: A Reinterpretation of Henry Simons's 'Rules versus Authorities in Monetary Policy,'" *Levy Economics Institute Working Paper Collection*, Levy Economics Institute of Bard College, Working Paper No. 713 (2012) (https://www.levyinstitute.org/pubs/wp_713.pdf).

Morozov, Evgeny. "Bizarre Freundschaften: Die neuen Rechten und Big Tech," *Süddeutsche Zeitung*, January 21, 2019, 11 (available at: https://www.sueddeutsche.de/digital/facebook-silicon-valley-populisten-kritik-morozov-1.4295480 under the title "Warum Europas Populisten Facebook lieben – und was in den USA anders ist").

—. *To Save Everything, Click Here: The Folly of Technological Solutionism*. New York 2013.

Morrissey, Brian. "Facebook gives new face to online ads," *Brandweek* 47/35 (2006), 11.

Mosco, Vincent. *The Digital Sublime: Myth, Power, and Cyberspace*, Boston 2004.

Müller, Jan-Werner. *Was ist Populismus? Ein Essay*, Berlin 2016.

Münker, Stefan. "Freiheit, die in Ketten liegt: Zur Philosophie der blockchain," *Zeitschrift für Medien- und Kulturforschung* 10/2 (2019), 117–126.

Münkler, Herfried. *Populismus in Deutschland: Eine Geschichte seiner Mentalitäten, Mythen und Symbole*, London 2012 [eBook].

Musil, Robert. *The Man Without Qualities*, ed. Burton Pike, trans. Sophie Wilkins, London 2017.

Nachtwey, Oliver and Timo Seidl. "Die Ethik der Solution und der Geist des digitalen Kapitalismus," *IFS Working Paper 11*, Institut für Sozialforschung, Frankfurt am Main, October 2017.

Nake, Frieder. "Das algorithmische Zeichen," in W. Bauknecht, W. Brauer, and Th. Mück (eds.), *Informatik 2001: Tagungsband der GI/OCG Jahrestagung 2001*, vol. 2, Konstanz 2001, 736–742.

Nassehi, Armin. *Muster: Theorie der digitalen Gesellschaft*, Munich 2019.

Nesvetailova, Anastasia and Carlos Belli, "Global Financial Governance: Taming Financial Innovation," in Sophie Harman and David Williams (eds.), *Governing the World? Cases in Global Governance*, London and New York 2013, 46–61.

Niehans, Jürg. *A History of Economic History: Classic Contributions, 1729–1980*, Baltimore and London 1990.

Nietzsche, Friedrich. *On the Genealogy of Morality and Other Writings*, 3rd edn. (Cambridge Texts in the History of Political Thought), ed. Keith Ansell-Pearson, trans. Carol Diethe, Cambridge (UK) 2017.

—. *Twilight of the Idols*, in idem, *The Anti-Christ, Ecce Homo, Twilight of the Idols – And Other Writings* (Cambridge Texts in the History of Philosophy), ed. Aaron Ridley and Judith Norman, trans. Judith Norman, Cambridge 2005.

Nosthoff, Anna-Verena and Felix Maschewski. *Die Gesellschaft der Wearables: Digitale Verführung und soziale Kontrolle*, Berlin 2019.

Novalis. *Notes for a Romantic Encyclopaedia: Das Allgemeine Brouillon* (SUNY series, Intersections: Philosophy and Critical Theory), trans., ed., and introd. David W. Wood, Albany (NY) 2011.

Ogorek, Regina. *Richterkönig oder Subsumtionsautomat? Zur Justiztheorie im 19. Jahrhundert*, Frankfurt am Main 1986.

Olschanski, Reinhard. *Ressentiment: Über die Vergiftung des europäischen Geistes*, Paderborn 2015.

O'Neil, Cathy. *Weapons of Math Destruction: How Big Data Increases Inequality and Threatens Democracy*, New York 2016.

Orléan, André. *Le Pouvoir de la finance*, Paris 1999.

Parker, Geoffrey G., Marshall W. Van Alstyne, and Sangeet Paul Choudary. *Platform Revolution: How Networked Markets Are*

Transforming the Economy – And How to Make Them Work for You, New York and London 2016.

Pasquinelli, Matteo. "Italian Operaismo and the Information Machine," *Theory, Culture and Society* 32/3, May 2015, 49–68.

Pentland, Alex. *Social Physics: How Good Ideas Spread. Lessons from a New Science*, New York 2004.

Perez, Carlota. *Technological Revolutions and Financial Capital: The Dynamics of Bubbles and Golden Ages*, Cheltenham (UK) and Northampton (MA) 2002.

Philipponnat, Thierry. *Le Capital: de l'abondance à l'utilité*, Paris 2017.

Piketty, Thomas. *Capital and Ideology*, trans. Arthur Goldhammer, Cambridge (MA) and London 2020.

—. *Capital in the Twenty-First Century*, trans. Arthur Goldhammer, Cambridge (MA) and London 2017.

Pircher, Wolfgang. "Die Inszenierung von Vertrauen: Zur Theatralität des Geldes," in Ralf Bohn and Heiner Wilharm (eds.), *Inszenierung und Ereignis*, Bielefeld 2015, 189–206.

Pistor, Katharina. *The Code of Capital: How the Law Creates Wealth and Inequality*, Princeton 2019.

Prantl, Heribert. "Das Finale nach dem Ende," *Süddeutsche Zeitung*, June 29, 2012, 2.

Preis, Tobias. *Ökonophysik: Die Physik des Finanzmarktes*, Wiesbaden 2011.

Priester, Karin. *Rechter und linker Populismus: Annäherung an ein Chamäleon*, Frankfurt am Main 2012.

Probst, Peter. "Ressentiment," in Joachim Ritter, Karlfried Gründer, and Gottfried Gabriel (eds.) *Historisches Wörterbuch der Philosophie*, Darmstadt 2007, Vol. 8, 921–924.

Procter, Robert N. and Londa Schiebinger (eds.). *Agnotology: The Making and Unmaking of Ignorance*, Stanford 2008.

Propp, Kenneth. "The Emerging EU Regulatory Landscape for Digital Platform Liability," *New Atlanticist* (Atlantic Council), October 22, 2019 (https://www.atlanticcouncil.org/blogs/new-atlanticist/the-emerging-eu-regulatory-landscape-for-digital-platform-liability/).

Pufendorf, Samuel. *The Whole Duty of Man, According to the Law of Nature*, trans. Andrew Tooke [1691], ed. Ian Hunter and David Saunders, Indianapolis 2003.

Reckwitz, Andreas. *The Society of Singularities*, trans. Valentine A. Pakis, Cambridge 2020.

Reichert, Ramon. *Das Wissen der Börse: Medien und Praktiken des Finanzmarktes*, Bielefeld 2009.

Reynolds, Matt. "The Strange Story of Section 230, the Obscure Law that Created Our Flawed, Broken Internet," *Wired*, March 24, 2019, 5–6 (https://www.wired.co.uk/article/section-230-communications-decency-act).

Rödl, Florian. "EU im Notstandsmodus," *Blätter für deutsche und internationale Politik* 5 (2012), 5–8.

Rushdy, Ashraf H. A. *After Injury: A Historical Anatomy of Forgiveness, Resentment, and Apology*, Oxford 2018.

Sahr, Aaron. *Das Versprechen des Geldes: Eine Praxistheorie des Kredits*, Hamburg 2017.

—. *Keystroke-Kapitalismus: Ungleichheit auf Knopfdruck*, Hamburg 2017. [A translation is scheduled to be published in 2022 as: idem, *Keystroke Capitalism: How Banks Create Money for the Few*, trans. Sharon Howe, London and New York (forthcoming)].

Sahr, Aaron, Friedo Kahrt, and Carolin Müller. "Staatliche Zahlungs(un)fähigkeit: Missverständnisse und Missverhältnisse monetärer Souveränität in Europa (II)," *Soziopolis*, January 28, 2020 (https://www.soziopolis.de/staatliche-zahlungsunfaehigkeit.html).

Samuelsen, Paul A. "A few remembrances of Friedrich von Hayek (1899–1992)," *Journal of Economic Behavior and Organization*, 69/1, 2009.

—. "Proof that Properly Anticipated Prices Fluctuate Randomly," in idem, *Collected Papers of Paul A. Samuelson*, vol. 3, Cambridge (MA) and London 1972, 782–790.

Santner, Eric L. "The Rebranding of Sovereignty in the Age of Trump: Toward a Critique of Manatheism," in William Mazzarella, Eric L. Santner, and Aaron Schuster, *Sovereignty, Inc.: Three Inquiries in Politics and Enjoyment*, Chicago 2020, 19–112.

Sartre, Jean-Paul. *The Family Idiot: Gustave Flaubert 1821–1857*, trans. Carol Cosman, vol. 1, Chicago 1981.

—. ibid., vol. 5, Chicago 1993.

Sauer, Ulrike. "Nichts als leere Versprechen," *Süddeutsche Zeitung*, April 27, 2020, 17.

Schäfer, Dorothea. "Facebook-Währung Libra: Nur ein genialer Marketingtrick?" *DIW Wochenbericht* 86/37 (2019), 688 (https://www.diw.de/documents/publikationen/73/diw_01.c.678080.de/19-37-5.pdf).

Schäffler, Stephan. *Mathematik der Information: Theorie und Anwendungen der Shannon-Wiener Information*, Heidelberg, Berlin, and New York 2015.

Scheler, Max. *Ressentiment* [1915], trans. William W. Holdheim, 5th corr. edn., Milwaukee (WI) 2010.

Schiller, Dan. *Digital Depression: Information Technology and Economic Crisis*, Urbana (IL) and Chesham (UK) 2014.

—. *How to Think About Information*, Urbana (IL) and Chesham (UK) 2007.

Schiller, Herbert I. *Information and the Crisis Economy*, Oxford and New York 1986.

Schmeling, Maik. "What Is Libra? Understanding Facebook's Currency," *SAFE Policy Letter* 76 (2019) (https://www.econstor.eu/handle/10419/204501).

Schnelle, H. "Information," in Joachim Ritter, Karlfried Gründer, and Gottfried Gabriel (eds.) *Historisches Wörterbuch der Philosophie*, Darmstadt 2007, 356–357.

Schoukens, Paul, Alberto Barrio, and Saskia Montebovi. "Social Protection of Non-Standard Workers: The Case of Platform Work," in Bram Devolder (ed.), *The Platform Economy: Unravelling the Legal Status of Online Intermediaries*, Cambridge (UK), Antwerp, and Chicago 2019, 227–258.

Scialom, Laurence. *La Fascination de l'ogre: Comment desserrer l'étau de la finance*, Paris 2019.

Scornos, Dina and Niels Bammens. "International Corporate Taxation of Digital Platforms," in Bram Devolder (ed.), *The Platform Economy: Unravelling the Legal Status of Online Intermediaries*, Cambridge (UK), Antwerp, and Chicago 2019, 327–362.

Scott, Bruce R. *Capitalism: Its Origins and Evolution as a System of Governance*, New York, Dordrecht, Heidelberg, and London 2011.

Seybold, Matt. "The Political Economy of The Confidence-Man," *Leviathan* 21/3, October 2019, 51–59.

Shapiro, Andrew L. *The Control Revolution: How the Internet Is Putting Individuals in Charge and Changing the World We Know*, New York 1999.

Shawcross, William. *Murdoch: The Making of a Media Empire*, New York 1997.

Shearer, Elisa and Jeffrey Gottfried. "News Use Across Social Media Platforms 2017," *Pew Research Center*, September 6,

2017 (https://www.pewresearch.org/journalism/2017/09/07/news-use-across-social-media-platforms-2017/).

Shroeder, John W. "Sources and Symbols for Melville's Confidence-Man," *PMLA* 66/4 (1951), 363–380.

Simanowski, Robert and Ramón Reichert. *Sozialmaschine Facebook: Dialog über das politisch Unverbindliche*, Berlin 2020.

Simons, Henry S. "Rules versus Authorities in Monetary Policy," *Journal of Political Economy* 44/1 (1936), 1–30.

Skidelsky, Robert. *Keynes: The Return of the Master*, New York 2009.

Slaughter, Anne-Marie. *A New World Order: Government Networks and the Disaggregated State*, Princeton 2004.

Slee, Tom. *What's Yours is Mine: Against the Sharing Economy*, New York and London 2015.

Slobodian, Quinn. *Globalists: The End of Empire and the Birth of Neoliberalism*, Cambridge (MA) and London 2018.

Smith, Adam. *The Theory of Moral Sentiments*, ed. Ryan Patrick Hanley, London 2009.

Smith, Vera C. *The Rationale of Central Banking and the Free Banking Alternative* [1936], Indianapolis 1990.

Sombart, Werner. *The Quintessence of Capitalism: A Study of the History and Psychology of the Modern Business Man* [1913], ed. Bryan S. Turner, trans. M. Epstein, London and New York 1998.

Sommer, Bernd. *Prekarisierung und Ressentiments: Soziale Unsicherheit und rechtsextreme Einstellungen in Deutschland*, Wiesbaden 2010.

Srnicek, Nick. *Platform Capitalism*, Cambridge 2017.

Staab, Philipp. *Digitaler Kapitalismus: Markt und Herrschaft in der Ökonomie der Unknappheit*, Berlin 2019.

Sten, Christopher W. "The Dialogue of Crisis in The Confidence-Man: Melville's 'New Novel,'" *Studies in the Novel* 6/2 (1974), 165–185.

Strange, Susan. *Mad Money: When Markets Outgrow Governments*, Ann Arbor 1998.

Streeck, Wolfgang. *Buying Time: The Delayed Crisis of Democratic Capitalism*, trans. Patrick Camiller, London and New York 2014.

Szabo, Nick. "Smart Contracts," 1994 (https://web.archive.org/web/20011102030833/http://szabo.best.vwh.net:80/smart.contracts.html).

Tarde, Gabriel. *The Laws of Imitation* [1890], trans. Elsie Clews Parsons, New York 1903.

—. *Psychologie économique*, vol. 1, Paris 1902.

Terranova, Tiziana. "Free Labor: Producing Culture for the Digital Economy," *Social Text* 18/2 (2000), 33–58.

Terzić, Zoran. *Idiocracy: Thinking and Acting in the Age of the Idiot*, trans. Michael Turnbull, Zürich (distrib. University of Chicago Press) (in press).

Thépaut, Yves. "Le Concept d'information dans l'analyse économique contemporaine," *Hermès. La Revue* 44/1 (2006), 161–168.

Thiel, Peter and Blake Masters. *Zero to One: Notes on Startups or How to Build the Future*, New York 2014.

Tilly, Richard. *Geld und Kredit in der Wirtschaftsgeschichte*, Stuttgart 2003.

Tischer, Daniel. "Cutting the Network? Facebook's Libra Currency as a Problem of Organization," *Finance and Society* 6/1 (2020), 19–33.

Tomšič, Samo. *The Capitalist Unconscious: Marx and Lacan*, London and New York 2015.

Tooze, Adam. *Crashed: How a Decade of Financial Crises Changed the World*, New York 2018.

Tréguer, Félix. "Wenn die Polizei Fieber misst," *Le Monde Diplomatique* (German edition), May 2020, 7.

Turner, Adair. *Between Debt and the Devil: Money, Credit, and Fixing Global Finance*, Princeton 2015.

—. *Economics after the Crisis: Objectives and Means*, Cambridge (MA) and London 2012.

Ullrich, Wolfgang. "Ganz ohne Einflussangst. Zur Karriere der Influencer," *POP: Kultur und Kritik* 12 (2018), 45–49 (https://www.uni-muenster.de/Ejournals/index.php/pop/article/view/2365/2250).

Varian, Hal R. "The Economics of Internet Search," in Johannes M. Bauer and Michael Latzer (eds.), *Handbook on the Economics of the Internet*, Cheltenham (UK) and Northampton (MA) 2016, 385–394.

Varoufakis, Yanis. *And the Weak Suffer What They Must? Europe's Crisis and America's Economic Future*, New York 2016.

—. *Adults in the Room: My Battle with the European and American Deep Establishment*, New York 2017.

—. *The Global Minotaur: America, Europe and the Future of the World Economy*, London and New York 2011.

Vasa, Alexandra and Philippe Roepstorff-Robiano. "Börsen-, Spekulations- und Inflationsroman," in Joseph Vogl and Burkhardt Wolf (eds.), *Handbuch Literatur und Ökonomie*, Berlin and Boston 2019, 566–580.

Vasudevan, Ramaa. "Libra and Facebook's Money Illusion," *Challenge*, 63:1 (2020), 21–39 (https://doi.org/10.1080/05775132.2019.1684662).

Vega, Don Joseph de la. *Confusión de Confusiones*, Universidad Nacional de Cuyo, Mendoza/Argentina 2013.

—. *Confusion de Confusiones: Portions Descriptive of the Amsterdam Stock Exchange* [1688], select., trans., and introd. Hermann Kellenbenz, Eastford (CT) 2013.

—. *Die Verwirrung der Verwirrungen: Vier Dialoge über die Börse in Amsterdam*, trans. and introd. Otto Pringsheim, Breslau 1919.

Virno, Paolo. *A Grammar of the Multitude: For an Analysis of Contemporary Forms of Life*, trans. Isabella Bertoletti, James Cascaito, and Andrea Casson, Cambridge (MA) and London 2010.

Vogel, Hans-Jochen. *Mehr Gerechtigkeit! Wir brauchen eine neue Bodenordnung – nur dann wird Wohnen auch wieder bezahlbar*, Freiburg 2019.

Vogel, Steffen. *Europas Revolution von oben: Sparpolitik und Demokratieabbau in der Eurokrise*, Hamburg 2013.

Vogl, Joseph. *The Ascendency of Finance*, trans. Simon Garnett, Cambridge (UK) and Malden (MA) 2017 [Translation of *Der Souveränitätseffekt*, Zürich and Berlin 2015].

—. *Kalkül und Leidenschaft: Poetik des ökonomischen Menschen*, Zürich and Berlin 2008.

—.*The Specter of Capital*, trans. Joachim Redner and Robert Savage, Stanford 2015 [Translation of *Das Gespenst des Kapitals*, Zürich and Berlin 2010].

Waschbüsch, Lukas. "Saftig ausgepresst," *die tageszeitung*, July 9, 2019, 21.

Wedel, Janine. *Shadow Elite: How the World's New Power Brokers Undermine Democracy, Government, and the Free Markets*, New York 2009.

Weinberger, David. *Too Big to Know: Rethinking Knowledge Now that the Facts Aren't the Facts, Experts Are Everywhere, and the Smartest Person in the Room Is the Room*, New York 2011.

Wetzel, Hubert. "Mobilisierung per App," *Süddeutsche Zeitung*, May 28, 2020, 7.

Wiener, Norbert. *Cybernetics or Control and Communication in the Animal and the Machine*, reissue of the 1961 2nd edn., Cambridge (MA) 1985.

Willmroth, Jan. "Die Null wird stehen," *Süddeutsche Zeitung*, July 26, 2019, 15.

Windolf, Paul. "Was ist Finanzmarkt-Kapitalismus?" *Kölner Zeitschrift für Soziologie und Sozialpsychologie* (Special Issue on "Finanzmarkt-Kapitalismus," ed. Paul Windolf), 45 (2005), 20–57.

Wittgenstein, Ludwig. *Über Gewißheit/On Certainty*, ed. G. E. M. Anscombe and H. G. von Wright, New York 1972.

Wylie, Christopher. *Mindf*ck: Inside Cambridge Analytica's Plot to Break the World*, London 2020.

Zara, Christopher. "The Most Important Law in Tech Has a Problem," *Wired*, March 1, 2017 (https://www.wired.com/2017/01/the-most-important-law-in-tech-has-a-problem/).

Žižek, Slavoj. "Genieße Deine Nation wie Dich selbst! Der andere und das Böse – vom Begehren des ethnischen Dings," in Joseph Vogl (ed.), *Gemeinschaften: Positionen zu einer Philosophie des Politischen*, Frankfurt am Main 1994, 133–164.

—. *The Ticklish Subject: The Absent Centre of Political Ontology*, London and New York 2009.

Zuboff, Shoshanna. *The Age of Surveillance Capitalism: The Fight for a Human Future at the New Frontier of Power*, New York 2019.

—. "Big Other: Surveillance Capitalism and the Prospects of an Information Civilization," *Journal of Information Technology* 30 (2015), 75–89.

Zuckerberg, Mark. Building Global Community, February 16, 2017 (https://www.facebook.com/notes/mark-zuckerberg/building-global-community/10154544292806634/).

2 Laws, rulings, reports, and programs

Bundeszentrale für politische Bildung. "Größere Finanzkrisen seit 1970," November 15, 2017 (https://www.bpb.de/nachschlagen/zahlen-und-fakten/globalisierung/52625/finanzkrisen-seit-1970).

Capgemini, *World Wealth Report 2011*, 22 Juni 2011 (https://www.capgemini.com/resources/world-wealth-report-2011/).

Citizens United v. Federal Election Commission, 558 U.S. 310 (2010) (https://www.fec.gov/resources/legal-resources/litigation/cu_sc08_opinion.pdf).

Commission on Global Governance, *Our Global Neighborhood: The Report of the Commission on Global Governance*, New York 1995.

Communications Decency Act, 47 U.S. Code § 230: Protection for private blocking and screening of offensive material (1996) (https://www.law.cornell.edu/uscode/text/47/230).

Directive 2000/31/EC of The European Parliament and of The Council of 8 June 2000 on certain legal aspects of information society services, in particular electronic commerce, in the Internal Market *(Directive on electronic commerce)* (https://eur-lex.europa.eu/legal-content/EN/TXT/PDF/?uri=CELEX:32000L0031&from=DE).

First National Bank of Boston v. Bellotti, 435 U.S. 765 (1978) (https://supreme.justia.com/cases/federal/us/435/765/).

Forum on Information and Democracy, *Working Group on Infodemics: Policy Framework*, November 2020 (https://informationdemocracy.org/wp-content/uploads/2020/11/ForumID_Report-on-infodemics_101120.pdf).

Gesetz über die Nutzung von Telediensten *(Teledienstgesetz – TDG) vom 22. Juli 1997* (Art. 1 in Gesetz zur Regelung der Rahmenbedingungen für Informations- und Kommunikationsdienste-Gesetz [*Informations- und Kommunikationsdienste-Gesetz – IuKDG*]) (https://www.lehrer.uni-karlsruhe.de/~za186/MMB/recht/gesetz.htm).

Gesetz zur Vereinheitlichung von Vorschriften über bestimmte elektronische Informations- und Kommunikationsdienste (*Elektronischer-Geschäftsverkehr-Vereinheitlichungsgesetz – ElGVG*), February 26, 2007 (https://www.buzer.de/s1.htm?g=TDG+1997&f=1).

Hearing before the United States House of Representatives Committee on Financial Services, October 23, 2019, Testimony of Mark Zuckerberg, Founder, Chairman and Chief Executive Officer, Facebook (https://financialservices.house.gov/uploadedfiles/hhrg-116-ba00-wstate-zuckerbergm-20191023.pdf).

International Money Fund. *External Evaluation of IMF Surveillance*. Report by a Group of Independent Experts, Washington 1999.

Libra Association Members. "An Introduction to Libra," White

Paper, June 18, 2019, 1–4 (https://www.scribd.com/document/413733914/LibraWhitePaper-en-US). [The original Libra White Paper.]

—. "Libra White Paper. Version 2.0," April 2020 (https://www.diem.com/en-us/white-paper/#cover-letter).

Treaty on European Union (Maastricht, February 7, 1992) (https://www.cvce.eu/content/publication/2002/4/9/2c2f2b85-14bb-4488-9ded-13f3cd04de05/publishable_en.pdf).

Index